Books by Richard O'Connor

Fiction

GUNS OF CHICKAMAUGA

COMPANY Q

OFFICERS AND LADIES

THE VANDAL

Nonfiction

THOMAS: ROCK OF CHICKAMAUGA

HOOD: CAVALIER GENERAL

SHERIDAN THE INEVITABLE

HIGH JINKS ON THE KLONDIKE

BAT MASTERSON

JOHNSTOWN: THE DAY THE DAM BROKE

HELL'S KITCHEN

WILD BILL HICKOK

PAT GARRETT

BLACK JACK PERSHING

GOULD'S MILLIONS

THE SCANDALOUS MR. BENNETT

COURTROOM WARRIOR: THE COMBATIVE CAREER
OF WILLIAM TRAVERS JEROME

JACK LONDON: A BIOGRAPHY

BRET HARTE: A BIOGRAPHY

AMBROSE BIERCE: A BIOGRAPHY

AMBROSE BIERCE
A Biography

Ambrose Bierce
A Biography

By RICHARD O'CONNOR

with Illustrations

Little, Brown and Company · Boston · Toronto
c 1967

Published simultaneously in Canada
by Little, Brown & Company (Canada) Limited

PRINTED IN THE UNITED STATES OF AMERICA

To Dale L. Walker
and Haldeen Braddy

Contents

Illustrations

AMBROSE BIERCE
A Biography

Introduction

"DEATH IS NOT the end," Ambrose Bierce once remarked. "There remains the litigation over the estate." The sardonic testament of that writer has been admitted to probate. His estate has been settled up, except for the final mystery of what happened after he vanished into revolutionary Mexico. Premeditated or not, his disappearance was in key with his character as a writer; he liked to leave a question or two unanswered. The surrogates of the literary court have estimated the worth of what he left us, and themselves have left a question or two unanswered. Usually, in those magisterial surveys of his time, which was that of the Genteel Tradition, he is assigned a rather humble niche suitable for a man who disdained the mainstream and clung to the eddying shallows. He wrote stories of the supernatural "in the manner of" Poe; he also turned out perhaps a half-dozen Civil War stories of some merit.

Beyond that he was an explosively controversial journalist, a critic of his times so merciless that the brilliant (but borrowed) metaphor of his embittered ex-protégé George Sterling of a man diligently "breaking butterflies on a wheel" is regarded as a just and conclusive verdict. (That charge of gibbeting nonentities was made posthumously, but Bierce had already answered it: "Satire, like other arts, is its own excuse and is not dependent for its interest on the personality of those who supply the occasion for it.") He is also conceded a misanthropy never equaled on this continent and rarely on any other; the role of "a minor prophet of hopelessness" in whom the Gothic was "no hothouse flower but a monstrous orchid" (Clifton Fadiman); an unregenerate reactionary whose writings had a "familiar fascistic ring" with their "insistence on discipline, law and order, and on the need for the control of the disorderly mob by an enlightened and well-washed minority" (Edmund Wilson). The latter conceded that Bierce's style was "sharp-edged and flexible . . . like the ribbon of a wound-up steel tape-measure," but its employment was seriously limited by the fact that death was his "only real character." He is dismissed as an oddity by the panjandrums who write three-volume biographies of his leading contemporaries, as a by-blow, an exotic remnant of the utilitarian age when America was industrializing itself and preparing to move out onto the world stage.

Thus Bierce has been left to the connoisseurs of such curiosa as Lafcadio Hearn, Pierre Loti, Arthur Machen and Sheridan Le Fanu. And yet he keeps popping up through the encrustation of literary history like one of his fictional corpses that won't stay buried. An excellent recent study of his work (Stuart C. Woodruff's *The Short Stories of Ambrose Bierce*) indicates one factor in his continuing attraction: "Bierce is like a kaleidoscope: the individual elements remain the same but they form a different pattern for each viewer."* Howard P. Lovecraft, a modern expert on the genre in which Bierce worked, wrote (in *Supernatural Horror in Literature*) that Bierce deserved a place "close to real greatness" and credited him with having written "some immortal tales" which form a "leading element" in American literature of the supernatural.

Critics closer to his own time thought his eventual position would be even greater. To Percival Pollard he was the "greatest tale-teller in America." Paul Jordan Smith nominated him as the

---

* One of the most remarkable television broadcasts of recent years was a French film based on "An Occurrence at Owl Creek Bridge," which CBS produced on its *Twilight Zone* series.

"greatest writer of the short story this country has yet produced." Wilson Follett considered him "a man of pure literary genius" and predicted that he would "emerge from the mists of his legend" as a "world figure" in literary history. Samuel Loveman noted that in Bierce's work "the evocation of horror becomes for the first time . . . an atmosphere definite and uncannily precise. Words, so simple that one would be prone to ascribe them to the limitations of a literary hack, take on an unholy horror, a new and unguessed transformation."

He has always been something special, certainly not one who appealed to the ingroup of his time. H. L. Mencken, who had good reason to look back to Bierce's influence on his own life and work, remarked (in *Prejudices: Sixth Series*) that "the reputation of Bierce has always radiated an occult, artificial, drug-store scent. He has been hymned in a passionate, voluptuous, inordinate way by a small band of disciples, and he has been passed over altogether by the great majority of American critics. Certainly it would be absurd to say that he is generally read, even by the intelligentsia." Least of all, one might add, by the intelligentsia.

It was his precise recollection of atmosphere, the limpid clarity of his description of physical setting that gave his Civil War stories such a startling air of realism. Mencken considered him the "first writer of fiction ever to treat war realistically." Certainly he was the first to show that heroism had no place in the scientific slaughter which war had become even in his time. Both in his short stories and in his nonfictional sketches he conveyed the reality of Shiloh, Stones River, Chickamauga, Kenesaw Mountain and Franklin as no other writer has. For the first time soldiers were represented as bewildered animals "dying," as Mencken noted, "like hogs in Chicago."

He also offended contemporary sensibilities by treating the former enemy, the Confederates, against whom he had fought and been critically wounded, as fellow sufferers. Waving the bloody shirt was more likely to gain popularity, North or South, in his time. In "A Bivouac of the Dead," he wrote: "They were honest and courageous foemen, having little in common with the

political madmen who had persuaded them to their doom . . .
They did not live through the period of honorable strife into the
period of vilification — did not pass from the iron age into the
brazen — from the era of the sword to that of the tongue and
pen. Among them there is no member of the Southern Historical
Society. Their valor was not the fury of the non-combatant; they
have no voice in the thunder of civilians . . . Not by them are
impaired the dignity and infinite pathos of the Lost Cause. Give
them, these blameless gentlemen, their rightful part in all the
pomp that fills the circuit of the summer hills."

He has been termed an "aristocratic radical," a position calculated to draw fire from all sides, and would write, "My allegiance
to republican institutions is slack through lack of faith in them as
a practical system of governing men as men are . . . [But] I will
call no man 'Your Majesty' or 'Your Lordship.' For me to meet
in my own country a king or nobleman would require as much
preliminary negotiation as an official interview between the
Mufti of Moosh and the Ahkoond of Swat." He meant every
word of it. Once he was "commanded" to the presence of
Empress Eugénie, who merely wanted to thank him for his
professional services as defender of her vanished realm and
beleaguered reputation, but he refused the invitation because his
sense of "republican independence" rebelled.

The black humor and grisly comedy of the man, though it
never found public favor, is part of a literary current that has run
strongly from its sources in the Colonial period. The writers most
successful in their own time have usually been those who expressed optimism over a happy ending for our dream as a nation.
Bierce's work, however, reflects a darker vision of America's
destiny — a vision that he shares, to a greater or lesser extent,
with Melville, Hawthorne, Poe, Stephen Crane, William Faulk-
ner and many contemporary novelists.

Thus, Bierce, for all his oddities, is part of a profound and
significant literary tradition. Clifton Fadiman, writing the introduction to a collection of Bierce's writings in 1946, predicted that
Bierce would "speak to us with added vehemence" when "the
time of the pessimists has come again" and there is widespread

repugnance for those "in the saddle." In this respect Mr. Fadiman considered Bierce, always a thunderous nay-sayer, "quite a
man of our time." The "purity of his misanthropy," Mr. Fadiman predicted, would cause his revival in any age in which
humanism, withering in wars hot and cold, would give way to
yearnings for a totalitarian state.

If he is rediscovered in the near future, it will likely be as the
first notable exponent of black humor in America. Prudish as he
was in anything written for publication, he would be offended at
inclusion in such raffish company. Anything bordering on the
pornographic evoked an outcry for rigid censorship and harsh
penalties from Bierce. Today's black humorists could, however,
meet him with profit. He is their natural father. As in all such
paternity cases there would be resentment and misunderstanding,
but the experience would be unforgettable.

> No one can deny that the most attractive figures in literature are always those around whom a world of lies and legend has been woven, those half mythical artists whose real characters become cloaked forever under a veil of the bizarre.
>
> — Dylan Thomas

ONE *The First Disaster*

A MBROSE BIERCE summed up his views on parentage and family life in a group of five stories aptly titled *Parenticide*. The crime, in his opinion, was entirely justifiable. His own parents were "unwashed savages," who could spare him little affection but were quick to punish him with a hickory switch or "such foreign bodies as they could lay their hands on," and religious fanatics into the bargain. His childhood was so squalid that he could rarely bring himself to recall it, though the hardscrabble farm on which he was raised later was memorialized in the following verse:

> *The malarious farm, the wet fungus-grown wildwood*
> *The chills then contracted that since have remained.*
> *The scum-covered duck pond, the pigstye close by it,*
> *The ditch where the sour-smelling house drainage fell*
> *The damp, shaded dwelling, the foul barnyard nigh it . . .*[1]

And so on through a dreary catalogue of backwoods squalor. Birth, as he defined it in his celebrated *The Devil's Dictionary*, was "the first and direst of all disasters." His own, he felt, was no exception, and was followed by a boyhood filled with hardship and disaffection, and a youth that dissolved into the four-year nightmare of war.

Actually it was all so typical of a boyhood on the Middle Border, in the middle of the nineteenth century, as to be banal, a condition Bierce resented more fiercely than any amount of hardship.

Ambrose Gwinett Bierce was born on June 24, 1842, in the settlement of Horse Cave Creek, Meigs County, Ohio. His parents were Marcus Aurelius Bierce and Laura Sherwood Bierce. Ambrose was the tenth of thirteen children born to the Bierces. Thanks to the extraordinary Bierce vitality, ten of them survived infancy, an amazing number considering the infant mortality rate on the frontier. Equally strange to their unimaginative neighbors was the fact that all the Bierce children were given names beginning with "A," because Marcus Aurelius loved poetry and alliteration. The children accordingly were named Abigail, the eldest, nineteen at the time of Ambrose's birth; Amelia, Ann Maria, Addison, Aurelius, Augustus, Almeda, Andrew, Albert, Ambrose, Arthur, and the twins, Adelia and Aurelia. The last three died in infancy.

On both sides of his house, Ambrose Bierce was descended from the earliest migrants to America from England. The Bierces first settled around Cornwall, Connecticut, and were accounted honest, hardworking, prolific yeomen with no great aptitude for success. Ambrose's paternal grandfather, William Bierce, was a farmer, miller and Revolutionary War veteran. His mother's family, the Sherwoods, also of Cornwall, were considered more intellectual and aristocratic; they were descended from William Bradford, who would surely have been dismayed at being one of the ancestors of the rebellious and impious Ambrose.*

---

* Bierce had little interest in matters of genealogy, which he defined in *The Devil's Dictionary* as "an account of one's descent from an ancestor who did not care to trace his own." Nor did he have any great respect for his Colonial ancestry. One of his parodies in verse read:

My country, 'tis of thee
Sweet land of felony,

Shortly after the turn of the nineteenth century a number of Cornwall families migrated to the Western Reserve, among them the Bierces and Sherwoods, and settled in Portage County, Ohio. Marcus and Laura were married in 1822, and shortly thereafter moved to Horse Cave Creek in southeastern Ohio.[2]

Poverty and religion, both of the extreme variety, were the two chief influences on Ambrose Bierce's childhood. His father was an unsuccessful farmer with an unseemly love of literature. A pioneer in the Western Reserve who adored Lord Byron, as Marcus Bierce did, and who spent part of his tiny cash income on books instead of barns, was not likely to enrich himself or even keep his family in comfort. A brooding, reticent man, who roused himself from contemplation only to cut a hickory switch and take after a misbehaving son, Marcus did not endear himself to his tenth child. Ambrose, in later years, did credit him with having incidentally instilled in himself a love of books. At the age of ten Ambrose had read Pope's translation of Homer in his father's small library, and he later admitted, "To his books I owe all that I have."

Otherwise Marcus had little influence on Ambrose. The dominant male in the Bierce family was Marcus's brother, Ambrose's uncle, Lucius Verus Bierce, who seemed to have acquired all the energy and ambition in that branch of the family. Lucius Bierce managed to work his way through Ohio University, obtained a law degree, practiced for a year before being elected district attorney of Portage County, and later was mayor of Akron for many years. A flaming patriotism periodically interrupted his political career. In 1837, he was a leading figure in the military campaign, dignified as the "Patriot War," which was undertaken by several hundred Americans to liberate Canada from an unpopular government; a cause that struck more fire in American hearts than Canadian. Lucius Bierce styled himself as "General"

Of thee I sing —
Land where my father fried
Young witches and applied
Whips to the Quaker's hide
And made him spring.

of the force of one hundred eighty men who invaded Canada, captured the city of Windsor, opposite Detroit, and burned the barracks there before a detachment of British regulars appeared on the scene and killed 130 of the invaders. Lucius was among the thirty Americans who escaped. It was a fiasco but "General" Bierce was a great popular hero in Ohio. He volunteered in 1846 but his company was disbanded before it could be sent to Mexico. Ever after Lucius was the number-one Fourth of July orator in the Western Reserve. His political and military distinction, and his flamboyant style, naturally won the admiration of his nephew Ambrose. Lucius himself married late in life and took sufficient interest in his brother's family to assist, later in Ambrose's youth, in attempting to curb his rebellious spirit.

By comparison with the swashbuckling Lucius, Ambrose's own father was a drab, dour, plodding figure. His mother, however, was a determined woman who dominated her husband and children — with the frequent exception of Ambrose — and laid down the law, domestic and moral. Despite her son's later reference to his parents as "unwashed savages," she insisted on neatness and cleanliness in all her children, as well as obedience and godliness. A woman with ten children to raise hasn't much time to explain her demands. If her manner was abrupt, even dictatorial, the other children accepted it as only natural. Ambrose, being more independent, sensitive and intelligent than any of his siblings, was inclined to contest matters — a tendency which led to frequent punishment, consequent resentment, and a determination to escape from parental discipline as soon as possible.

If there was one circumstance that Ambrose resented more than any other, it was the pervasive religious influence of his home and countryside. His parents were fervent Congregationalists; praying, hymn-singing and Bible-reading were integral parts of their home life; the Sabbath was observed with a mournful rigidity. The whole Western Reserve, in fact, was gripped by an obsession with religion, with a transplanted Puritanism. Ambrose often had to be switched for sneaking away from home on Sundays and observing the Sabbath after his own whimsical fashion. From time to time roaming evangelists appeared in the community to flay backsliders and remind everyone that the fires of hell were waiting for those addicted to drinking, dancing, card-playing and other vices. Young Ambrose particularly resented the revival meetings and the hysteria they aroused, and there rapidly formed in his impressionable mind the contempt for religion, as manipulated by latterday Christians, that increased with the years. Once, according to his brother Albert, he and Ambrose disrupted a revival meeting by driving an old white horse through the campground and scattering the assemblage.[3]

His only intimate in the family circle was his brother Albert, with whom he was on the closest terms to the end of his life. Albert would join him in the mischief-making that so often caused his father or mother to resort to corporal punishment. The other children were docile, and in other ways so different that Ambrose must have seemed like a changeling. One sister, Almeda, absorbed so much of the atmospheric piety that she spent most of her life as a missionary in Africa. His brother Addison became a circus strongman. Otherwise the Bierce children were content to marry, settle down near their parents and lead blameless, if stodgy, lives. His brother Andrew lived with their parents until they died.

Ambrose was the biological sport, the odd one. Early in boyhood his nights were haunted by dreams in which apparitions, ghostly lights, fantastic shapes and phantasmagoric scenes appeared; a dream life which later became transmuted into a bizarre form of literature. One dream that kept recurring was of traveling over a fire-blackened landscape until he came to a huge deserted building. He wandered through its rooms, menacingly shadowed and empty, until he came to a chamber in which a weird light was glowing. In the dream it seemed that the light signified eternity. Later he tried to explain its significance in Nietzschean verse. Humanity was dead, all the angels and devils were "cold enough at last," and "God lies dead before the great white throne!"

Perhaps some of his boyhood preoccupation with a world that existed in another, more nightmarish dimension he could glimpse only in dreams — an unseen dimension that haunted him to the end of his life and formed a spectral background to some of his best work — was a reflection of what he heard from his elders in the backwoods community. Calvinism, reinforced by periodic camp meetings, was being threatened by a new force that many regarded as unholy. The Western Reserve, during Ambrose's boyhood, was overrun by the Spiritualist movement, which gathered devotees in every town and village. Despite the direst warnings from their pastors, they met in "spirit rooms" to commune with the departed and receive messages on the "spiritual telegraph."

The cause célèbre of the American Spiritualist movement was the Abby Warner case, which created an uproar throughout the Western Reserve. Ambrose was nine years old at the time and read of it in his father's newspapers. Abby Warner was an eighteen-year-old orphan, illiterate and subnormal mentally but possessed, her guardians claimed, of amazing powers as a medium. To demonstrate her talent, she was taken to St. Timothy's Episcopal Church in Massillon, Ohio, during services. Parishioners in surrounding pews kept hearing a rat-a-tat noise in the section occupied by Abby despite the fact that she kept her hands folded primly in her lap. The rapping continued even after a plea from the altar that she and/or her ghostly accomplices cease the "disturbance." Next day Abby was arrested on charges of having "disturbed a Christian assembly in the solemn act of public worship." Overflow crowds attended her trial, which was thoroughly covered by the newspapers. She was found not guilty after witnesses testified she had no visible connection with the noises which caused so much consternation at St. Timothy's. The confrontation between the alleged spirit world and orthodox Christianity, so neatly arranged by Abby's sponsors, succeeded in "planting Spiritualism in almost every household in the Western Reserve," according to a historian of the movement.[4]

Perhaps it was to escape such unwholesome emanations that the Bierce family, a few months later, moved westward. More likely it was in search of better land, a more promising future. They settled on Walnut Creek, three miles south of Warsaw in northern Indiana. It was then heavily forested, thick with oak, maple and hickory. The Bierces took over an eighty-acre plot about a mile from the Walnut Creek settlement with its church, sawmill and log-cabin schoolhouse and set about the long and laborious job of clearing it for farming.

Ambrose was an angelic child in appearance, with light blue eyes and golden curls, a proper little sissy at first glance; but his tendencies were toward deviltry, truancy and other waywardness; he was a Huck Finn with little interest in the rudimentary education offered by itinerant schoolmasters, who also believed that a brisk tattoo on the seat of small boys' pants was a great help in the learning process, or in the Sunday school of the Presbyterian church in the settlement. He ran wild with his brother Albert in the rolling countryside, the deep woods, the shore of Goose Lake and the banks of the Tippecanoe River a few miles away from their home; as wild, that is, as their watchful mother would permit. Later Albert would recall that he and Ambrose "did not make life as pleasant for her as we might have, yet I know that I always loved her and still love her memory."[5] No such tender statement was ever made by his brother Ambrose.

The older he grew, the more time Ambrose spent with his father's books. Except for Albert, he did not join other children in their games and had begun to regard himself as somewhat superior to them, just as his father held himself aloof from the untutored farmers of the district. He refused to join in the games during recess; baseball and other sports, as he later wrote, were no more than "the last shifts of intellectual vacuity militant against the Siren song of natural stagnation."[6] Yet he did not stagnate; the natural beauty of the great Indiana forest, the miracle of the changing seasons attracted him more than organized play. Outside home and school he spent his time roaming the woods, sometimes with Albert, sometimes alone. Neither then nor later did loneliness hold any terrors for him; it seemed a natural state for a boy, and later a man, who was not greatly charmed by human society.

For such a boy the mythical — even such a commonplace myth as Santa Claus — naturally was a strong attraction. Almost half a century later he recorded his undiminished anger over being cheated by that genial legend of childhood. He recalled asking "a woman to whom I was bound by ties of blood and affection"— apparently his mother — whether there was really a Santa Claus. He would not have resented it, he said, if she had come out with the truth. Instead she insisted on the reality of Santa Claus. Later, on learning the truth, he felt doubly bilked and resented it with a passion that was excessive. He then "proceeded forthwith to detest my deceiver with all my little might and main. And even now I cannot say that I experience any consuming desire to renew my acquaintance with her in that other life to which, she also assured me, we hasten hence."[7] That would seem a rather long time to brood over disillusionment about Santa Claus, but Ambrose Bierce had a long, fierce and vindictive memory. True forgiveness, he believed, was something that never happened.

He entered his early teens a rather sullen, withdrawn and introspective boy. By then two of his older sisters had married and left the family farm and his older brothers were taking much of the burden off Marcus Bierce. Ambrose walked three miles to high school in Warsaw every weekday, a slender handsome boy with piercing blue eyes that mirrored the dissatisfaction he found in the life around him. He was no joy to his teachers. His own thoughts and speculations were more important to him, even in the classroom, than the lessons they tried to drum into him by rote. Few important American writers have distinguished themselves in school or have attempted to prolong the educational process; their real school is the wider world and their way of learning is more intuitive than formal; they are born dropouts.

Many years later, for his friend and publisher Walter Neale, he recaptured his feelings as an adolescent. "Youth sees the nasty world stretched out before him. He can go far in no direction without stepping into a cesspool. To him it is astonishing that his predecessors have not cleaned it up."[8] Youth, it seemed to him, was something to be gotten over as quickly as possible, with adulthood the only goal worthwhile. He would not seek to prolong it any more than he would his droning, dreaming hours in the Warsaw high school. The picnics, hayrides, country dances and sleighing parties which delighted his contemporaries held no attraction for him.

At fifteen, in fact, he decided to anticipate manhood by a few years and live on his own. He left the farm at Walnut Creek settlement, never to return except for brief visits. Apparently this decision was made with the approval of his parents, since he began working and living in Warsaw, only a few miles away. He became the printer's devil on the *Northern Indianan* and boarded at the home of its editor, Reuben Williams. Learning to set type and doing all the dirty work around the back shop of a rural newspaper was, in those days, almost the classic beginning for an American writer. There is no evidence that he had already decided upon a writing career, but his literate boyhood must have pointed him in that direction.

About the same time gentler and more satisfying feminine influences than those offered by his mother and sisters, for whom he apparently had shockingly little feeling, touched his life. One was a girl his own age named Bernie Wright, whom he called Fatima or Tima, a pretty girl with a sense of humor. She was more or less his sweetheart, his first "real love affair," as he later told Walter Neale. He was also involved at the same time with "a woman of broad culture . . . well past seventy . . . still physically attractive, even at her great age," according to his account to Neale.[9] Bierce stoutly maintained that, in addition to discussing books and other aesthetic matters with the Warsaw lady, there was a physical side to their intimacy. (It may have been that Bierce confided more openly to Neale than anyone else, but the publisher's account of Bierce's confessions is considerably racier — and perhaps more suspect — than those of other friends. Others regarded Bierce as something of a prude where sexual matters were concerned; it was only Neale who pictured him as discussing his amatory past with great frankness and frequent gusto.)

That supposed clandestine affair with a woman old enough to be his grandmother or even great-grandmother is no less hazy than the events which caused him to bolt from his job as

printer's devil at the *Northern Indianan*. Local legend had it that
he decided to leave Warsaw because he was falsely accused of a
theft — from whom or under what circumstances is still a mystery. At any rate he was cleared of suspicion a short time later.
The accusation itself was such an affront to a seventeen-year-old
with his touchy pride that he decided to leave the town and the
state. Either that decision or the accusation of theft — or more
likely his long record of rebelling against parental authority —
impelled his father and mother to call his Uncle Lucius into
consultation. Ambrose would listen to Uncle Lucius; the whole
world did, it seemed.

Lucius Bierce's decision was that Ambrose should be sent to a
military academy, where discipline would be applied with imper-
sonal force. Accordingly he was dispatched to the Kentucky
Military Institute for a year, which may have been one of the
best things that happened to him. He quickly acquired an erect,
soldierly bearing that marked him for the rest of his life. He also
learned enough of drill and tactics, and of map reading and
making, to enable him to be commissioned an officer at a very
youthful age after the Civil War broke out and to be attached to
a division commander's staff as topographical officer.

At the end of a year, either by agreement with his uncle or
without it, he left the academy and returned to Warsaw.[10] The
benefits of his brief immersion in academic and military discipline were not immediately apparent. He refused to return to his
parents' home and instead hung around Warsaw picking up
whatever odd jobs he could to support himself. For a time he
worked in a brickyard. Then, in the eyes of his family, he sank a
lot lower. Now eighteen years old, a husky and handsome youth,
he went to work at Faber's store-saloon: the same sort of
establishment as Abraham Lincoln had apprenticed himself to,
half clerk and half bartender, over in backwoods Illinois. Faber's
was a general store in one section, a barroom in the other.
Ambrose was employed as general factotum in the saloon section.
Here the small-town sports gathered to drink and play cards. It
was Ambrose's job to serve them beer, wine, liquor or cider and
fetch sandwiches and drinks to the card tables. This proximity to

card-playing and liquor-drinking and general dissipation, all abhorred by his straitlaced family, made him an outcast among the respectable people in town as well as on the farm at Walnut Creek settlement. He never went home any more and held himself aloof from the townspeople. Most considered him a surly specimen who would never amount to much. Even Bernie Wright found him hard to understand, a quick-tempered, moody, jealous suitor. She was a gay, flirtatious young thing, had not promised herself to Ambrose, and could not help resenting his unwarranted possessiveness. Who did he think he was? That was one question which, if asked, Ambrose Bierce would have been starkly unable to answer. He hadn't the faintest idea who he was or where he was heading — and the question would vex him to the end of his life.

In the spring of 1861 he was only one of thousands of restless, disaffected American males who must have heard the echo of Fort Sumter's guns with a feeling almost of relief, of joyous anticipation. The question of identity, of what to do with his life could be held in suspension. He was only too glad to trade in the dirty white apron of the youth who hustled drinks and sandwiches for the boys in the back room at Faber's for a Union-blue soldier's uniform. And besides that break with the humdrum, marked-for-failure life in Warsaw the war was an outlet for his repressed idealism. Even later in life, when he was given to masking his emotions and playing so beautifully the role of the cynic, he would not disguise the crusading enthusiasm with which he marched off to war. "At one time in my green and salad days, I was sufficiently zealous for Freedom to engage in a four years' war for its promotion. There were other issues involved, but they did not count much for me."[11]

By "Freedom," he apparently meant not only the preservation of the Union but the destruction of the institution of slavery. Unlike many Indianans, particularly those who were Democrats or members of the pro-Confederate Knights of the Golden Circle, the Bierce family was strongly antislavery. None more so than his Uncle Lucius, whom he came close to idolizing. When

John Brown moved west to Kansas to begin his bloody campaign against slavery and all its manifestations, Lucius Bierce obtained the arms and ammunition of a disbanded company of the state militia and turned them over to him. During Brown's visit to Akron, Mayor Bierce also gave him the sword and pistol he had carried in the Patriot War years before. And on December 2, 1859, when Brown fell before a firing squad after his assault on the Federal arsenal at Harpers Ferry, Lucius Bierce delivered a eulogy before a mass meeting in which he predicted that the volley was the first fusillade of a civil war. He closed his oration in words that were widely published in the North:

"The tragedy of Brown's is freighted with awful lessons and consequences. It is like the clock striking the fatal hour that begins a new era in the conflict with slavery. Men like Brown may die, but their acts and principles will live forever . . . It is one of those acts of madness which history cherishes and poetry loves forever to adorn with her choicest wreaths of laurel."[12]

At the outbreak of war Lucius Bierce proved he was more than a master of rhetoric. Among the first to answer President Lincoln's call for 75,000 volunteers, he organized, equipped and drilled two companies of marines; then, being in his sixties and unable to take a more combative role, he delivered them to the navy yard in Washington.

That call for volunteers was issued April 15, 1861. Four days later his nephew Ambrose, the second man in his county to volunteer, answered the call by enlisting as a private in Company C, Ninth Indiana Volunteer Infantry, commanded by Colonel Robert Milroy. A short time later his brother Albert enlisted in the Eighteenth Battery, Ohio Light Artillery.

Company C was sent to Indianapolis on April 25 and joined the rest of the regiment at the state fairgrounds, which had been converted into Camp Morton. It was regimental opinion that they would shortly march south, fall upon the boastful but craven Confederates and shatter the Confederacy well before their three-month term of enlistment was up.

Just in case something went wrong, Ambrose wanted to be remembered as something besides a saloon roustabout. He sent

Bernie Wright a long and delirious poem protesting his love and displaying a command of language no mere taproom hustler could boast.

> . . . *Thy love, dear girl, is worth eternal woe,*
> *And wouldst thou knew whose heart thus yearns for thee*
> *And if thou knew couldst deign to pardon me*
> *Two moments sweet I've been in paradise*
> *Thy lips have twice met mine and only twice.*[13]

He sent Bernie the poem anonymously, but since he addressed her as Fatima or Tima and no one else did, she would have no trouble divining who the author was. Such moments of coyness were rare in his life. The next would come fifty-two years hence when he would march off to another war far to the south.

ON EACH SIDE of the Civil War there were hundreds of thousands of combatants, yet the only great Civil War novel was *The Red Badge of Courage*, written by a man born six years after the war ended. The greatest shorter fiction, and the first to describe the circumstances of war realistically, was Ambrose Bierce's. He was the only writer of note to have served in the Civil War armies. The war which produced four Presidents of the United States was strangely reluctant to allow any literary talent to survive. And besides, in a day when drafted civilians could evade service by hiring substitutes, men of the educated class, from which most writers then came, were able to stay out of uniform. Among his contemporaries only Mark Twain served briefly with the colors — the Confederacy's — and he demobilized himself without consulting his superiors after falling out of a hayloft while on maneuvers.

War was the making of Bierce as a man and a writer. Without that experience he probably, as his townspeople predicted, would have amounted to little more than a small-town newspaperman, a courthouse-square cynic grumbling his life away. With it, something coalesced in his mind and imagination, gave him a viewpoint, goaded him toward describing — in the most precise and coolly recollected detail any participant has managed — what he felt and experienced. "War — Bierce's Civil War, the great educational nightmare of his formative years — was the perfect metaphor for him," Marcus Cunliffe has written. "In its very nature war entailed horror. Civil War produced ironies and coincidences of a sort which may seem relatively slick in the tales of civilians. Brother *did* kill brother, actually and figuratively. And, not able to believe that either side was wholly in the right, Bierce transcended his habitual cynicism. The futility had for him overtones of authentic tragedy."[1] The only literary works of classic proportions that came out of the Civil War were Bierce's short stories and General Ulysses S. Grant's *Memoirs*. Both were native Ohioans and both had severe personal problems; but Grant became the towering, then crumbling hero of the Gilded Age while Bierce was its most caustic and persistent critic.

Bierce, at eighteen going on nineteen, immediately showed that he had a greater aptitude for military than for civilian life. The Ninth Indiana, after a month's drilling in the mud of the Indianapolis fairground, was shipped by rail to the Virginia border, the section now a part of West Virginia. Two days after reaching Grafton, on June 3, 1861, it skirmished with Confederate troops as part of a brigade commanded by General George B. McClellan. Five weeks later the Ninth again went into action and drove the enemy off Girard Hill, where the Confederates had dug themselves in behind breastworks. During this brief but bitter action, according to the correspondent of the Indianapolis *Journal*, Bierce and another private named Boothroyd distinguished themselves by charging up the hill to "within fifteen paces of the enemy's breastworks when Boothroyd was wounded in the neck by a rifle ball paralyzing him. Bierce, in open view of the enemy, carried poor Boothroyd and his gun without other assistance, fully twenty rods, balls falling around him like hail." The Ninth proceeded to take the town of Philippi, then skirmished again with the enemy at Carrick's Ford.[2]

The ninety-day enlistment period ended late in July, and Bierce and his comrades were sent back to Indiana to be mustered out. The war, of course, still had not been won; other Union forces had done more retreating than advancing. The blood-dimmed prospect of a long war confronted the nation.

Still a burning patriot and undismayed by what he had seen of war, Bierce immediately reenlisted in the Ninth and was given the rank of sergeant-major. He was now a blooded veteran, able to swagger in front of the new recruits. "We were regarded by the others with profound respect as 'old soldiers.' We gave ourselves, this aristocracy of service, no end of military airs; some of us even going to the extreme of keeping our jackets buttoned and our hair combed. We had been in action, too; had shot off a Confederate leg at Philippi, 'the first battle of the war,' and had lost as many as a dozen men at Laurel Hill and Carrick's Ford, whither the enemy had fled in trying, Heaven knows why, to get away from us. We now 'brought to the task' of subduing the Rebellion a patriotism which never for a moment doubted that a rebel was a fiend accursed of God and the angels — for whose extirpation by force and arms each youth of us considered himself specially 'raised up.' "

Again the Ninth was marched into the Cheat Mountain region of Virginia. That spur of the Alleghenies ever afterward seemed an enchanted land to Bierce, interminable ridges, purple valleys slumbering in shadow, a land in which "it seemed always afternoon." To the flatlanders from Indiana and Ohio, who had never seen a hill higher than a church steeple, it was "a perpetual miracle," fragrant with spruce and pine, bedecked with laurel — "real laurel, as we understood the matter, whose foliage had been accounted excellent for the heads of illustrious Romans and such . . ."[3]

The Ninth was ordered to take the summit of Cheat Mountain "to guard the pass through which nobody wanted to go." Winter came, and the opposing forces glowered at each other from their respective summits, the Union brigade guarding the northern exit of the Staunton-Parkersburg turnpike, the Confederates the southern end of the pass. Most of the time was spent trying to keep warm, but "we had a bit of war now and again." One bit was the attack on Buffalo Mountain, where the main enemy force was camped. The Union brigade advanced in two columns, hoping to encircle and trap the enemy. It didn't come off, and the brigade was "most gloriously thrashed." As Bierce later succinctly described the tactical situation, "The enemy, in enjoyment of that inestimable military advantage known in civilian speech as 'surrounded,' always beat the attacking columns one at a time or, turning redhanded from the wreck of the first, frightened the other away." Marching back to their own winter quarters in defeat, Bierce's regiment came across the scene of a recent skirmish, where wild hogs were eating the Union dead. Bierce and his comrades immediately slaughtered the rooting swine. In describing that grisly scene he could not resist adding humor to Grand Guignol: "They had eaten our fallen, but — touching magnanimity! — we did not eat theirs." On that sullen, slogging retreat, Bierce recalled, the summer patriots were turned into winter veterans. "We were as patriotic as ever, but we did not wish to be that way."[4]

It was in the Cheat Mountain region that Bierce later set the scene for one of his most memorable short stories, "A Horseman in the Sky." It was the story of a well-born young Virginian who defied his father's wishes and joined the Union army. One day he was on sentry duty, fell asleep at his lonely mountain outpost, and awakened to see a mounted Confederate officer on the rim of a cliff across the valley. He was struck by the beauty of the horse and man outlined against the clear blue sky. "The figure of the man sat the figure of the horse, straight and soldierly, but with the repose of a Grecian god carved in the marble which limits the suggestion of activity." He knew it was his duty to fire and thus destroy this work of art. He did. Later his sergeant insists on a full report. The sentry is forced to confess that the "horseman in the sky" was his father.

In February 1862 Bierce's regiment was ordered to leave the "enchanted mountains" and entrain for Nashville to join General Don Carlos Buell's Army of the Cumberland. A military crisis had arisen in the west; the Confederates had been driven out of Nashville but were regrouping, with reinforcements, in northern Mississippi to assume the counteroffensive. The Army of the Ohio, commanded by Grant, had pursued and taken up positions at Pittsburg Landing on the Tennessee River. On its arrival in Nashville the Ninth Indiana was assigned to General William Nelson's division, General William B. Hazen's brigade. General Hazen, soon to become Bierce's personal idol, "my commander and my friend, my master in the art of war," was a professional soldier and a strict disciplinarian who sweated some of the carefree habits out of the Volunteer regiment. Hazen was a prickly character, brave, hot-tempered, on testy terms with his superiors, "the best-hated man I ever knew . . . his very memory is a terror to every unworthy soul in the service."[5]

On April 6, the battle of Shiloh broke out when the Confederates launched the most violent attack of the war thus far against Grant's divisions at Pittsburg Landing. The Army of the Cumberland was immediately ordered to join the battle line, marching up the Tennessee on the double to be ferried across the river on two small steamers. Bierce's division was in the vanguard. It was dusk "but on the heights above, the battle was burning brightly enough; a thousand lights kindled and expired in every second of time. . . . Fleeting streaks of fire crossed over to us by way of welcome. . . . There were deep, shaking explosions and smart shocks; the whisper of stray bullets and the hurtle of conical shells; the rush of round shot." Above them, at the mouth of a creek, were two toylike Federal gunboats firing up the bayou and holding off the Confederate attack on the Union's left flank . . . "twenty gunners beating back an army because a sluggish creek had been pleased to fall into a river at one point rather than another." Crossing over the Tennessee on one of the steamboats with his regiment, Bierce encountered a woman on the deck whom he would never forget. "She was a fine creature, this woman; somebody's wife. Her mission, as she understood it, was to inspire the failing heart with courage; and when she selected mine I felt less flattered by her preference than astonished by her penetration. How did she learn? She stood on the upper deck with the red blaze of battle bathing her beautiful face, the twinkle of a thousand rifles mirrored in her eyes; and displaying a small ivory-handled pistol, she told me in a sentence punctuated by the thunder of great guns that if it came to the worst she would do her duty like a man. I am proud to remember that I took off my hat to this little fool."[6]

The Ninth Indiana took up a position on the Union left between Owl Creek and the Tennessee River, a small plateau covered by a rain-drenched forest, past endless rows of tents which were "constantly receiving the wounded, yet were never full; they were continually ejecting the dead, yet were never empty." The Army of the Cumberland had arrived just in time — two more hours would have been too late — to bolster Grant's army and keep it from being driven into the Tennessee. All night decimated regiments were withdrawn, shattered ones reorganized, fresh ones marched to the front. "The night was now black-dark; as is usual after a battle, it had begun to rain. Still we moved; we were being put into position by somebody. Very often we struck our feet against the dead; more frequently against those who still had spirit enough to resent it with a moan. These were lifted carefully to one side and abandoned . . ."

When morning came, the Ninth was drawn up in battle formation — but where was the battle? The regiment moved forward to contact the enemy; "no braying of brass to apprise the enemy, no fifing and drumming to amuse him; no ostentation of gaudy flags; no nonsense. This was business." They passed over fields littered with broken bodies, dead horses, wrecked caissons and ammunition wagons. They came across a Union sergeant with a ghastly head wound which exposed the brain. "One of my men, whom I knew for a womanish fellow, asked if he should put his bayonet through him. Inexpressibly shocked by the cold-blooded proposal, I told him I thought not; it was unusual, and too many were looking."[7]

It appeared that the Confederates were retreating to their base at Corinth. But, as the Ninth learned shortly, the enemy still had a sting in its tail. Bierce's company took up a position in a clearing. "Then — I can't describe it — the forest seemed all at once to flame up and disappear with a crash like that of a great wave upon the beach — a crash that expired in hot hissings, and the sickening 'spat' of lead against flesh. A dozen of my brave fellows tumbled over like ten-pins. . . . We had expected to find, at most, a line of skirmishers similar to our own. . . . What we had found was a line of battle, coolly holding its fire until it could count our teeth. . . . We got back, most of us, and I shall never forget the ludicrous incident of a young officer who had taken part in the affair walking up to his colonel, who had been a calm and apparently impartial spectator, and gravely reporting, 'The enemy is in force just beyond this field, sir.' "

The Ninth Indiana and a companion regiment of Hazen's brigade withstood a counterattack by Confederate forces that outnumbered them two to one. On Hazen's orders the Ninth pulled back to a line of rail fence to await the Confederate infantry. "A great gray cloud seemed to spring out of the forest into the faces of the waiting battalions. It was received with a crash that made the very trees turn up their leaves." The Confederates fixed bayonets for the charge, but were cut down by a blast of musketry from the Union regiments. "Lead had scored its oldtime victory over steel; the heroic had broken its heart against the commonplace. . . ." All day the Confederates attacked and withdrew in waves. At one point the Union line was about to crack, then a regiment in reserve moved up to bolster them. There was a final counterattack, this time by the Union regiments, and the Confederates were swept back beyond the positions from which they had stormed down on Grant's army the day before. Shiloh, bloody Shiloh, was ended. "Then for the first time we note that the silence of the whole region is not comparative, but absolute. Have we become stone deaf? See; here comes a stretcher-bearer, and there a surgeon! Good heavens! a chaplain!"

Looking back on it twenty years later, when he wrote that account, the battlefield acquired "so airy a grace" that he wished he could recapture the moment of victory at Shiloh. He was one of those rare men with a genuine lust for battle; artillery was symphonic music for him, musketry and the roar of assaulting columns its delightful counterpoint. Ambrose Bierce would never feel so alive as in the midst of war and death. To be plunged back into those scenes, he wrote, "I will willingly surrender another life than the one that I should have thrown away at Shiloh." Even as he recalled the terrors of that day at Shiloh, he could not forget the "moon-gilded magnolia" and how "unfamiliar constellations burned in the Southern midnights." Horror was one side of the coin, beauty the other. He would always find them inseparable, sometimes indistinguishable.[8]

In another war, Bierce would have been one of those soldiers said to have "found a home in the army." The privations were nothing compared to the change and chanciness of military life. His days around Warsaw seemed unbearably drab and predictable in comparison. He was, then and always, a thoroughgoing romantic, an adventurer, to whom death and danger were the spice of life. There was an element of the desperado in his character; later it would be expressed in carrying a loaded pistol on mundane streets and a readiness to issue or accept challenges to a duel. Right to the end, he would seek the unquiet life.

His superiors were quick to observe that Bierce was the stuff of a good infantry officer. Shortly after the campaign against Corinth he was given a field commission as a second lieutenant. Soon after that he was mentioned in general orders for gallantry in guiding a relief column to a brigade in an exposed position and risking his own life by drawing enemy fire away from the reinforcements.

Oddly enough, popular as he had been in the company while a private and noncommissioned officer, his lieutenancy was viewed by his comrades as an intolerable affront to them. An Elkhart, Indiana, newspaper reported that complaints had been received from Company C that Bierce's appointment was "very obnoxious," especially since the company until then had been allowed to elect its own officers.[9] Obviously such an unmilitary, if democratic, process as election of commissioned officers could not be maintained during a long and costly war, but the soldiers of the Civil War armies, believing themselves citizens before they were warriors, were bitterly reluctant to yield up the privilege. In Bierce's case, his comrades were annoyed by a haughtiness of manner, partly acquired at the Kentucky Military Institute, and a bearing that would have done credit to a West Pointer. He wasn't one of those easygoing types who try to be a buddy to the men who serve under them. The moment he was handed his commission he became as peremptory as any Prussian sprig on the parade ground at Potsdam and expected to be obeyed with alacrity, and no furtive grins, by men who had been calling him "Brose" an hour before.

On the day after Christmas 1862, the Army of the Cumberland marched out of Nashville and into another nightmarish battle at Stones River, where the Confederate army under General Braxton Bragg came out of its winter camp at Murfreesboro to confront the Union forces. They were about evenly matched, and evenly they shed blood in the thickets bordering the river. At a climactic stage of the battle the Ninth Indiana was posted behind a railroad embankment when the Confederates unleashed a furious counterattack. The Ninth held firm, but its commander, Major J. D. Braden, an Elkhart blacksmith in civilian life, fell seriously wounded while directing the defense of the position.

Years later Major Braden would recall the incident for an Elkhart newspaperman. Lieutenant Bierce, he said, had always seemed "cold and unapproachable" to others in the regiment. When Braden was shot in the head, however, and seemed to be "choking in my own blood," Bierce lost all his reserve. "He knelt beside me," Major Braden recalled, "and gripped my hand in what we both thought was a last goodbye. I tell you he was crying like a little girl."[10]

Lieutenant Bierce picked up the major and carried him to safety under heavy fire.

Next day it appeared that the Army of the Cumberland had won the battle, but at a cost that almost made such victories prohibitive.

With an odd sense of detachment, Bierce could always find a measure of humor in the wreck of battle. Shortly after the battle of Stones River, when the army was tidying up various post-action affairs, a cavalry officer was courtmartialed for desertion in the face of the enemy and was sentenced to face a firing squad.

To save unnecessary labor, he was blindfolded and placed astride his coffin so he would fall neatly into it when the volley struck him. Just before the firing squad lined up, the officer insisted on conferring with its commander. The latter shook his head and the execution proceeded. Later Bierce, who did not shy away from such spectacles, asked the officer in charge of the firing squad what the condemned man asked of him. Cavalryman to the end, it seemed, he had asked that a saddle be placed under him on the coffin.[11]

In February 1863, Bierce was promoted to first lieutenant and attached to the staff of the brigade commander, General Hazen, as his acting topographical officer. Map-drawing, learned at the military academy, was one of his considerable talents along with a sharp eye for terrain and an ability to make tactical use of it.

The semisuccess of Stones River encouraged General William S. Rosecrans, now commanding the army, to drive Bragg's Confederates farther south. Ahead was some of the bitterest fighting of the war. The Army of the Cumberland drove ahead so relentlessly that the enemy was forced out of Chattanooga, a strategic railroad center, and his situation grew so critical that he was heavily reinforced by divisions from the Army of Northern Virginia. Despite the fact that Bragg was growing stronger in retreat, the Federal army continued its headlong advance. "We knew well enough that there would be a fight: the fact that we did not want one would have told us that, for Bragg always retired when we wanted to fight and fought when we most desired peace." By then Rosecrans's communications to the rear were disorganized and his three army corps scattered over the mountainous countryside.

Thus on September 20, 1863, the battle of Chickamauga began, and none in that war was harder fought. The reinforced Confederate army struck the Union forces when they were scattered in pursuit formation. As with most battles, it started with the sort of groping, hesitant gestures of belligerence Bierce described so aptly in one of his short stories: "The army's weapons seemed to share its military delinquency. The rattle of rifles sounded flat and contemptible. It had no meaning and

scarcely roused to attention and expectancy the unengaged parts
of the line-of-battle and the waiting reserves. Heard at a little
distance, the reports of cannon were feeble in volume and
timbre; they lacked sting and resonance. The guns seemed to be
firing with light charges, unshotted . . ."[12]

It didn't take the Confederates long to warm up. They drove a
wedge between the Union corps, and the Army of the Cumberland was soon fighting for its existence. One difficulty in the
Union command was that many of its generals were politically
ambitious. The army's chief of staff was the Ohioan James A.
Garfield, and there were others, equally aware that the road to the
White House might lead from the battlefields, who were intriguing against each other and the commanding general. The latter,
General Rosecrans, was in such a state of nerves that he would be
one of the first to flee the field for Chattanooga.

Bierce's own chief, General Hazen, had nothing but contempt
for most of his peers and superiors. "Grant, Sherman, Sheridan
and a countless multitude of the less eminent luckless had the
misfortune, at one time or another, to incur his disfavor, and he
tried to punish them all. . . . He convicted Sheridan of falsehood, Sherman of barbarism, Grant of inefficiency. He was
aggressive, arrogant, tyrannical, honorable, truthful, courageous
— a skillful soldier, a faithful friend and one of the most
exasperating of men. Duty was his religion, and like the Moslem
he proselyted with the sword. His missionary efforts were directed chiefly against the spiritual darkness of his superiors in
rank, though he would turn aside from pursuit of his erring
commander to set a chicken-thieving orderly astride a wooden
horse, with a heavy stone attached to each foot."[13] The only one
of the army's senior commanders for whom Hazen had any
respect was General George H. Thomas, a heavy-set, bearded
Virginian called "Pap" by his troops, a stolid, deliberate man
whose rocklike integrity as a man and a soldier was to be
demonstrated later that day. Bierce, a faithful echo where Hazen
was concerned, also considered General Thomas one of the few
honest, decent figures in high command.

Hazen's brigade was one of those lying in an exposed position

on the Union left when the Confederate army launched its
attempt to break up the Army of the Cumberland and destroy it
division by division. Early in the fight Hazen's batteries began
running out of ammunition, and Bierce was sent to forage for
some. "Finding an ordnance train I obtained from the officer in
charge a few wagons loaded with what I wanted, but he seemed
in doubt as to our occupancy of the region across which I
proposed to guide him. Although assured that I had just tra-
versed it, and that it lay immediately behind Wood's division, he
insisted on riding to the top of the ridge behind which his train
lay and overlooking the ground. We did so, when to my aston-
ishment I saw the entire country in front swarming with Confederates; the very earth seemed to be moving toward us! They
came on in thousands, and so rapidly that we had barely time to
turn tail and gallop down the hill and away, leaving them in
possession of the train . . . By what miracle that officer had
sensed the situation I did not learn, for we parted company then
and there and I did not see him again."[14]

That, in fact, was the assault column Bragg drove into the
Union lines. The whole Union right wing broke up and fled,
some for the rear, some to the left, where General Thomas's
corps was still intact. Bierce was among those who elected to
continue the resistance, though he disclaimed any credit for valor
in doing so. "There was no great heroism in it; that is what every
man should have done, including the commander of the army.
We could hear Thomas's guns going — those of us who had ears
for them — and all that was needful was to make a sufficiently
wide detour and then move toward the sound. I did so myself,
and have never felt that it ought to make me President. [The
sideswipe was directed at Garfield, who also joined Thomas in
that critical hour, and used it to good political effect.]" Bierce
was utterly disgusted at the way high officers led the pell-mell
retreat on the roads back to Chattanooga. ". . . on my way I
met General Negley, and my duties as a topographical officer
having given me some knowledge of the lay of the land offered to
pilot him back to glory or the grave. I am sorry to say that my
good offices were rejected a little uncivilly, which I charitably

attributed to the general's obvious absence of mind. His mind, I think, was in Nashville, behind a breastwork."[15]

Perhaps that ride through the thickets bordering Chickamauga creek provided the inspiration for his short story "Chickamauga." The story concerns a child who strayed into the woods from his home near the creek before the battle began. The boy was "playing soldier" when real war erupted all around him. Yet the six-year-old, preoccupied with his own game, played on. "The fire beyond the belt of woods on the farther side of the creek, reflected to earth from the canopy of its own smoke, was now suffusing the whole landscape. It transformed the sinuous line of mist to the vapor of gold. The water gleamed with dashes of red, and red, too, were many of the stones protruding above the surface, but that was blood; the less desperately wounded had stained them in crossing. On them, too, the child now crossed with eager steps; he was going to the fire." The child, still uncomprehending, came across dead men in the woods. "He waved his cap for their encouragement and smilingly pointed with his weapon in the direction of the guiding light — a pillar of fire to this strange exodus." The boy ran on until he reached the clearing where his home had stood. The pillar of fire came from the burning house in which he had lived. Nearby was his mother's body, the top of her head blown off. "The child moved his little hands, making wild, uncertain gestures. He uttered a series of inarticulate and indescribable cries — something between the chattering of an ape and the gibbling of a turkey — a startling, soulless, unholy sound, the language of a devil. The child was a deaf mute."

Bierce found the remnants of the Army of the Cumberland, Thomas's corps and various units which had fled to their left instead of the rear, holding a fairly strong position on Snodgrass Hill. He reported to General Thomas, who immediately attached him to his staff as an aide and dispatch rider. A short time later, by one of those freakish coincidences of war, the Eighteenth Ohio Light Artillery, in which his brother Albert was a battery commander, came galloping up to the new battle line. He and Albert held their first reunion since the start of the war while

Albert continued to direct the fire of his battery. Their conversation was interrupted momentarily when one of Albert's gunners was killed by a sniper. The brothers propped the corpse against a nearby tree.

As the tempo of the battle increased, with Confederates falling in windrows before the blasts of Union batteries well sited on the brow of Snodgrass Hill, his commander came up with what was left of their brigade. The singleminded Hazen's first remark to his staff officer was to inquire what had happened to the ammunition he'd sent Bierce for.

The only assignment General Thomas gave his temporary aide was to ride out the back-country road leading to the rear of Snodgrass Hill and keep a lookout for reinforcements. Gordon Granger's reserve corps had been posted in Rossville, several miles to the rear of the battle line, and it was expected that that doughty general would come to Thomas's assistance as soon as he realized what had happened. Snodgrass Hill by then was enveloped by the greatly superior Confederate forces, who felt that victory was in their grasp. If the Southern army could manage to surround Thomas's position and annihilate its defenders, the Confederacy would win its greatest victory of the war. Thomas's problem was to find enough infantry to extend his lines and protect the row on row of field guns, fired over open sights as fast as the gunners could swab them out and reload, which were taking an exorbitant toll of every Confederate assault column that presented itself on the slopes of Snodgrass Hill. It was therefore urgent that Granger's reserve divisions be brought into the horseshoe-shaped perimeter as swiftly as possible. The sun was setting; the enemy attacks were growing more furious and desperate; the Union army might be saved if it could hold out until nightfall.

So Bierce waited on the country road for the first signs of General Granger's approach, with orders from Thomas to deploy on the right flank of the Union position. "This was the way of it," Bierce wrote later. "Looking across the fields in our rear (rather longingly) I had the happy distinction of a discoverer. What I saw was the shimmer of sunlight on metal: lines of

troops were coming in behind us! The distance was too great, the
atmosphere too hazy to distinguish the color of their uniforms,
even with a glass. Reporting my momentous 'find' I was directed
by the General [Thomas] to go and see who they were. Galloping toward them until near enough to see that they were of our
kidney I hastened back with the glad tidings and was sent again,
to guide them to the general's position . . . It was General
Granger with two strong brigades of reserve, moving soldier-like
toward the sound of heavy firing."

With dusk falling, it became apparent that the defenders of
Snodgrass Hill couldn't hold out much longer. Both rifle and
artillery ammunition were so low that "had the Confederates
made one more general attack we should have had to meet them
with the bayonet alone. I don't know why they did not; probably
they were short of ammunition. I know, though, that while the
sun was taking its own time to set we lived through the agony of
at least one death each, waiting for them to come on." Night fell,
and the Union defenders' blood was curdled by a last defiant
Rebel yell from the thickets beyond the slopes of Snodgrass
Hill — "the ugliest sound that any mortal ever heard — even a
mortal exhausted and unnerved by two days of hard fighting,
without sleep, without rest, without food and without hope."[16]

After Chickamauga the battered Army of the Cumberland
withdrew to the defenses of Chattanooga, where they were
placed under siege by the Confederates. The siege lines were
loose enough to allow the Union army to be reinforced by Grant
and Sherman at the head of the Army of the Tennessee, which
had recently succeeded in taking Vicksburg. The Union strategy
was for its combined armies to break out of Chattanooga and
drive the enemy southward to his western citadel of Atlanta. The
breakthrough point was to be Missionary Ridge, fortified by the
Confederates and looking down on the Federal divisions maneu-
vering for the assault on its heights.

On November 24, 1863, the battle began with Pap Thomas
now in command of the Army of the Cumberland. Grant's idea,
as commander of the joint operation, was that his own army

would take Missionary Ridge while Thomas's army, in effect, ran interference for it. As it turned out, the Army of the Cumberland, furious over its semidefeat at Chickamauga, took the initiative from its commanders and stormed straight over Missionary Ridge, over the Confederate rifle pits, trenches and gun positions.

During a crucial phase of the battle, just before the Cumberlanders made their unordered and astonishing breakthrough, Bierce happened to be at general headquarters. Lordly as spectators at a sporting event, the generals were gathered on a hilltop watching the action in the amphitheater below: Grant, Sherman, Sheridan, Thomas — the victorious quadrumvirate of the Civil War gathered on one spot for the first and last time — as well as Granger, Wood and Bierce's own chief, Hazen. Bierce was amused to observe that the great chieftains, like ordinary mortals, resorted to alcohol in a moment of stress; that they were not totally occupied by weighty matters of strategy. A bottle of whiskey passed from one eminent bearded mouth to the other. "They looked upon the wine when it was red, these tall fellows — they bit the glass. The poisoned chalice went about and about." Of General Grant, he recalled, "I don't think he took enough to comfort the enemy — not more than I did myself from another bottle — but I was all the time afraid that he would, which was ungenerous, for he did not appear at all afraid that I would. This confidence touched me deeply." But then, as he also noted, it was a drinking man's war; "we did shed the blood of the grape and the grain abundantly during the war."[17]

Later in the day, presumably well braced for any violent encounters with the enemy, he was ordered by General Hazen to keep an eye on Colonel James C. Foy's Twenty-third Kentuckians and make sure they didn't stray out of the line of advance. It wasn't that the Kentuckians were craven, but their colonel was something of an eccentric. Several months earlier the regiment wandered off during a minor battle and Bierce was sent to find it. The regiment was "found about one-half mile away, utterly isolated and marching straight to kingdom come. Foy had not the slightest notion of where he was going to. 'What are you doing here, Colonel?' I asked, biting my lips to keep from laughing. He looked at me for a moment in a helpless and bewildered way, then pulled on a grave face and replied: 'Oh, I'm sort o' flankin' 'em.'" At Missionary Ridge, Bierce stayed with the regiment long enough to see its red battle flags fluttering in perfect alignment with the rest of Wood's division as it led the charge over Missionary Ridge.[18]

Early that winter, with hostilities practically in abeyance, Bierce was granted the first leave of his career. A first lieutenant at twenty-one, wearing a long dragoon's moustache, he went home to Warsaw, a considerable fellow at last in that small Indiana town. Considerable, too, in the eyes of Bernie Wright. In December 1863, around Christmastime, the lighthearted girl announced her engagement to Lieutenant Bierce. During the holiday season she, her fiancé and her sister Clara, acting as chaperone, attended various social functions around Warsaw. A few months later, when he had returned to the army, he wrote Clara Wright that he valued her almost as much as her sister. "You always seemed to think, Clare, that I never cared for you except as Tima's sister — a sort of unnecessary evil." At that, Bierce might have done better with the less frivolous Clara, who apparently took him, and his frequently grim moods, more seriously than the fun-loving, flirtatious Bernie.

In the same letter to Clara he expressed uneasiness over his relations with Bernie: "Ask Tima why I get no more letters from her. Have I offended her? I may have written something as heartless and cruel as I used to say to her. If I have I hope she will forgive me . . . Do you think there is a probability of my letters getting into other hands than hers? The thought troubles me very much." A few paragraphs down, he pointedly asked, "Is Joe Williams at W. [Warsaw]? The less you have to do with him the better you will please me."[19]

Obviously Bierce returned to duty a troubled and querulous suitor. There is no doubt that he was in love with Bernie — somewhat grandiloquently he wrote Clara that he would "renounce the whole world . . . throw away every ambition" for Bernie — but his possessiveness only irked his fiancée, who must have thought him an idiot for offering so much in return for so little.

By then a Union army group commanded by Sherman and including the Army of the Cumberland was engaged in its arduous campaign through northern Georgia, grappling every few miles down the railroad with the skillfully commanded enemy (General Joseph E. Johnston had replaced Braxton Bragg). Johnston kept retreating, but also was taking a heavy toll of the attacking Union forces. It was during the early stages of the Atlanta campaign that Bierce learned how callous and casual high commanders could be about the lives of their men. This lesson in military history was administered in the course of an engagement known as Pickett's Mill. General Sherman decided to attempt an end run around the Confederate army and attack it from the rear. Hours were lost in deploying the attacking force through a heavily wooded area, more than enough time to alert the enemy and allow him to make his own dispositions. Hazen's brigade was shrunken by casualties, down to a mere fifteen hundred men, yet it was selected to lead the attack. On receiving his orders from his superiors, Bierce noted, Hazen never "uttered a word . . . Only by a look which I knew how to read did he betray his sense of the criminal blunder." Bierce added:

"That, then, was the situation: a weak brigade of fifteen hundred men, with masses of idle troops behind in the character of an audience, waiting for the word to march a quarter-mile uphill through almost impassable tangles of underwood, along and across precipitous ravines, and attack breastworks constructed at leisure and manned with two divisions of troops as good as themselves."

The brigade, which would have numbered eight thousand at full strength, was slaughtered as soon as it emerged from the tanglewood and came within gunshot of the enemy lines. Even so Hazen's regiments advanced to within twenty paces of the Confederate fieldworks. "It is the perception — perhaps unconscious — of this inexplicable phenomenon [that Hazen's men got as far as they did without a single one actually leaping upon the enemy breastworks] that causes the still unharmed, still vigorous and still courageous soldier to retire without having come into actual contact with his foe," Bierce observed. "He sees, or feels, that he *cannot*. His bayonet is a useless weapon for slaughter; its purpose is a moral one. Its mandate exhausted, he sheathes it and trusts to the bullet. That failing, he retreats. He has done all that he could do with such appliances as he has."[20] By the time Hazen's brigade fell back almost seven hundred men had been killed, wounded or captured — almost half its strength. Bierce titled his account of that minor battle "The Crime at Pickett's Mill"; it constituted an indictment of the army commander, Sherman, and the corps commander, General Oliver O. Howard. Henceforth Bierce's patriotism would be not unalloyed by cynicism. He would be a military buff all his life, but he had a low opinion of generals who didn't even try to find out what they were sending their troops up against. Undoubtedly the event also contributed to his lifelong contempt for those established in power, whether military or civil, and his willingness to be always an outsider, a highly vocal and caustic critic of all in positions of authority.

A much more personal and deeply scored lesson in how men would use their power to their own ignoble ends was administered to Bierce a few weeks later when the Union armies confronted the enemy in a heavily fortified position at Kenesaw Mountain. The Confederates under Joe Johnston, a diligent fortifier, had converted Kenesaw Mountain into a fortress, employing thousands of Negroes and Georgia militia to cut fire lanes, dig deep trenches and build breastworks. They had also extended their lines to surrounding high ground to make a flanking maneuver difficult. An argument broke out among the Union commanders on how to assault the massive position. Thomas of the Army of the Cumberland urged that the enemy be outflanked. But that would take time and Sherman, the army group commander, was an impatient man; other than tactical considerations, or the safety of his troops, evidently weighed upon him. There was an election coming; General McClellan, favoring a comparatively soft line toward the Confederacy, was running against Lincoln; and in Washington it was felt that a great victory in the west, the destruction of Joe Johnston's army or the capture of Atlanta, might be the decisive factor. Also, according to a war correspondent at Sherman's headquarters, Sherman was disgruntled because Grant, now in command of the Army of the Potomac, was getting all the attention. Against the protests of his subordinates Sherman decided that a quick frontal assault would be launched against Kenesaw Mountain.

Late in June 1864, with the Army of the Cumberland leading the assault, the Union armies jumped off against the mountain "ringed with fire." In less than an hour, with hardly a dent made in the Confederates' defenses, twenty-five hundred Union soldiers had fallen. Among them was Ambrose Bierce. The only account of how it happened came from his immediate superior, General Hazen, who reported that on June 23 he had sent Bierce to direct the advance of the brigade's skirmish line: "While engaged in this duty, Lieut. Bierce was shot in the head by a musket ball which caused a very dangerous and complicated wound, the ball remaining within the head from which it was removed sometime afterwards."

The bullet had struck Bierce in the temple and then coursed around the side of his skull. He was carried out of the woods to a horse-drawn ambulance, which carried him to the railroad. There were no hospital trains then; the wounded were regarded almost as an expendable nuisance, and nursing was left to drunks and misfits hired by the Sanitary Commission. Bierce's head was bound up at a field hospital. Then he was placed aboard one of a long line of flatcars hauling the wounded back to the base hospitals in Chattanooga. They were protected only by tarpaulins. No one treated them on the long ride back to Chattanooga. Bierce afterward remembered that he regained consciousness on the jolting flatcar under a moon that shone with a cold merciless clarity. The moonlight bothered him more than the pain of his head wound. Later, when he awakened again, rain was falling; men were moaning and cursing all around him.

He spent about a month in the base hospital in Chattanooga, then was given a long furlough and went back home to Indiana. He still suffered considerably from pains in his head, which was still heavily bandaged when he returned to Warsaw, eager to straighten things out with Bernie Wright. Apparently the hero with a shattered head didn't appeal to her as much as the dashing officer of the previous winter. They quarreled, possibly over reports which had reached Bierce of her undoubtedly innocent flirtations. Undoubtedly, too, he knew they were innocent; but in one with his fierce pride the faintest suggestion of disloyalty from someone he loved was unbearable. And undoubtedly when the engagement was broken it was the best thing that could have happened to both parties. Ambrose didn't think so, and relieved his feeling in bitter, callow verse which referred to "tears of hopeless prayerless pain" and to his heart as a "gloomy cell of misery — heated toy of woman's art."[21]

On the surface it may have seemed merely another rustic romance, this one involving a wounded hero and a freckled flibbertigibbet, but after that Bierce never quite lost his suspicion of women as fickle and heartless. The simple, lighthearted country girl left a mark on him out of all proportion to her weight as a human being. Bernie Wright sank into small-town obscurity, unwittingly having contributed, in the years to come, to some of the bitterest antifeminist phrases ever written.

Bierce paid a very short visit to the family farm outside Warsaw. His brother Augustus later recalled that Ambrose came out one day with his head "all tied up." He moped around Warsaw, eager for the end of his medical furlough, and finally returned to duty in September before he was well enough for active service. His head still felt as though it had been "broken like a walnut." For the time being he was capable only of limited service "being then, as for many years afterward, subject to fits of fainting, sometimes without assignable immediate cause, but mostly when suffering from exposure, excitement or excessive fatigue."[22]

By September Atlanta had fallen to the Union armies which, however, failed to capture the opposing army. Sherman had set off on his march through Georgia, and Thomas, with a depleted Army of the Cumberland, was left to the dismal task of chasing after the Confederate army now commanded by General John B.

Hood. This pursuit resulted in much marching and counter-marching, all of it futile. Late in October, Bierce and his outfit were down in Alabama on the Coosa River. One Sunday, having little to do around headquarters, he and several companions decided to take a canter through the countryside. Unfortunately they wandered into the territory of a locally famous guerrilla chieftain named Jeff Gatewood, were ambushed and got separated in fleeing from the trap.

Bierce hid on an island in the swamp until sunset and was just leaving his hideout when he heard the click of a rifle being cocked. A moment later he was taken prisoner. Later he recounted:

"The history of this great disaster to the Union arms is brief and simple. A Confederate 'home guard' hearing something going on upon the island, rode across, concealed his horse and still-hunted me. And, reader, when you are 'held up' in the same way may it be by as fine a fellow. He not only spared my life, but even overlooked a feeble and ungrateful after-attempt upon his own (the particulars of which I shall not relate), merely exacting my word of honor that I would not again try to escape while in his custody. Escape! I could not have escaped a new-born babe.

"At my captor's house that evening there was a reception, attended by the elite of the whole vicinity. A Yankee officer in full fig — minus only the boots, which could not be got on to his swollen feet — was something worth seeing, and those who came to scoff remained to stare. What most interested them, I think, was my eating — an entertainment that was prolonged to a late hour. They were a trifle disappointed by the absence of horns, hoof and tail, but bore their chagrin with good-natured fortitude . . . No restraint was put upon me; my captor even left me with the women and children and went off for instructions as to what disposition he should make of me. Altogether the reception was a pronounced success, though it is to be regretted that the guest of the evening had the incivility to fall dead asleep in the midst of the festivities, and was put to bed by sympathetic and, he has reason to believe, fair hands."

Next morning he and another prisoner — "a most offensive

brute, a foreigner of some mongrel sort, with just sufficient command of our tongue to show that he could not control his own"— were taken on a long ride to the nearest army post. That night, however, while the others slept in a house along the way, Bierce slipped off and made his escape. He fled through swamps and thickets all that night and the next day, hiding when bloodhounds were loosed, feeding off raw sweet potatoes and persimmons, until he reached his own camp at Gaylesville. He stumbled into the circle of firelight outside the headquarters tent. " 'What is it, Cobb?' said the chief, who had not taken the trouble to rise. 'I don't know, Colonel, but thank God it is dead!' It was not."[23]

The final great battle in which Bierce was involved was at Franklin, Tennessee, during the last days of November 1864. By then the Army of the Cumberland had established itself at Nashville, where it awaited the last-hope onslaught of Hood's Confederate army. Bierce was serving on the staff of a division which, with several others, was almost cut off by Hood's swift advance. The Union divisions, confronted by three enemy corps, pulled back northward to Franklin before the enemy attacked the last day of November. It had all the signs of a last stand; behind them was the Harpeth River with all its bridges blown, and behind it the town of Franklin. "A mere bridgehead," Bierce called it. "It did not look a very formidable obstacle to the march of an army of more than forty thousand men."

Yet it was a most tranquil scene as the Union infantry lay in their shallow trenches. "Sleep was in the very atmosphere. The sun burned crimson in a gray-blue sky through a delicate Indian summer haze, as beautiful as a day-dream in paradise. If one had been given to moralizing one might have found material a-plenty for homilies on the contrast between that peaceful autumn afternoon and the bloody business that it had in hand."[24]

Bierce, not having entirely recovered from his ordeal in escaping Confederate capture or the head wound that preceded it, was largely a spectator at the battle.

In the opening phase the Confederates tore a huge gap in the Union line, which was repaired only by repeated counterattacks.

"Such devil's work does not last long, and we had the great joy to see it ending. . . . Slowly the mobile blur moved away from the town, and presently the gray half of it dissolved into its elements, all in slow recession. The retaken guns in the embrasures pushed up towering clouds of white smoke; to east and to west along the reoccupied parapet ran a line of misty red till the spitfire crest was without a break from flank to flank."

Then, as night fell, "The assailants began to give way. There was no general retreat; at many points the fight continued, with lessening ferocity and lengthening range; well into the night. It became an affair of twinkling musketry and broad flares of artillery; then it sank into silence in the dark."[25]

The Union divisions were permitted to disengage and continue their retreat to the defenses of Nashville. Two weeks later the Army of the Cumberland came storming out and shattered Hood's Confederates, the only army to be destroyed in the field during the Civil War.

The war ended the following spring. In the months between, Bierce slowly recuperated in the army's winter quarters at Huntsville, Alabama. At twenty-three he was a temporary captain in a temporary army. Civilian life stretched ahead of him without any great joy in the prospect. The war had been his education; he would always look back upon it as the high point of his life, and a quarter-century later would write:

"It was once my fortune to command a company of soldiers — real soldiers. Not professional life-long fighters, the product of European militarism — just plain, ordinary, American, volunteer soldiers, who loved their country and fought for it with never a thought of grabbing it for themselves; that is a trick which the survivors were taught later by gentlemen desiring their votes."[26]

THREE *Without a Carpetbag to His Name*

"I WAS ONE of those poor devils," Bierce once said, "born to work as a peasant in the fields, but I found no difficulty in getting out." True enough. A grateful government eased his passage from peasantry to gentry. Congress itself insisted that, since he was a commissioned officer, he must also be a gentleman. Not only that, but the President breveted him a major in recognition for his "distinguished" services. No one could deny that as a gentleman certified by Congress, with distinction attested to by the President, he was entitled to something better in civilian life than he had before. A brevet major could not be expected to go back to serving beer and sandwiches in the back room of Faber's or even to rejoin his family in working their farm.

The thought of returning to Warsaw apparently never crossed his mind. Bernie was still an aching memory, and the only member of the family he esteemed was his brother Albert, who did return to Warsaw, went into business, failed and soon would join his younger brother in California.

Bierce was given permission to resign his commission shortly before the war ended, but he didn't leave the government payroll. Probably through General Hazen's good offices, he jumped immediately into a job with the Treasury Department agency charged with confiscating enemy property. It was not a pleasant duty. He was stationed in Selma, Alabama, whose racial troubles of a century later may well have been heightened by memories of its destruction in the closing phase of the Civil War. General James Wilson's cavalry corps had descended upon the small city and literally destroyed it. Drunken cavalrymen looted and burned without interference from their officers; eight hundred horses and mules had been driven into the town and wantonly killed, leaving a stench that hovered over the town for months. When Bierce arrived to take up his duties as a Treasury agent, it was "little better than a ruin . . . the work begun by the battery had been completed by the torch. The conflagration generally was attributed to the negroes, who certainly augmented it, for a number of those suspected of the crime were flung into the flames by the maddened populace." Every Northerner was "horribly hated." Bierce himself was regarded as a carpetbagger or worse, since it was his task to seize what was left in the scorched and plundered countryside.[1]

As he explained his duties, which he frankly stated were "exceedingly disagreeable," he was one of a number of "agency aides" working under the special agent for that district. "In the Selma district the property that we were expected to seize and defend as best we might was mostly plantations (whose owners had disappeared; some were dead, others in hiding) and cotton. The country was full of cotton which had been sold to the Confederate Government, but not removed from the plantations to take its chance of export through the blockade. It had been decided that it now belonged to the United States. It was worth about five hundred dollars a bale — say one dollar a pound. The world agreed that that was a pretty good price for cotton."[2]

Bierce, rigorously honest for all his newly acquired cynicism about men and their motives, was plunged into a whirlpool of intrigue, violence and corruption. Cotton was being smuggled out on small steamboats navigating the Alabama and Tombigbee Rivers with pilots who received one hundred dollars a day for their services; the difficulty was in transferring it to deep-water vessels in Mobile Bay with a dozen gunboats on constant patrol.

The solution of Southerners and Northerners alike engaged in smuggling out cotton confiscated by the Treasury was bribery. The cotton runners bribed Treasury agents to hand over blank shipping permits signed by the agents. And when bribery wouldn't work the smugglers resorted to removing the unbribable by knife or gun. Obviously the way for a Treasury agent to stay alive, and even prosper in the process, was to accept the situation and its emoluments.

To be stiff-necked, as Bierce and a few others were, was to invite assassination. Alabama was under martial law, of course, but as Bierce pointed out, that was effective "only within areas covered by the guns of isolated forts and the physical activities of their small garrisons." He later wrote about his service in Alabama as a sleuth for the Treasury in often facetious terms, but his life was constantly in danger and he and his few incorruptible associates could only rely on the "immemorial laws of self-preservation and retaliation, both of which were liberally interpreted."

His own immediate superior, Captain Sherburne B. Eaton, also a former member of General Hazen's staff, arrived in Selma "just in time to act as sole mourner at the funeral of his predecessor — who had had the bad luck to interpret his instructions in a sense that was disagreeable to a gentleman whose interests were affected by the interpretation." Shortly after Bierce himself took up his duties two United States marshals, who had been helping the local Treasury agents confiscate cotton, were found in a ditch outside of town with their throats slashed. It was not at all rare, Bierce said, for his associates to disappear while out on a cotton-seizing mission. "Really the mortality rate among the unacclimated in the Selma district at that time was excessive. When my chief and I parted at dinner time (our palates were not in harmony) we commonly shook hands and tried to say something memorable that was worthy to serve as 'last words.' We had been in the army together and had many a time gone into battle without having taken that precaution in the interest of history."[3]

The special agents of the Treasury, Bierce admitted, were "not altogether spotless." He may not have been referring to his own superior, but one of Eaton's accountings to the Treasury read:

Cotton sold	$15,963.01
Total Receipts	$27,779.48
Total Expenses	$27,779.48

Bierce himself resisted temptation with a staunchness that would have won the dour approval of his Puritan ancestors.

At one time he was devoting all his investigative talents to tracking seven hundred bales of cotton which were supposed to have been cached near Selma. Two gentlemanly fellows approached him with hints that they knew where the cache was located. There followed a long feeling-out period in which Bierce and the two men took turns wining and dining each other. "We had early come to an understanding and a deadlock. Failing to get the slenderest clue to the location of the cotton I offered them one-fourth if they would surrender it or disclose its hiding-place; they offered me one-fourth if I would sign a permit for its shipment as private property."

Neither side would yield, despite lashings of champagne and sluicings of brandy. He and the two men finally conceded mutual defeat after an "unusually luxurious" farewell dinner. The cotton, if the cache really existed, and it probably did, was never found, but Bierce couldn't help "feeling a certain tenderness for men who know and value a good dinner."[4]

Another tempter was a rascal named Jack Harris, who divided his time between cotton-smuggling and serving as an undercover agent for the Treasury in exposing his rivals in the trade. He was a Californian with one of those unabashedly villainous characters, overlaid by a raffishly genial personality, whom Bierce could never wholeheartedly disapprove of; a swarthy, black-bearded bucko who was "ignorant with an ignorance whose frankness redeemed it from offensiveness, vulgar with a vulgarity that expressed itself in such metaphors and similes as would have made its peace with the most implacable refinement. He drank hard, gambled high, swore like a parrot, scoffed at everything, was openly and proudly a rascal, did not know the meaning of fear, borrowed money abundantly, and squandered it with royal disregard."

One day Jack Harris came to Bierce with a proposal. He knew

where a thousand bales of cotton were stashed, he said, and had made plans to smuggle it out of the country. All he needed was a little cooperation from Bierce, who was in charge of the Selma district during one of Eaton's frequent sojourns in New Orleans. Harris even entrusted Bierce with the details of his scheme. He had a steamboat ready, which would travel the river at night and pick up the cotton at various landings. Bierce knew he wouldn't impress the adventurer by expressing high moral outrage at the proposal, which included a generous cut for Bierce if he cooperated by signing some blank shipping permits, so he warned Harris that he would never be able to get his thousand bales out of Mobile Bay even if he managed to ship the contraband downriver. "He was astonished and, I think, pained by my simplicity. Did I think him a fool? He did not purpose — not he — to transship at all: the perfected plan was to dispense with all hampering formality by slipping through Mobile Bay in the black of the night and navigating his laden river craft across the Gulf to Havana! The rascal was in dead earnest, and that natural timidity of disposition which compelled me to withhold my cooperation greatly lowered me in his esteem, I fear." Bierce was not greatly surprised, years later, to hear that Jack Harris perished on the notorious *Virginius's* filibustering expedition against Cuba.[5]

His life as an agent of the Reconstruction that was markedly failing to reconstruct was not all stern duty, prowling the ruined plantations for hidden treasure, and rejecting proposals for his corruption. Fraternizing with ex-Confederates was often more enjoyable than being in the company of fellow Northerners, particularly of the carpetbag variety. He became friendly with two brothers named Charles and Frank, who had been Confederate officers, "glorious fellows . . . well-educated, brave, generous, sensitive to points of honor." The friendship was more valuable to Bierce than to the two brothers, for "an army with banners could not have given me the same immunity from danger, obstruction or even insult in the performance of my disagreeable duties." He began spending most of his off-duty time with Frank and Charles and their friends, and had come to feel an intense regret for having killed so many equally estimable men "in the criminal insanity that we call battle."

One night he and the brothers were returning home on a dark street when they noticed that they were being followed. Their shadow stopped when they stopped, turned when they turned, and seemed intent on dogging their footsteps. Finally they went back and cornered him with a demand that he stop following them. The stranger persisted. As they continued up the street, Bierce felt Frank's hand slip into his pocket and remove the pistol he was carrying. A moment later Frank turned suddenly and fired one shot. Their shadow went down with a bullet in his leg. Next day the man, who never explained his actions, had the shattered leg amputated. Bierce and the brothers paid his medical expenses, his hotel bill and his transportation back to Mobile. In addition, they were summoned before "an old gentleman of severe aspect," who was functioning as magistrate though as Bierce later learned he had no legal commission to undertake such duties. Frank was fined five dollars for disorderly conduct.

Bierce's opinion of the Reconstruction kept sinking the longer he stayed in the conquered South and the more he saw of the Federal measures to keep the wounds inflicted by war open and angry. There was a chivalrous element in Bierce's character, no doubt nurtured by the romantic literature he had absorbed in boyhood and youth, which took offense at the harsh treatment imposed on the recently beaten enemy. The issues which had brought on the war, he began to see, were not quite so simple, so purely a matter of right versus wrong, as he had been led to believe. During the war he had been disillusioned by the way high officers sacrificed the lives of their men, often through carelessness but more often in their eagerness to outshine a rival, to grab the glory in the reflection of which they hoped to attain political power after the fighting stopped. Now he saw some of the loudest idealists, who had proclaimed that the war had been fought to abolish slavery, enriching themselves at the expense of the former slaveholders and indulging their darker instincts by inflicting unnecessary punishment on the helpless ex-enemy.

His visits to occupied New Orleans, which had fallen under

the military rule of the bullet-headed General Sheridan, only reinforced his belief that the Union army, urged on by the Radical Republicans whose vengeful activities were no longer checked and restrained by President Lincoln, was tarnishing its war-won laurel by ruthlessly repressive measures. Bierce often journeyed to New Orleans to see ex-Captain Eaton, his superior, who found it more pleasant there than at his nominal head-quarters in Selma. General Sheridan, as proconsul of Louisiana and Texas, had imposed new laws which allowed only Negroes, carpetbaggers and the few Louisianans who had remained loyal to the Union to cast their ballots in any city or state elections. The result was a race riot in which thirty-eight Negroes were killed and forty-six injured. Sheridan and his paladins were also involved in a heated controversy over control of a four-million-dollar appropriation which was made to repair the levees wrecked during the war.

He loved New Orleans, its graceful streets and Creole charm, and would always value it above all other American cities. The activities of the Federal officers of the occupation outraged him all the more because of their ruinous effect on that gracious civilization. Thirty years later he wrote that what he witnessed in New Orleans and elsewhere in the occupied South contributed heavily to his disenchantment with humanity and his disengagement from the theory that it was guided by any sort of principles. "Time was, in that far fair world of youth where I went a-soldiering for Freedom, when the moral character of every thought and word and deed was determined by reference to a set of infinitely precious 'principles'— infallible criteria — moral solvents, mordant to all base metals, and warranted by the manufacturers and vendors to disclose the gold in every proposition submitted to its tenets. I have no longer the advantage of their service, but must judge everything on its own merits — each case as it comes up."[6]

Perhaps to escape temporarily from the misery and corruption he saw all around him, he embarked on a trip to Panama during a slack period in the affairs of the Selma district agency. Already conscious of a literary urge but rather poorly equipped to express it in the way of spelling and syntax, he kept a journal in which he recorded his impressions of Central America. On landing at Colon, "the first object that attracted my attention . . . was a groop of Cocoa Palms with the nutes thick upon them. The next thing that impressed me was the free and easy impudence of the black boys asking to carry my luggage . . . Filith universal the rude cleanliness in the dresses of the women formed a pleasing contrast . . . The throngs of great black buzzards sitting on every roof and tree, and hopping fearlessly about the offal strewn streets was in keeping with the general appearance." He took the train to Panama City across the Isthmus. "Tropical in earnest . . . everything growing so luxurious and on so jigantic a scale." Panama was "a quaint old town almost crowded into the sea. By the Mountains, sentinells were stationed at every car. They were slovenly negroes and looked quite unservisable . . ."[7] Yet in a few years, through a rigorous process of self-education, he made himself into the most meticulous of craftsmen and a stylist with firm control of the language.

Shortly after his return from Panama he received a letter from General Hazen offering him a post with an expedition Hazen had been ordered to undertake, exploring, surveying and mapping the country between Nebraska and California. Bierce would be attached to the party as "engineer officer," a quaint designation for a young man with no engineering experience or qualification whatever; his real purpose would be to act as Hazen's dog robber and companion. Or as Bierce himself put it, "to amuse the general and other large game." Hazen, in return, would attempt to secure a captaincy in the regular army for Bierce. The latter had no greater ambition, at the moment, then obtaining such a commission, which was far grander than a brevet major in the Volunteers. A professional soldier's career seemed the most he could expect out of life. Bierce accepted, with alacrity.

Meanwhile, late in 1865, he applied for relief from his post in the Treasury Department. Apparently he had to wait for several months until the bureaucrats in Washington chewed over his request to depart with honor, shuffled his papers from office to office, and lengthily considered the matter of his replacement.

While he was waiting to take leave of his duties as a Treasury hawkshaw, he had a last brush with the desperadoes who infested the swamps and bayous looking for an opportunity to plunder. So far he had escaped assassination, partly because the natives had come to consider him a decent enough fellow for a Yankee; but his comparative popularity couldn't save him from the organized bands of ex-soldiers who "did not consider themselves included in the surrender and conscientiously believed it both right and expedient to prolong the struggle by private enterprise."

Thus he became involved in a violent attempt at hijacking on one of the dark rivers which flow through the back country of southern Alabama. He and Eaton had collected six hundred bales of cotton, worth several hundred thousand dollars at the going price on the cotton-starved world market, and were taking it down the Tombigbee on a steamboat. Toward dusk they stopped at an army post on the river and picked up a dozen soldiers under command of a sergeant to act as their armed escort. Armed, but as they were to learn a short time later, ammunitionless. They were just rounding a bend in the river where the channel pushed them close to the left bank when they were fired upon from the brush lining the stream.

"The din of the firing, the rattle and crash of the missiles splintering the woodwork and the jingle of broken glass made a very rude arousing from the tranquil indolence of a warm afternoon on the sluggish Tombigbee," he would remember in later years. "The left bank, which at this point was a trifle higher than the hurricane deck of a steamer, was now swarming with men who, almost near enough to jump aboard, looked unreasonably large and active as they sprang from cover to cover, pouring in their fire."

The pilot had deserted the wheelhouse, the boat was drifting with the current, and bales of cotton from its deck were falling overboard. The captain and engineer were in hiding. Eaton ran to fetch and deploy the "armed" escort, which was found to have embarked without a cartridge among them.

That left the job of defending the boat against a boarding party from the shore to Ambrose Bierce, or at least that was the way he told it years afterward. "I happened to be on the hurricane deck, armed with a revolver, which I fired as rapidly as I could, listening all the time for the fire of the soldiers — and listening in vain." Bierce had to admit to himself that the situation was "somewhat grave." For him and Eaton, "capture meant hanging out of hand." The only favorable aspect was that the boat was drifting toward the mouth of a bayou; once they reached it, the hijackers would be unable to jump on board. Bierce searched out the captain, engineer and pilot; found them cowering in their cabins; and marched them back to their posts of duty with a now-empty pistol at their ears.

He then returned to the hurricane deck, which had been barricaded with bales of cotton, reloaded and continued to trade fire, at an increasing range, with the hijackers in the brush.

All this time he had been conscious that another gun, which sounded like a "small cannon," had been fired at frequent intervals from somewhere up forward on the boat. The slackening fire from the shore gave him the opportunity to find out who his unseen ally was — the only other man who had defended the boat. "While issuing a multitude of needless orders from the front of the hurricane deck I looked below, and there, stretched out at full length on his stomach, lay a long, ungainly person, clad in faded butternut, bareheaded, his long, lank hair falling down each side of his neck, his coat-tails similarly parted, and his enormous feet spreading their soles to the blue sky. He had an old-fashioned horse pistol, some two feet long, which he was in the act of sighting across his left palm for a parting shot at the now distant assailants." Thanks to his help, and Bierce's quick action, the boat's capture had been prevented and the casualties kept down to several men wounded. Then Bierce remembered that the man was a returning Confederate soldier who had been allowed to hitch a ride downriver to Mobile.

Bierce, after counting fifty-odd bullet holes in the pilothouse alone, went down to thank him, knowing that his natural sympathies would have been with the guerrilla band which had tried to hijack their cargo.

"But," Bierce added, "how the devil does it happen that *you* fight *that* crowd?"

"Well, Cap," the ex-soldier said, "I allowed it was mighty

clever in you-all to take me on, seein' I hadn't ary a cent, so I thought I'd jist kinder work my passage."[8]

Early in July 1866, Bierce joined General Hazen in Omaha for the survey westward. It did not promise to be a pleasure jaunt. Hazen was a vigorous young man of thirty-six and always inclined to dispense with the amenities. Their expedition would include, besides the two officers, only a cook and a teamster. Along the way they would occasionally pick up a cavalry escort at the nearest post when they came to a stretch of territory where the Indians were reported particularly restive about the increasing incursion of the white race. That summer the fighting tribes of the plains were, in fact, growing more hostile daily, and General Sheridan would shortly be summoned from his task of civilizing the Southerners to "pacifying" the dissident tribesmen with the assistance of that other eminent social worker, George Armstrong Custer. The railroads — Union Pacific moving west, Central Pacific inching east from Sacramento — had not yet been joined with the ceremonial gold spike in Utah. Between Nebraska and California was trackless Indian country. As Bierce put it, "I left the one road a few miles out of the Nebraskan village and met the other at Dutch Flat, in California." The only friendly faces they would see along the way, he thought, were those of the Mormon colony in Salt Lake City and various rude cavalry forts "where ambitious young army officers passed the best years of their lives guarding livestock and teaching the mysteries of Hardee's tactics to that alien patriot, the American soldier."[9]

General Hazen and his three-man "expedition," the report of which (written by Hazen) would be published by Congress, set out on the hot dusty wagon road leading up the Platte to Fort Kearney. It was "bordered with bones — not always those of animals — with an occasional mound, sometimes dignified with a warped and rotting headboard bearing an illegible inscription," such as "He done his damnedest." It was that brief postwar lull before hundreds of thousands of settlers, soon to be encouraged by the linking up of the railroads, came bursting out of the comparatively cramped East, North and South. But now the first pioneers were largely a memory. "Westward the course of empire had taken its way, but excepting these poor vestiges it had for some fifteen hundred miles left no trace of its march."

Bierce was enthralled by Court House Rock on the North Platte; "tipsy with youth, full-fed on Mayne Reid's romances, and now first entering the enchanted region that he so charmingly lied about, it was a revelation and a dream."[10] Once they had passed that landmark of the earlier western migration, he began making topographical maps of the territory they traveled through, the first he sketched being in the Dakotas as they stopped to inspect several forts. Hazen's written report and Bierce's maps, however, were such sketchy efforts that one suspects that the real purpose of the expedition, from the viewpoint of their superiors, was to get Hazen out into the wilderness and away from any publicity outlets into which he might pour his opinions on the way Grant, Sherman and Sheridan had conducted their campaigns. Hazen undoubtedly had the goods on them, having sat in high councils throughout the western campaigns, and worse yet was reckless enough to break the military code of silence in such matters. The news that Hazen, Bierce and party had been ambushed, fileted and barbecued by the hostiles would undoubtedly not have been an occasion for full mourning among their high-ranking colleagues.

When the party reached Fort Smith at the foot of the Big Horn Mountains, it was ordered in what Bierce called a "master stroke of military humor" to return to Washington by way of Salt Lake City, San Francisco and Panama. Instead General Hazen, whose tendency toward insubordination was shocking in a West Pointer, struck off on his own, turned northwestward and headed for Fort Benton up the Missouri in Montana Territory. Outside Fort Smith they encountered what Bierce described as a herd of buffaloes with an unusual proclivity: grazing on human hair. "We had to guard our camp at night with fire and sword to keep them from biting us as they grazed. Actually one of them half-scalped a teamster as he lay dreaming of home with his long fair hair commingled with the toothsome grass. His utterances as the well-meaning beast lifted him from the ground and tried to shake the earth from his roots were neither wise nor sweet, but they made a profound impression on the herd, which, arching its multitude of tails, absented itself to pastures new like an army with banners."[11]

General Hazen was contemptuous of the danger posed by hostile Indians, and almost seemed annoyed when they refused to attack his small party, now augmented by a cavalry detail and a guide named Jim Beckworth who had once been a Crow chief. The Indians' refusal to challenge his party indicated to Hazen that the typical tribesman was "a dirty beggar and thief who murders the weak and unprotected but never attacks an armed foe." His colleagues would soon find that the general underestimated the Indian.

Bierce apparently did not. Deep in Sioux country he had the eerie feeling that the Indians might attack as the party huddled around the campfire. As he described the scene and his feelings one night on the trail:

"The flame of a campfire stands up tall and straight toward the black sky. We feed it constantly with sagebrush. A circling wall of darkness closes us in; but turn your back to the fire and walk a little away and you shall see the serrated summitline of snow-capped mountains, ghastly cold in the moonlight. They are in all directions; everywhere they efface the great gold stars near the horizon, leaving the little green ones of the mid-heaven trembling viciously, as bleak as steel.

"At irregular intervals we hear the distant howling of a wolf — now on this side and again on that. We check our talk to listen; we cast quick glances toward our weapons, our saddles, our picketed horses: the wolves may be of the variety known as Sioux . . ."

Unapprehensive but curious, General Hazen asked their guide, "What would you do, Jim, if we were surrounded by Indians?"

"I'd spit on that fire," Beckworth replied.[12]

Nevertheless, occasional qualms aside, Bierce loved the West, and even more the idea of the West and its spacious freedom. Landscapes empty of humanity generally appealed to him. When those great spaces were constricted and the frontier shrank year by year, he was resentful of his fellow countrymen who ended that freedom, "riparian tribes once infesting the lowlands of Ohio and Indiana and the flats of Iowa," as he called them.

They were entertained with enthusiasm at the army posts along the way, the festivities at Fort Phil Kearney made poignant in retrospect by the fact that even as Hazen's expedition was traversing that country the Indians were "gathering their clans into one great army for a descent upon the posts we had left behind; a little later some three thousand of them moved upon Fort Phil Kearney, lured a force of ninety men and officers outside and slaughtered them to the last man."

The pleasurable aspect of that outing on the great plains diminished suddenly as they pushed on into the mountains, where game and water were much scarcer. "Where we swam the Yellowstone we had an abundance of both, for the entire river valley, two or three miles wide, was dotted with elk. There were hundreds.

"As we advanced they became scarce; bear, deer, rabbits, sage-hens, even prairie dogs gave out too, and starvation was a welcome state: our hunger was so much less disagreeable than our thirst that it was a real treat . . . If in all that region there is a mountain I have not climbed, a river that I have not swum, an alkali pool that I have not thrust my muzzle into, or an Indian that I have not shuddered to think about, I am ready to go back in a Pullman sleeper and do my duty."[13]

They staggered into Fort Benton, "a sorry-looking lot," and spent some days there recuperating for the next leg of their journey. No doubt, looking back on it, the pleasanter aspects of that journey were all the more poignant for the fact that the country would soon be spoiled forever; mining camps were springing up all over isolated Montana, and settlers would soon follow the adventurers and prospectors. The settlers already there seemed a scurvy lot, especially in comparison with the soldiers who protected them. "I have marked the frontiersman's terror-stricken hordes throng tumultuous into the forts before the delusive whoops of a dozen lurking braves. I have observed his burly carcass scuttling to the rear of the soldiers he defames, and kicked back into position by the officers he insults. I have seen his scruffy scalp lifted by the hands of the squaws, the while he pleaded for his worthless life, his undischarged weapon fallen from his trembling hands. And I have always coveted the privilege of a shot at him myself."[14] Heaven knows where he saw all that; when he crossed the plains and mountains in '66 none of the forts he and his companions visited were under attack by anything more vicious than mess waiters popping open the champagne, nor were there any settlers scuttling for the safety of those outposts.

From Fort Benton they traveled north to Helena, then south to Virginia City, and on to Salt Lake City. Mormonism was still generally unpopular in the United States, but Hazen and Bierce agreed it worked admirably as a politico-religious system for settling a new territory. Next to the Jews and the Chinese, Bierce considered the Mormons the worthiest "large class of people" in the melting pot. The attitude toward them elsewhere, he thought, was traceable to guilt over the persecutions inflicted on the Mormon settlers as they struggled westward through the lynch-minded Middle Border. The treatment given the Mormon migrants, he said, was "one of the most hateful and sneaking aggressions that ever disgraced the generally straightforward and forthright course of religious persecution."[15]

It was growing late in autumn as the Hazen expedition crossed into Nevada, paused to inspect Fort Churchill, twenty-five miles from the boomtown of Virginia City, then pushed on to skirt Lake Tahoe and negotiate the Sierra passes before winter closed in. Travelers in that country, that late in the season, were always spurred on to surmount the passes by the memory of the horrible fate of the Donner party less than twenty years before Bierce and his companions climbed the mountain barrier.

Their last bivouac before descending into California's more hospitable valleys was made, in fact, on the site of the Donner party's cannibalistic winter in the high pass. Bierce was naturally in his element spending the night in that once-ghastly vale. In his account of it much later he recalled the "flickering lights and dancing shadows" cast by their campfire. Around it, for the first time, he heard the story of the Donner party and its grim, if necessary, subtraction. As the meat roasted over the fire, he imagined that "I could detect something significantly uncanny. The meat which the Donner party had cooked at that spot was not quite like ours. Pardon: I mean it was not like that which we cooked."[16]

FOUR

San Francisco: First Interlude

EXHILARATION must have mounted in Bierce the day, late in 1866, the Sacramento River boat he and his companions were traveling on, approaching its destination, negotiated the Carquinez Strait and steamed into the waters of San Francisco Bay. Humped on the horizon was San Francisco, even then a fabled city with its legend of overnight fortunes, millionaires in red flannel undershirts and Nob Hill mansions with stables built of marble. It is doubtful, however, that he realized his fate lay in that city on the hills.

There was bad news awaiting Hazen and Bierce when they picked up mail and messages at the Presidio. The general had promised that he would secure Bierce a captaincy in the regular army, perhaps not quite realizing how much his abrasive personality had limited his influence in the bureaus of the War Department. A message from the adjutant general's office stated that Bierce could be offered a commission only as a second lieutenant in the Fifth Infantry. Both Hazen and Bierce were outraged. "Ingratitude," said Bierce, "more strong than traitors' arms, vanquished me."[1]

Actually it wasn't so much "ingratitude" as an oversupply of officers left over from the Civil War. Just then the "benzine boards," army tribunals formed to thin out the officers' corps, were in session. Practically every serving officer had to take a sharp reduction in rank, no matter how much glory he had won or influence he had acquired. Even Custer, with Sheridan and Grant as his patrons, had to trade in the twin stars of a major general for the silver leaves of a lieutenant colonel as the status of officers was adjusted from Volunteer to Regular; there were brigadiers "busted" to second lieutenants, colonels reduced to sergeant's stripes, and many were simply discharged. Bierce, as a brevet major, was rather fortunate to be offered a commission at all.

Perhaps during their months in the wilderness Hazen and Bierce hadn't heard of the benzine boards or their indignation wouldn't have been so great. Bierce decided to reject the offer and make his way in civilian life; thus he "parted from Hazen more in sorrow than in anger," and stayed in San Francisco.

Later he wrote mockingly of what might have happened if he had stayed in the army. "I have thought since that this may have been a youthful error: the Government probably meant no harm, and if I had served long enough I might have become a captain. In time, if I lived, I should naturally have become the senior captain of the Army; and then if there were another war and any of the field officers did me the favor to paunch a bullet I should become a junior major, certain of another step upward as soon as a number of my superiors equal to the whole number of majors should be killed, resign or die of old age — enchanting prospect!"[2]

Actually he might have found a more tranquil life if he had stayed with Hazen and returned to Washington as ordered, and might have encountered less personal tragedy if he had fled from San Francisco in any case. He would have served out his years, perhaps never rising above the rank of captain, during the army's long slumber (and deterioration) between the Civil War and the Spanish-American War. It is easy to imagine him as a growingly cantankerous disciplinarian in the lonely frontier forts, an elderly company commander given to overindulgence in books and whiskey and reminiscence of Chickamauga and Missionary Ridge. Perhaps it was the intuitive glimpse of just such a fate that made him seize the opportunity to turn down the army's offer. If character is destiny, Ambrose Bierce was never made to wither away in the obscurity of a peacetime army.

From Clark's Landing, where Bierce disembarked from the Sacramento River packet, to the heights of Nob Hill, San Francisco throbbed with life and energy. It had come out of the Civil War prosperous from helping supply the Union armies and from the rivers of silver and gold flowing down from the California foothills and the Nevada desert. Of San Francisco in the late Sixties, Bayard Taylor, himself a certified forty-niner, wrote in *El Dorado*, "The very air is pregnant with the magnetism of bold, spirited, unwearied action, and he who but ventures into the outer circle of the whirlpool, is spinning, ere he has time for thought, in its dizzy vortex."

The newcomer, however, took some time to reach the "dizzy vortex" of the city's social and intellectual life. First he had to find a job. Officers at the Presidio tipped him off that the post of night watchman at the United States Mint was open. His excellent record as a confiscator of enemy property in Alabama certainly would recommend him to the Treasury Department. A short time later he was awarded the post, which paid fifteen hundred dollars a year and certainly did not greatly tax the energies of a man of twenty-five. He shared rooms with a fellow Treasury employee named Elisha Brooks, who later testified that his fellow workers found Bierce an oddly self-sufficient character with a prickly sense of pride and dignity. Fellowship wasn't in his line, as his fellow soldiers had learned, though he could unbend and thaw out quickly enough in a barroom.

Even then, in what he called his "green and salad days," he was bitterly contemptuous of beliefs other people held sacred. The "Bitter Bierce" of later legend had even then begun his crystallization. Bierce, said Elisha Brooks, was a pleasant enough companion "if you could tolerate his denunciation of all religions and his habit of using the most offensive language in speaking of matters that people usually regard as sacred. He would never allow you to differ from him in his views of religious or sacred matters . . ."[3]

Early in 1867, while employed at walking the corridors and grounds of the Mint at night with his dark lantern and service revolver, he made up his mind to become a writer. That ambition had, of course, been stirring in him since boyhood. Doubtless it was revived and invigorated by the literary atmosphere of San Francisco in those postwar years, when the city became the hothouse of the "new" Western school of writing which was then imposing itself on the consciousness of the nation, just a little weary of the cold elegance and rigidly formal style of the literary Brahmins of Boston. The reading public was demanding something livelier, if cruder; fresher and truer to life, if less elevating. And San Francisco of the late Sixties was well-equipped to supply the demand. Mark Twain was a lank, red-haired journalist even then turning from police court assignments to a more literary form of expression. Bret Harte, the well-tailored, slightly supercilious young New Yorker who had come out before the war and wandered the foothills in the last stages of the gold rush, was secretary to the superintendent of the Mint and winning recognition, even in the East, for his satirical sketches in the San Francisco periodicals. Joaquin Miller and Charles Warren Stoddard were contributing verse to those same journals. Ina Coolbrith was being acclaimed as the greatest female poet since Sappho. Prentice Mulford, Clarence King and others were making their mark. The *Californian*, the *Golden Era*, the *News-Letter* and even the columns of the daily newspapers were the proving ground of this new and more forceful school of Western writing. San Francisco itself was culture-conscious, as proud of a Harte or Twain as of its silver magnates.

A few months after Bierce went to work at the Mint, according to Brooks, he began bringing home stacks of books from the library. He was conscious of his deficiencies in formal education and was cramming himself with literature and history. Brooks afterward recalled for a Bierce biographer that he waded through Gibbons's multivolumed history of the decline of the Roman Empire and expressed approval of the Englishman's style. Burke, Spencer and Pope were other guideposts in his attempts to attain a style of his own. In rehearsal for a literary career, he wrote a number of tracts defending atheism, which went unpublished but which he circulated among his fellow employees at the Mint with all the fervor of his missionary sister distributing Bibles to the African heathen.

He also drew sketches and cartoons for the amusement of his friends and co-workers. The 1867 election campaign attracted his waspish pen, which produced a series of cartoons ridiculing the pretensions of the candidates on both sides. A fellow employee collected them, divided them into two sets, and sold them to the rival parties to be published and used against each other. Outraged when he heard about it, Bierce cooled down only after his unofficial agent split the eight-hundred-dollar takings with him. After that, however, he quit cartooning; the possibility of being nailed by a libel suit evidently persuaded him that it was safer to confine his talent for satire and ridicule to the written word.

Between working, reading and writing, he found time to explore the fascinating, cosmopolitan city. It was an endless spectacle: the carriages driving to Cliff House; Lillie Coit, the unconventional society belle, dashing off to fires under a big brass helmet as the honorary member of Knickerbocker Fire Company No. 5; corner loafers setting upon the Chinese and beating them up or cutting off their pigtails; the lecture halls crammed with messiahs offering spiritual, social and economic panaceas to overflow audiences; the mining speculators thronging Montgomery Street; budding demagogues making their pitch from soapboxes in the vacant sandlots near City Hall. When the notorious Juan Salazar was publicly hanged, Bierce, of course, was on hand. "The sheriff," he later wrote, "performed his peculiar duties with a skill and dignity that made one rather covet the distinction of being hanged by him. Salazar assisted with intelligent composure, and the spectators, who had repented of his crime, endured his death with Christian fortitude and resignation."[4]

He also spent a lot of time hanging around the bar and public rooms of the Russ House, a four-story wooden hotel that occupied the block on Montgomery between Pine and Bush Streets. The hostelry was favored by ranchers, cattlemen, big-time gamblers; not the best people, perhaps, but the people who knew how to live the best. One of the hotel's shops was the Diamond Palace, a jewelry store entirely paneled by mirrors described by a local historian as "*the* jewelry store of the town, the one at which the wives, daughters and — not infrequently — the mistresses of affluent citizens indulged their taste for . . . pearl necklaces, gem-studded coronets and diamond tiaras."[5] The free-wheeling atmosphere, like that of the St. Charles in New Orleans, appealed enormously to young Bierce. He soon gave up rooming with the staid Elisha Brooks and moved into the Russ House himself.

By late in 1867, less than a year after his arrival on the coast, Bierce had begun writing for publication. His first acceptable efforts were bits of verse published in the *Californian*, one a highly romantic poem with an "opal chalice brimming gold," another attempting a definition of the mystery of life and an explanation of pain, "the payment in blood for each wish we attain."

He soon came to the reluctant but sensible conclusion that he was not capable of writing serious poetry, but would never cease to regard himself as an expert on the work of others. His talents, he decided, were more adaptable to the wildly humorous and hyperbolic efforts of such new writers as Bret Harte and Mark Twain. Their style has been described by the late Idwal Jones as "a fusion of the whimsical and the bombastic," combined with a studied irreverence toward established people and institutions. San Francisco editors encouraged all sorts of assaults on the beliefs of their stuffier fellow citizens. Bret Harte was busy condemning the fashionable habit of blaming the Chinese for everything that went wrong, the glorification of outlaws, and even the sainthood accorded the forty-niners, whom Harte claimed were simply "damned fools who landed here when the water came up to Montgomery Street." Twain was equally vigorous in defacing the long-worshiped totems of respectable San Franciscans. James W. Watkins, the managing editor of the San Francisco *News-Letter*, a literary weekly to which Bierce was soon to become a star contributor, even attacked the city itself as situated on a foggy strait, intolerant in its attitudes, crime-ridden and smugly provincial. California boosterism did not thrive on the printed page around San Francisco.

Well and good for Ambrose Bierce, who was all too eager to fill the role of naysayer, critic, gadfly, deflater of the collective ego. If it was satire they wanted, Bierce was confident that his pen had a cutting edge equal to any. It was necessary, of course, to abandon his early models. Later he claimed that he read Twain to "sharpen lethiferous wit against bovine humor." Toward his other mentor, Harte, whom he came to dislike personally for his lordly manner, he was more grateful. Harte's humor was "incomparable," and though the "flight of his genius" was always confined to a narrow space "it beats the air with as strong a wing as when it first sprang away."

During the spring and summer of 1868, Bierce was selling articles and essays to the *Californian*, the *Golden Era* and the *Alta California*. The subjects of these short journalistic pieces ranged from the Piute Indians he had seen in Utah to "The Tresses of the Fair Ladies."

During this period he also began contributing to the *News-Letter*, the satirical weekly, particularly its "Town Crier" page, which featured brief stinging paragraphs directed at the more pompous personalities around the Bay and jolting little essays on the more obnoxious foibles of the citizenry. The *News-Letter* was published by F. A. Marriott, an Englishman who had been editor of the London *Illustrated News* and *Morning Chronicle*, and edited by a veteran of New York and London journalism, James Watkins. Its forte, supposedly, was polite malice and sophisticated humor. By summer of 1868, however, most of the readiest wit in town was being employed in turning out the first issues of the *Overland Monthly*. The chief wit, Bret Harte, was himself employed as the *Overland*'s editor and had enlisted Twain, Stoddard, Coolbrith, Mulford and all the most promising young talent in and around town.

Marriott and Watkins realized that if they hoped to keep their readership against this new monthly competition they would have to enliven the "Town Crier" page, which was the *News-*

Letter's chief editorial asset. The more or less established talent wasn't available, so editor Watkins began culling the various contributors of "Town Crier" paragraphs. The brightest, if not the most polished, were submitted by one A. G. Bierce (Bierce's byline of the moment, since he equally detested his first name and his second, Gwinett). More in despair than in hope, perhaps, Watkins sent a note to Bierce asking him to drop around the *News-Letter* office. Bierce did so immediately; no editor had as yet considered him interesting enough to summon.

Watkins took an immediate liking to young Bierce and decided that he could be groomed to supply most of the "Town Crier" page. Thus began Bierce's real education as a professional writer. Watkins, a gentle and scholarly man for a roving journalist, and one with an unusual appreciation of the English language, its precise and proper employment, labored over every sentence Bierce submitted. He saw that Bierce possessed the savagery necessary to the unsparing social critic; also the intrinsic wit. What the young man needed to learn was how to control them. To be effective he had to learn to use the cutting edge of his sword rather than the flat of it.

Watkins insisted that the tyro read Swift and Voltaire to learn what could be done with controlled savagery, and Thackeray's sketches in *Punch* for a smooth style that would make his criticisms of the local scene more palatable to readers less indignant than their author. He also pointed out to Bierce that to be compelling his work must possess an interior rhythm that would carry the reader along with its cadence; for this he recommended a re-reading of Shakespeare's dramatic blank verse. Vulgarity must be pruned out — this was a tendency Watkins had noticed in Bierce's paragraphs attacking contemporary mores with more vigor than taste. Good taste could not be taught, must be acquired, but was essential. Bierce, in brief, must lay down the bludgeon and find a more delicate weapon.

Then and later Bierce looked upon Watkins as his literary commander, as General Hazen had been his military preceptor. In both men, undoubtedly, though unconsciously, he was looking for a substitute for his real father, the wife-dominated failure whom he could never respect. He soaked up everything Watkins could teach him, and later said with considerable exaggeration that Watkins was "one of the greatest writers of English that ever lived."[6] Years after both men had parted from the *News-Letter* and from each other, Watkins continued to read Bierce's work with an editorial eye. In a letter to Bierce written in 1874 he shrewdly noted that Bierce's method was that of the great French satirists and epigrammatists, but behind it was "the real English (or American) thought, and you give us the net result of its processes phrased with the Frenchman's wit and point and epigram."

Bierce began contributing regularly to the *News-Letter* in midsummer of 1868, and the "Town Crier" columns took on a new pungency. Since the contributions to that page were all anonymous it is impossible to single out Bierce's, but many were indubitably marked by his unbuttoned style.

In December of 1868, when Watkins decided to return to New York, Bierce had proved such an apt pupil in his one-man school that he replaced Watkins as managing editor and conductor of the "Town Crier" page. Publisher Marriott apparently gave his twenty-six-year-old editor free rein; his own interests, now that the *News-Letter* was a profitable operation, were centered on the Aerial Steam Navigation Company. The weekly's profits, in fact, supported the company and made it possible for Marriott to continue experimenting with a steam-driven airplane. In 1869 Marriott exhibited his Flying Aviator, a model of his dream plane, at the Mechanics Fair, but like the Zeppelins, triplanes and other oddities of the age of aerial pioneering it was superseded by less fanciful designs.

Unrestrained by Watkins's principle that good taste should be more important than even the most devastating witticisms, the columns of the *News-Letter* under Bierce's editorship were soon shooting off Roman candles that lighted up the San Francisco literary scene and were observed from afar. The *Nation* called the Town Crier the "most impudent and most irreverential person on the Pacific Coast" with "a Rabelaisian audacity which stands abashed at but very few things indeed." The New York *Arcadian* observed that the *News-Letter* was "pervaded by a new and puzzling flavor that was a combination of eccentric wit and utterly unconventional form." In England, the *Saturday Review* and the *Spectator* were quoting some of Bierce's more pungent paragraphs. San Francisco itself became immediately aware of a Town Crier whose weekly message was "expressed with the outspokenness of a Rabelais, the irreverence of a Heine, and the misanthropy of a Swift."[7] Many of Bierce's observations were palatable only to those who agreed that pain, violence and death could be uproariously funny; it took an Olympian sense of humor indeed to appreciate many of Bierce's essays in the macabre.

Street crimes were all part of the passing show in postwar San Francisco. Butchertown thugs and Market Street dandies alike delighted in maiming each other. Their activities were reported in detail in the daily newspapers, of course, but Bierce recounted them on the "Town Crier" page with the lip-smacking gusto of a connoisseur. A sampling of his comments during 1869 included:

"The Italians continue their cheerful national recreation of stabbing one another. On Monday evening one was found badly gashed in the stomach, going about his business with his entrails thrown over his arm.

"A man in Vermont was recently hanged by the neck until he was dead, dead, dead, and for the trifling offense of stealing another's shirt. He had previously removed the head that the garment might not be soiled with hair oil.

"One day last week a woman at the Brooklyn Hotel attempted to refute some imputations against her character by passing through an ordeal of arsenic. She was speedily pumped dry by a meddling medico, and her chastity is still a bone of contention.

"Ratsbane is winning golden opinions upon all sides, as a perfectly safe and efficacious specific for life's fitful fever.

"On last Sunday afternoon a Chinaman passing guilelessly along Dupont Street was assailed with a tempest of bricks and stones from the steps of the First Congregational Church. At the completion of this devotional exercise the Sunday-scholars retired within the hallowed portals of the sanctuary, to hear about Christ Jesus, and Him crucified."

Religious institutions, and the activities of their practitioners, also came under the Town Crier's sustained and highly skeptical scrutiny. This was not as daring as it may seem, since California journalism had long been permissive on the subject of atheism. Ribbing a clergyman was considered fair game in many periodicals, though they were rarely drubbed with such calefactory enthusiasm as Bierce brought to the task. Religious belief, he asserted, was definable only as "the church member's ticket entitling him to a reserved seat in the dress circle of heaven, commanding a good view of the pit." A Methodist publishing company in the throes of a scandal over missing funds also drew his unsympathetic attention, and he advised its overseers that it "will never be decently managed until the elect are all turned out, and it passes into the hands of secular thieves who have sense enough to cover up their rascalities with something more opaque than the cloak of religion."

He also offered mock prayers for the benefit of the pious in his congregation. "O, Lord, who for the purposes of this supplication we will assume to have created the heavens and the earth before man created Thee; and who, let us say, art from everlasting to everlasting; we beseech Thee to turn Thy attention this way and behold a set of the most abandoned scalawags Thou hast ever had the pleasure of setting eyes on." The Town Crier also prayed that "in consideration of the fact that Thou sentest Thy only-begotten Son amongst us, and afforded us the felicity of murdering him, we would respectfully suggest the propriety of taking into heaven such of us as pay our church dues, and giving us an eternity of exalted laziness and absolutely inconceivable fun. We ask this in the name of Thy Son whom we strung up as above stated. Amen."[8]

In a section of the "Town Crier" page titled "Telegraphic Dottings" he offered brief comments in acerb juxtaposition that served as a rundown on the previous week's events: "Secretary [of the Treasury] Boutwell has great difficulty in ascertaining the condition of financial affairs. Let him do it by making his annual report; that's the usual way.–.–.Carl Schurz allowed himself to gently drift over Niagara Falls. It was the wrong Carl Schurz after all. [Schurz, a Civil War general, later Secretary of the Interior, had incurred Bierce's hostility.].–.–.The usual catalogue of casualties and inequities. Men shot, women stewed, children mangled. Most of these incidents occurred in Chicago.–.–.Pioneers are doing well. Only three died of delirium tremens, and two got choked with lies of '49.–.–.The average morality of the country has been increased by the death of two Kentucky sheriffs, killed in action.–.–.Stedman, Collector of Internal Revenue at New Orleans, behind in his accounts $600,000. He'll do.–.–.Governor Walker of Virginia is inaugurated. There! That's the last we shall hear of him until he is arrested for stealing.–.–.The usual miners' strike.–.–.[President] Grant in Wheeling. He put the wrong end of the cigar in his mouth and has not spoken a word for a week.–.–.Administration will follow a course in Cuban matters based on public opinion. Ba-a! Ba-a!"

In the local section of his dot-dash résumé of the week's misfortunes and tragicomedies, he would record: "Woman fell in the sewer. Sweets to the sweet.–.–.Man hanged himself in his barn.–.–.63 persons went to Heaven in July.–.–.187 couples married in July. The nights have been uncomfortably warm.–.–.Successful abortion. The woman died.–.–.Several babies staved off .–.–.Mr. Bancroft is about to build a new sty on Market Street.–.–. French priest has abandoned the errors of the Romish for those of the Protestant Church.–.–.Olympic [Club] muscle men elected performing and executive apes.–.–.The weekly rape is of a milder nature. Money will settle it this time.–.–.An insurance company was robbed. Tit for tat.–.–.Assorted incendiarism.–.–. Miscellaneous grand larceny.–.–.Young ruffians insult school girls. School girls like it.–.–.Frightful atrocities of Chinese. Theft and murder of a hen.–.–, Pioneer's going East. Our credit is ruined."

He lashed out in all directions as the *News-Letter*'s resident moralist and social critic. The smell of graft, though perfumed by protestation of progress and civic betterment, was quick to reach his nostrils. "The Nicholson pavement," he observed, "is still being laid upon divers of our streets. Will someone kindly inform us what private arrangements the supervisors have with the company? Twenty-eight cents per superficial foot leaves a handsome profit, and it is useless to attempt to convince us that it all goes to the contractors." Childhood was anything but sacred as far as the Town Crier was concerned. "The fact that boys are allowed to exist at all is evidence of a remarkable Christian forbearance among men — were it not for a mawkish humanitarianism, coupled with imperfect digestive powers, we should devour our young, as Nature intended." The athletes who held forth at the Olympic Club drew only his contempt, as did all forms of organized games, "manly arts, noble games and national sports." For athletes, he said, he had all the "lofty compassion of an owl for a blind puppy in a dark cellar."

Nor did his fellow journalists, or their calling, escape his scorching invective. Michael H. De Young, publisher of the *Chronicle*, was simply "a liar, a scoundrel and, perhaps, a coward." He picked up a quotation from a pompous editorial in the *Call*, "The best bond is a man's unsullied reputation." Bierce agreed, but "how the deuce can he have one in a city that boasts six daily newspapers, averaging three columns of local matter each? The thing is impossible."

Antifeminism was another favorite theme on the "Town Crier" page. Male readers were warned that "There is positively no betting on the discreet reticence of any woman whose silence you have not secured with a meat-ax."

Those in public office were kept under a particularly watchful eye, and the Town Crier's tendency to blab must have made miserable the home life of many an office holder. A delegation of prominent citizens, he reported, went down to greet a shipload of prostitutes from China. The sing-song girls were put up at a leading hotel (the Occidental, oddly enough) by their greeters, and were being shown the sights of San Francisco by the mayor and members of the board of Supervisors.

Something of a scandal erupted over the charges that a candidate for the board of education — which Bierce constantly railed at, along with the ineptness of the public schools — had been consorting with a prostitute. The man should be elected, he declared; it would result in a victory for morality because "No respectable harlot who cares for her reputation would continue her acquaintance with a man who had been elected to the Board of Education."

The editorial barbs he threw around town, his enthusiastic adoption of the role of devil's advocate, did not lessen his personal popularity. On the contrary, he became something of a celebrity, not only in literary circles but in more socially exclusive ones. It didn't frighten hostesses that he was becoming known as "the wickedest man in San Francisco." He was accounted one of the handsomest men in town, with almost angelic good looks. He was a six-footer, with an erect carriage, a mop of curly golden hair, a sweeping gunfighter's moustache, fierce blue eyes and baby-pink cheeks. There was no doubt of his "magnetism," as it was then called. One admiring female claimed she could *feel* his presence from ten feet away. He was so cleanly that one of his male friends said that "Ambrose looks as if he shaved all over every day." And he had enough vanity to dress as well as any man in town, except possibly Bret Harte, the artistic delight and financial ruin of more than one tailor.

A clever young writer in those days was relentlessly lionized, not only in the literary salons of Russian Hill but in the drawing rooms of neighboring Nob Hill; but Bierce felt easier in the company of fellow journalists and writers. His prankishness and occasionally heavy bouts with the bottle could be given freer play at the bar of the Russ House and others frequented by members of his calling. Among his favorite companions were Jimmy Bowman, a hard-drinking and determinedly Bohemian writer, and Charles Warren Stoddard, who was achieving success under Bret Harte's tutelage. Stoddard was a wispy youth with a delicate manner; "such a nice girl," as Mark Twain called him. Yet he must have been made of sterner stuff than Twain believed in order to be accepted as a fellow tankard-man by the likes of Bierce and Bowman.

One New Year's Eve, Bierce and two other young men, after drinking the night away, decided to strike Christianity a cracking blow. Atop one of the hillsides in Golden Gate Park was a huge wooden cross erected by the pious during the Christmas season. The trio, equipped with ropes and kindling, climbed the hill swearing to destroy that symbol of slavish devotion. When morning came, and friends to whom they had boasted of the project went to see what had happened, the three were found tangled in the ropes and bound to the cross. In their drunken incompetence, they had tied the ropes to themselves, then to the cross, and had tried to haul it down like a three-mule team. Instead they ended up roped to the cross like a trio of Christian martyrs. Roaring with laughter, their rescuers drew the obvious, ironic parallel.[9] Bierce didn't think it a bit funny. Like most devotees of the practical joke, he resented being the object of humor.

With the two leading literary nabobs of San Francisco Bierce was now on fairly friendly terms, more so with Harte than with Twain. Harte, as editor of the *Overland Monthly*, contracted with Bierce to write a series of sketches titled "The Grizzly Papers" and signed "Ursus" for that periodical. He also accepted Bierce's first published short story, "The Haunted Valley," significantly enough an essay into the macabre, which told how a psychopath went about frightening a lonely miner to death. When Harte wrote his celebrated poem "Plain Language from Truthful James," which became better known as "The Heathen Chinee," he thought it wasn't worthy of being published in the *Overland*, which he was trying to cast in the image of the *Atlantic Monthly*. He took the poem to Bierce, in whom friendship triumphed over editorial acquisitiveness. Bierce told Harte he'd be a fool not to publish it in the *Overland*. Harte took his advice, Bierce later claimed, and the result was national fame for Harte and the *Overland*.[10]

With Twain, to whom he had a stronger personal resemblance, his relations were a bit edgier. The first time he met Twain, as he would frequently recall for his intimates, was in the offices of the *News-Letter*. The lank, red-headed Twain strolled in and looked around the outer office with disdain.

"Young man," Twain drawled, himself in his early thirties, "this room is so nude I should think you and the owner would be ashamed of yourselves."

Bierce kept on working.

"Young man," Twain said, "where is the owner?"

"Somewhere around town," Bierce replied. "He'll be back shortly."

"Young man," said Twain, glowering at Bierce, "are you sure he is not in that next room drunk?"

Bierce insisted that he wasn't covering up for his employer, that publisher Marriott would return soon, and asked if there was anything he could do for the caller.

"I've come to repay Marriott a loan," Twain explained.

"You could leave the money with me."

"Young man," Twain demanded, staring intently at Bierce, "look me in the eyes and speak as though you were talking to your God. If I gave you that money are you sure your employer would ever see it?"

That broke the ice, and Twain chatted amiably until Marriott returned.

A year or two later, however, when Twain married the daughter of a wealthy burgher of upstate New York, Bierce sternly took him to task in his role of Town Crier:

"Mark Twain, who, whenever he has been long enough sober to permit an estimate, has been uniformly found to bear a spotless character, has got married. It was not the act of a desperate man — it was not committed while laboring under temporary insanity; his insanity is not of that type, nor does he ever labor — it was the cool, methodical, cumulative culmination of human nature working in the heart of an orphan hankering for someone with a fortune to love — someone with a bank account to caress. For years he has felt this matrimony coming on. Ever since he left California there has been an undertone of despair running through all his letters like the subdued wail of a pig in a washtub . . .

"Well, that genial spirit has passed away; that long, bright

smile will no more greet the early barkeeper, nor the familiar
'Chalk it down'* delight his ear. Poor Mark! he was a good
scheme, but he couldn't be made to work."[11]

Perhaps Bierce would have liked to retract that uncharitable
judgment of Twain as a fortune hunter — which, on the evidence, he was not — a short time later when he himself married
well above his financial and social station. But perhaps not.
Ambrose Bierce was rarely overtaken by the impulse to retract

In one of his occasional forays into polite society Bierce met
Ellen, known as Mollie, Day. She was several years younger than
he, a sweet-tempered, sentimental girl with a mass of dark blonde
hair. Hyperbole being one of the prime ingredients of legend-
making, she was often to be identified as a "beautiful society
girl." This was inexact. She had a rather long, intelligent face
and handsome dark eyes, and undoubtedly was more attractive
than the average, but she was not a beauty. Nor was she a
member of the Instant Aristocracy of Nob Hill; her father
unfortunately had made more money for other men of the forty-
niner days, as a mining engineer, than he did for himself. He
prospered in time, but wealth, to be socially certifiable, had to be
gained in those first few years of the gold rush. Thus the Days
did not rank with the Fairs, Crockers, Baldwins, Stanfords,
Floods and Mackays, whose wealth stemmed impeccably from
the Comstock Lode or the railroads. But they still ranked well
above the young man who rejoiced in the title of Town Crier.
And for all its reputation for being breezily informal — for all
the Eastern sneers that hands which had once gripped the pick
handle or slaved over a washboard now clenched dollar Havanas
or lorgnettes — San Francisco society was rigidly caste-conscious.

Mollie herself was born in Galena, Illinois, then the lead-
mining center of the United States. Her father, Captain Holland
H. Day (the title more or less a courtesy dating from an Indian
campaign in which he had participated), had worked as a
superintendent in the Galena mines. He came out to California

---

* Modern translation: "Put it on my tab."

as a mining engineer, not a prospector, early in the Fifties and superintended other men's mines in Trinity and Placer Counties. When gold was discovered in Nevada, by which time he had brought his family to California, he superintended the Savage mine, then the famous Ophir and the Central mines. Apparently he wearied of enriching other men while only drawing a decent salary himself and he began to buy up and develop mining properties in Utah. One mine, the Tintic, struck a fairly good vein and Captain Day prospered accordingly. He was not, however, in the "Big Four" class and probably not even a millionaire. A kindly, unpretentious man, he was content to have struck it rich enough to guarantee the well-being of his family.

That wasn't quite enough to satisfy Mrs. Day, who was an ambitious woman with social aspirations. If she couldn't make the climb to Nob Hill (from respectable but unglamorous Folsom Street) on her own, perhaps her vivacious daughter Mollie would assist through an advantageous marriage. She saw to it that Mollie was thoroughly groomed as matrimonial bait for the eligible youth of Nob Hill; was taught to sing and play the piano in refined fashion and cultivated the other social graces. Captain Day's opinion of such aspirations may have been indicated by the fact that he preferred to stay in Utah most of the time feasting his eyes on the slag heaps of the Tintic mine rather than on the more glamorous of the seven hills of San Francisco.

Bierce and Mollie Day began seeing a lot of each other at the summer resort of San Rafael, across the Golden Gate in Marin County. Mollie was a highly romantic girl who would naturally be attracted to a young man who professed to be cynical, atheistic, rebellious, moody, and who in the bargain was breathtakingly handsome, an ex-officer with a head wound which fortunately hadn't disfigured him. Adolphe Danziger, much later his protégé and biographer, claimed that Bierce "was not so madly in love with her as she was with him," that she was "inordinately jealous" of other women.[12]

During the summers of 1870 and 1871 Bierce saw much of Mollie, with whom he went boating, picnicking, strolling in the hills above the Bay. Usually they had his friends Charles Stoddard and Ina Coolbrith, the poetess, as chaperons. He also was her escort in the city at card parties, musicales and other respectable functions.

On this growing attachment Mrs. Day undoubtedly, and forthrightly, placed her stamp of disapproval. Ambrose Bierce, the harum-scarum journalist, wasn't the man she wanted her only daughter to marry. Evidently her son James, a meddlesome fellow who also earned Bierce's unremitting dislike, joined her in attempting to persuade Mollie that she would be throwing herself away on a troublemaking scribbler. Even if they didn't consider Bierce the "wickedest man in San Francisco," they didn't believe that he would enhance the Day social position; nor — even more correctly — that he would make her happy in the long run. The Bierce characteristics that seemed so romantic to Mollie were exactly those which Mrs. Day and her son regarded with suspicion, if not repugnance. Doubtless they had heard the rumor that the reason Bierce suffered from asthma, an increasing burden on his health, was that he had gotten himself drunk, wandered into a cemetery and spent the night sleeping in the chill fog with a gravestone for his pillow.

Rather early in Bierce's courtship, if it was that at the moment, Mrs. Day evidently did her best to discourage Mollie from seeing him. Early in 1870 there was a highly personal and rather plaintive note in one of Bierce's "Town Crier" columns: "Mollie — tell your mother not to relax her efforts to keep you from writing to us. The chances are that the old lady is right."[13]

The "old lady," however, was not successful in dissuading her daughter, who was usually gentle and submissive but could be determined in something so important to her. In November of 1871, while Bierce was staying in San Rafael because the air was easier on his clogged bronchial tubes, Mollie came to see him and other friends. A letter Bierce wrote his friend Stoddard indicated how happy, almost giddy, he was over his successful courtship. He had missed seeing Stoddard before his departure because he had had to meet the train on which Mollie arrived. "I had arranged a nice card party with the ladies and you don't know how much beauty, and youth, and virtue, and similar stuff, you missed by not remaining another night." He signed it, "Entirely yours (lucrative monopoly!)."[14]

A few days after that meeting in San Rafael, Captain and Mrs. H. H. Day formally announced the engagement of their daughter to A. G. Bierce, Esq.

A month later, on Christmas Day 1871, they were married in the Day home with only the Day family and a few friends present. The matriarch had not abandoned her misgivings, but Captain Day came down from Utah for the occasion and gave the marriage his wholehearted blessings. Bierce would always value his mild-mannered father-in-law above most men.

The brief ceremony was performed by the only cleric Bierce could abide even for the few minutes it took to read the marriage lines. This was the Reverend Horatio Stebbins of the First Unitarian Church, of whom Bierce had written a few kind words — "a better preacher, a more liberal man, a profounder theologian and altogether a more desirable person to have around" — but added the cautionary sentence, "Be careful that we do not catch thee tripping."[15]

Captain Day's wedding present was handsome indeed: all the expenses of a trip to and extended stay in England, which would be their honeymoon. Probably Bierce was not advised, immediately, that his mother-in-law would share that sojourn. Following the ceremony, however, Bierce and his bride went to San Rafael, unfashionable though the season was for that summer colony. They would stay there until it was time to go to England a few months hence.

In bulletins from the honeymoon cottage Bierce assured his bachelor friends in San Francisco that marriage wasn't so bad after all, and even admitted to being happy. He and Stoddard had quarreled over some trifling matter — trifling to Bierce, at any rate — and he wrote his friend asking that Stoddard not hold a grudge over the "hard words" that had passed between them, since they "didn't amount to a row of bent pins" and he was sure that "Mollie has forgotten it." The note ended with a plea. "Don't be an ass and harbor malice. (Do asses harbor malice, I wonder?)" He also invited Stoddard to bring Ina

Coolbrith and Joaquin Miller, the determinedly picturesque "Sweet Singer of the Sierras," and "come on up."[16]

It would be some years before Bierce would write of a bridal couple:

> They stood before the altar and supplied
> The fires themselves in which their fat was fried.
> In vain the sacrifice! — no god will claim
> An offering burnt with an unholy flame.[17]

FIVE

A Sea Change or Two

ON THE LAST "Town Crier" page to appear under his authorship, in March of 1872, Bierce published what was both a farewell to his readers and a threat to return if they needed his ministrations in the future; it also constituted his credo as a moralist-journalist: "The Town Crier does not seek a wider field for his talents. The only talents that he has are a knack at hating hypocrisy, cant, and all sham, and a trick of expressing his hatred. What wider field than San Francisco does God's green earth present? . . .

"Be as decent as you can. Don't believe without evidence. Treat things divine with marked respect — and don't have anything to do with them. Do not trust humanity without collateral security; it will play you some scurvy trick. Remember that it hurts no one to be treated as an enemy entitled to respect until he shall prove himself a friend worthy of affection. Cultivate a taste for distasteful truths. And, finally, most important of all, endeavor to see things as they are, not as they ought to be."

And if the San Francisco he had served as an editorial monitor failed to benefit from his strictures, he would again take up the "whip of the satirist" and it would "fall upon your shoulders as a snowflake settles against the rocky side of Mt. Shasta."[1]

When he left, however, he probably had little intention of

returning, no matter how badly San Francisco fell into error. Captain Day's wedding present would take him and Mollie to England and allow him time to establish himself as a writer; thus his honeymoon might well result in permanent expatriation. Now that the Union Pacific and Central Pacific had joined rails in Utah and were bringing out migrants by the thousands, it was perversely fashionable for the promising California writer to go the other way. Twain had departed eastward several years before. Bret Harte, wearing the laurel so quickly won and so quickly to wither, had made what William Dean Howells called a "princely progress" to Boston and New York one year before, and would spend the last third of his life in permanent English exile. Joaquin Miller, regarded as something of a fraud in San Francisco, both for his spectacular claims as a frontiersman and his pretensions as a poet, was the toast of Mayfair in his boots and buckskins. Prentice Mulford had also settled down in England, and Charles Stoddard would join him there shortly.

For all of them, Bierce no less than the others, London had become the capital of a literary dream world, a place where a writer would find greater honor and perhaps greater reward than in money-obsessed America. London at this time was what Paris would be to the writers of the 1920's and 1950's. If there were as yet no foundations to provide grants for travel and living expenses, talented Americans at least knew that, once they arrived, they would be welcomed and cozened. If an American writer ever starved in London during that period, he did so in decent obscurity. Fleet Street held its arms open wide in welcome and, as Harte and others were to learn, the English publishers were prejudiced in their favor. Beside London, even New York was drab and provincial.

Among Bierce's assets, other than his father-in-law's money, were letters of introduction from Marriott to his old comrades in Fleet Street. His hopes were also bolstered by the fact that English periodicals had frequently quoted his comments in the "Town Crier" columns, and while he wouldn't bring with him the fame of a Twain or Harte he had a small but glittering reputation as a master of invective.

On their way east he and Mollie stopped off at Elkhart, Indiana, where his parents and some of his brothers and sisters now lived. A day or two later they proceeded to New York and sailed for Liverpool, then on to London. The center of the British Empire, they found, was every bit as exciting and en-chanting as advertised, its welcome as warm as a handsome young American couple could expect.

They would settle somewhere in the countryside, where his mother-in-law would soon join them for an unconscionably ex-tended visit, but first they wanted to sample the throbbing life of London's cafés, restaurants and concert halls. On his own Bierce also joined in the local sport of pub-crawling, at which he had become adept on San Francisco's saloon circuit, and explored the journalistic hangouts on Fleet Street and the alleys opening off it.

In very short order he had plunged into London's literary life and established himself as one of its bright young men. He took to England as the English apparently took to him. Anglophilia would be one of the few enthusiasms that endured throughout his life. "For nearly all that is good in our American civilization we are indebted to England; the errors and mischiefs are of our own creation. In learning and letters, in art and the science of government, America is but a faint and stammering echo of England."[2] Though seldom found lacking in self-esteem, he later wrote that he "felt himself a pygmy among Titans" in England. He was never happier than there, in London first and then outside it, at least until Mrs. Day appeared and took up residence with them.

In later years Bierce would inveigh against the perils of the Bohemian life to his young disciples, but he quickly immersed himself in it when he reached London. One of his letters of introduction evidently was to Tom Hood, son of a celebrated father and himself editor of the weekly *Fun*, a man famous for his liquor capacity and ringleader of a group which gathered in the bar of the Ludgate Hill railroad station. Among the members were Captain Mayne-Reid, a literary idol of Bierce's boyhood; George Augustus Sala, a newspaperman and former foreign cor-respondent who had published a biography of Hogarth; William

Black, a novelist later knighted; Clement Scott; Harry Leigh; Tom Robertson; and, occasionally, W. S. Gilbert, who supplied the words to Arthur Sullivan's music. They were hard drinkers for the most part, but Bierce was able to maintain his reputation as "an eminent tankard-man," a title he frequently and insistently rejoiced in. Although he later referred to them in a nostalgic afterglow as the intellectual peers of the earlier habitués of the Cheshire Cheese, his companions at the Ludgate Hill pub were mostly hacks and newspapermen. To Bierce, Sala and Hood were the most impressive. Sala was a great raconteur and had the superficial brilliance of a journalist who had been around. "It was said that he could make an after-dinner speech in eighteen languages," Bierce would recall. "I can testify that he could eat the dinner in any language known to man."[3]

The favorite sport among the Fleet Street regulars was putting each other down. Occasionally, of course, Bierce was the butt of their jesting. In later years he frequently told of a discussion with Hood, Sala and others about a man then on trial on charges of homosexuality.

"I never heard of such a crime before," Bierce admitted to the others.

"What the gentleman means is this," Tom Hood cracked. "He never before heard that it was a crime."[4]

Bierce was usually able to give as good as he got. One day while he was still living in London, Robert Todd Lincoln, the late President's son, arrived on a visit. Bierce went to call on him at the American legation. "That evening," he would later recall, "I met Sala at dinner. While in America during the Civil War Sala had attended some kind of function at the White House, and in relating it to the London paper he represented he had brutally lampooned his hostess (Mary Todd Lincoln) through two or three columns. With that in memory, I thought I would spoil the flavor of his soup for him by way of revenge.

" 'Oh, Sala,' I said carelessly, 'I believe you met Bob Lincoln once — I've just seen him. He inquired if you were in town — fancy he's hot about that White House letter.'

"Sala looked as distressed as I could have desired.

" 'I suppose he has a bowie-knife in each boot leg,' he said gravely. 'Please go to him tomorrow morning and tell him that it was a typographical error.' "[5]

Assuming the pseudonym of "Dod Grile," Bierce began writing for Hood's *Fun* and another humorous weekly, *Figaro*, which was edited by an American named James Mortimer, who was also a member of the Ludgate Hill tavern group. For *Fun* he produced a series of humorous sketches titled "Fables of Zambri the Parsee, as Translated by Dod Grile" and published between July 1872 and March 1873. For *Figaro* he wrote a column "The Passing Showman," somewhat in the style of his "Town Crier" page in San Francisco.

This work immediately attracted attention. Among those who admired it was William E. Gladstone, the intermittent prime minister, a sobersided gentleman of the sort not ordinarily to be found among those who appreciated Bierce. Gladstone, in a newspaper interview, mentioned having read a collection of Bierce's sketches and proclaimed them a work of genius. There must have been a risible side to Gladstone's nature not remarked by his biographers.[6]

Another whose fancy was caught by Bierce's sketches was John Camden Hotten, a book publisher — or "pirate," as Mark Twain declared — who called on Bierce late in July 1872 and suggested a more formal publication of his work. The result was *The Fiend's Delight*, published later that year in the paperback edition then sold largely in railway stations. It consisted mainly of items from his San Francisco "Town Crier" columns, with some added material, and was published under the name of Dod Grile. And it failed to enrich him, since it was Mr. Hotten's theory that publication was reward enough for a writer.

In the introduction to *The Fiend's Delight*, Bierce blamed the "diabolic" spirit of some of the grislier sketches on the fact that he had acquired "Mr. Satan" as his collaborator:

"The atrocities consituting this 'cold collation' of diabolism are taken mainly from various California journals. They are cast in the American language, and liberally enriched with unintelligibility. If they should prove incomprehensible on this side of the

Atlantic, the reader can pass to the other side at a moderately extortionate charge. In the pursuit of my design I think I have killed a good many people in one way or another; but the reader will please to observe that they were not people worth the trouble of leaving alive. Besides, I had the interests of my collaborator to consult. In writing, as in compiling, I have been ably assisted by my scholarly friend, Mr. Satan; and to this worthy gentleman must be attributed most of the views herein set forth. While the plan of the work is partly my own, its spirit is wholly his; and this illustrates the ascendancy of the creative over the merely imitative mind."

He added the more pious sentiment that "I shall be content with the profit." But his other collaborator, Mr. Hotten, took care of that matter; perhaps the publisher was in even closer league with Mr. Satan.

One of *The Fiend's Delight* sketches which particularly titillated the Victorians who had become weary of "inspiring" literature concerned a farm boy who brought his father's severed head in from the meadow, where an unfortunate accident with the mowing-machine had occurred.

" 'Where did you get it?' asks the mother.

" 'Why, ma, that's pap's.'

" 'John,' and there was just a touch of severity in her voice, 'when your mother asks you a question you should answer that particular question. Where did you get this?'

" 'Out in the medder, then, if yer so derned pertikeller . . . the mowing-machine lopped it off.'

" 'My son, the gentleman whom you hold in your hand — any more pointed allusion to whom would be painful to both of us — had punished you a hundred times for meddling with things lying about the farm. Take that head back and put it down where you found it, or you will make your mother very angry.' "

During his three years in Britain, once his father-in-law's wedding present was used up, he had to struggle to keep one jump ahead of his creditors. The money he got from *Fun* and *Figaro* evaporated rather quickly. It was barely sufficient, he said, to "whet the whistle of the 'Gang,' " meaning his friends at the bar of the Ludgate Hill station, "for there was an unwritten law of 'treat,' and unless the barmaid was willing not to keep a vivid memory of my demands, I had to stay away. Fortunately I did not stay away."

When the Bierces decided to leave London for the countryside, however, it wasn't so much the distractions of the Gang that caused the move as Mollie's pregnancy and Bierce's asthma, which had grown worse in London's fogs. They lived for several months in Bristol, where their son Day was born in December 1872. At first he was rather pleased with fatherhood, and admitted that it was "sweet to have a baby in the house." Bierce, like many artists, however, was ill-equipped for paternity; the child becomes an encumbrance, a distraction from work, and finally less real than the creatures of his imagination. As an excuse for this lack of paternal feeling, he wrote fifteen years later that it was all a gyp perpetrated by women; only a fool felt any lasting pride of fatherhood. "What is there to be proud of? It is a tradition of grannies and midwives, promoted by the vanity of girls and adopted by cackling bachelors as a cat-call of derision."[7]

From Bristol the Bierces moved to Bath early in 1873. With that ancient town as a base they traveled around and saw the literary England Bierce had long dreamed about. They had already visited Stratford-on-Avon while living in London, and Bierce had written an account of the visit for the *Alta California* which ended: "I did not visit Charlecot, where Shakespeare stole the deer, nor did I extend my pilgrimage to the crabtree under which Will and his guzzling companions lay drunk. For me it is sufficient that he *did* steal a deer, and that he *did* get drunk."[8]

Bath and its associations delighted him even more. He wrote Stoddard, who was soon to leave San Francisco for his own fling in England, that Bath was the most charming town he had ever seen. "Every street has its history, every foot of the lovely country its tradition. Old Roman, and even Druidic, remains are as plentiful as green peas. You are aware that Bath was the stamping ground of Pope, Fielding, Smollett, Warburton, Malthus, Beau Nash, Ralph Allen — 'who did good by stealth and blushed to find it fame' — and a lot of worthies whose haunts I frequent and over whose graves I shed judicious drops and try to fancy myself like them. I don't succeed."[9]

The presence of presumably friendly ghosts did not, however, inspire him to any great effort. He was doing just enough work for *Fun* and *Figaro* to meet expenses "at this somewhat expensive place. It does not require much of my time either." He didn't intend to look for any "permanent work," he continued in a letter to Stoddard, since "my object in coming was to loaf and see something of the country — as Walt Whitman expressed it, when the paralysis had, as yet, invaded only his brain, 'to loaf and invite my soul.' "[10]

A few months later, with concealed bitterness, he announced in another letter to Stoddard, "My mother-in-law is here." She stayed almost a year, presumably welcome to her daughter but definitely not to her son-in-law. Probably Mrs. Day was only too quick to point out to Mollie that Bierce had not been properly broken to matrimonial harness. He wandered off to London at every possible opportunity, and undoubtedly returned in worse shape than when he left. The banality of having a mother-in-law problem must have irked him considerably, even though Mollie, whose disposition was trusting and sentimental and who had the amiable personality of her father, was not inclined to apply bit and curb on her mother's advice. Yet the first hairline of the split between Bierce and his wife that was to widen into a chasm was undoubtedly visible then. It was not necessarily a mismating — Mollie the life-loving, Ambrose the relentless cynic who thought life was a bad joke that endured from birth to death — but Bierce was wretched husband material. He chafed at the necessary restrictions of marriage. He never did understand women, nor did he make a serious attempt to: not as the elderly brute so maliciously described by the young novelist Gertrude Atherton as making a grab for her and attempting to kiss her beside a pigsty; not as the young husband with a beautiful and loving wife. He had no patience with feminine idiosyncrasies. In addition he was so inhibited that later he would boast that no woman had ever seen him naked. A cynic who claimed that all human activity was a farce, yet would quibble over certain matters like a Puritan dominie, must have been difficult to cope with, let alone understand.

At the same time he could roar with bawdy laughter when the old doctor who delivered their firstborn replied to Mollie's complaint that she had been hoping for a daughter: "Well, Madam, at his age it really doesn't make much difference."

He escaped from Mollie's hurt and puzzled eyes, and his mother-in-law's censorious frowns, by going to London and frolicking on Fleet Street. Later that year both Stoddard and Twain appeared in the city and he renewed his friendship with the one and his acquaintance with the other. Bierce was spending a month in Paris when Stoddard arrived, so he left a letter of instructions on how Stoddard was to conduct himself in the snags and eddies of the London literary world. Perhaps the unworldly young man who once had signed his poems "Pip Pepperpod" needed that shrewd advice, though he may have resented its admonitory tone.

Bierce advised the new arrival that he had asked Tom Hood to look after him, that Hood was a sterling fellow but "he has the worst lot of associates I ever saw," men who weren't fit to untie Stoddard's shoelaces. Meeting those scapegraces — presumably he meant the Gang at the Ludgate Hill taproom — was unavoidable, but Stoddard was admonished "(1) don't gush over them; (2) don't let them gush over you; (3) don't accept invitations from them; (4) don't get drunk with them; (5) don't let them in any way monopolize you; (6) don't let them shine by your reflected light." Bierce admitted he had done all those things; however, "I don't mind biting and stinging, but you would — particularly if done in the dark."

The gay lads of Fleet Street, he said, "will be very good, but upon the implied understanding that you are not to compete with them in their pitiful struggle." He should cultivate Englishmen whose work he had admired, but was warned that "an American reputation is easily made by a third-rate Englishman."

Literary London, he explained, was "divided into innumerable cliques." If Stoddard became involved in one of them, the others would shun him in annoyance. "You will, by the way, be under a microscope here; your slightest word and most careless action noted down, and commented on by men who cannot understand how a person of individuality in thought or conduct can be other than a very bad man . . . keep your own counsel, don't make speeches at clubs, avoid any appearance of eccentricity, don't admire anything and don't disparage anything; don't eat mustard on mutton!"

Stoddard could hardly have been blamed if he had fled back to America after receiving that picture of London literary life. Nor was the final injunction any more reassuring. "I am hand in glove with some hundreds of them, and they think they are my intimate friends. If any man says he is, or acts as if he were, avoid him, he is an imposter. This letter is *strictly confidential*, and when I come back I shall ask you to hand it to me."[11]

By this time Bierce was becoming a personage, at least along Fleet Street. A second collection of his San Francisco columns, *Nuggets and Dust*, was as well received as *The Fiend's Delight*, though it caused Bierce an unusual attack of modesty. "Do you know," he wrote Stoddard, "I have the supremest contempt for my books — as books. As a journalist I believe I am unapproachable in my line; as an author, a slouch!"[12] Evidently he was convinced that short, thrusting satirical sketches were and always would be his line. If it was a comparatively paltry one, confining him to weekly journalism, he seemed to have no great ambition to extend himself, and by way of recompense would speak harshly of the novel as an art form.

The winter of 1873 he was celebrated enough as a satirist to be one of the guests of honor at a banquet given by the White Friars Club in Mitre Court, Fleet Street. The esteem in which he was held was attested by the fact that the other two honored guests were Mark Twain and Joaquin Miller, who was regarded as a genius at self-advertisement if nothing else. Though the other two were more famous, Bierce was hailed as "one of the most original and daring humorists this age has produced." Miller was a great embarrassment to Twain and Bierce, who were well aware that the English — perhaps with a touch of malice —

were eager to accept Miller as a very typical American. Miller showed up in music-hall regalia, hair flowing to the shoulder, buckskin jacket, red sash, huge knife in his belt as though he might have to hack his way through savage tribesmen to reach Mitre Court. While the others goggled — and Bierce and Twain tried to ignore him as they would a child showing off for his elders — Miller picked up a fish by the tail and swallowed it whole. Bierce experienced his own moment of embarrassment when called upon for a few words. He told his fellow banqueters of the time he first met Twain in the offices of the *News-Letter*. The others watched Twain for his reaction. Twain cavalierly refused to smile at the anecdote; the others took their cue from him, and Bierce sat down to funereal silence. No doubt he would have greatly liked to kick both Miller and Twain up Fleet Street after those festivities ended.

Despite his warning to Stoddard against falling in with them, Bierce himself frequently repaired to the boozy goodfellowship of the Ludgate Hill tavern and the Fleet Street Gang whenever homelife palled or luck went against him. One day he went to the Highgate residence of John Camden Hotten, his publisher, to brace him for a hundred-pound advance. Hotten gave him a postdated check. Bierce took it to the Ludgate Hill pub, which was unable to cash it. Sala and others at the round table reserved for them suggested that Bierce hasten back and demand a cash advance on the postdated check. When Bierce returned to Highgate, he was informed that "the rascal had died of eating a pork pie, to beat me out of my money." After "having pinched the body and ascertained that it was indubitably lifeless," he called a cab and hastened "furiously bank-ward." His only hope was to cash the check before the bank learned of Hotten's death.

Unfortunately, along the way he stopped off at the Ludgate station bar to report the news to Hood, Sala and others who were inclined to rejoice at the news of any publisher's departure. They celebrated with a number of drinks, then fell to composing "questionable epitaphs" in Hotten's honor. Naturally they expected Sala to supply the most suitable one. His wit had been renowned ever since the night he heard that a prominent watchmaker was to be knighted on the coming honors list. Sala had gone out to Cheapside, banged on the watchmaker's door in the middle of the night, and shouted up to him at an upstairs window: "Watchman, what of the night?"

Sala did not let them down. His epitaph read:

HOTTEN

ROTTEN

FORGOTTEN

Bierce lingered so long over drinks and epitaphs that it was close to the bank's closing time when he finally drove up.

"We can't pay this," Bierce was told. "Mr. Hotten is dead."

"You don't say so! When did you learn that?"

"A half-hour ago."

Concocting those mock-epitaphs, Bierce recounted, "cost me one hundred pounds sterling."[13]

The experience did not discourage him from taking his place regularly at the Fleet Street Gang's table. Only on one occasion of record was his amiability severely tested — and that was by an outsider, a wealthy Englishman who had been trying for some time to meet the author of *The Fiend's Delight*. The man finally cornered Bierce at the Ludgate Hill pub, took the chair next to his, and slapped down a twenty-pound note to "help along" with the bar tab.

Bierce glowered at the intruder-admirer, covered his twenty pounds with a shiny new guinea, and snarled: "Take it, sir, and buy yourself a fish stall at Covent Garden."

Throughout his three-year stay in Britain, Bierce was closest to and fondest of Tom Hood, the only one of the pub crowd whom he visited at his home. Hood was quieter and more reflective than most of the Fleet Street types, and was in declining health. Bierce would recall how he used to talk the nights away with Hood at his home in a suburb beyond the Crystal Palace. "Back of his odd little house was this odd little garden, and here we were accustomed to burn our cigars after which we commonly passed the entire night in a room upstairs, sipping grog, pulling at our pipes, and talking on all manner of things."

Hood shared Bierce's fervent interest in the supernatural. "Tom had in him a vein of what in another would be called superstition, but it was so elusive in character and whimsical in manifestation that I could never rightly assign it a place . . ." They gravely, and with apparent affirmation, considered the matter of ghosts. The last night they ever saw each other, corporeally at least, they agreed that whoever died first would attempt to get in touch with the other.

Bierce was out in the country when word reached him that Hood had died. That evening he went for a walk and brooded over his friend's untimely death. Returning home along a War-wickshire lane, he suddenly felt — or felt that he felt — the unseen presence of Tom Hood. "I need not attempt to describe my feelings; they were novel and not altogether agreeable. That I had met the spirit of my dead friend; that it had given me recognition, yet not in the old way; that it had then vanished — of these things I had the evidence of my own senses. How strongly this impressed me the beating of my heart attested whenever, for many months afterward, that strange meeting came into my memory."[14]

A somewhat livelier and more persistent ghost, that of the Second Napoleonic Empire, enlisted his attention before he left England. The quasichivalric role he played as defender of an exiled empress was inflated beyond lifelike proportions in later years when the Bierce legend really started forming. It was not quite true that he buckled on armor, or fought duels on her behalf. In fact, Bierce had a robust democratic antipathy for royalty of all makes, in or out of power, and he was not the sort of visiting American described by Daisy, Princess of Pless, as "tumbling over each other to be the first to glow, and swell, under the smile of royalty."

Early in 1874, Bierce and his family, which still included his mother-in-law, were living in Leamington, Warwickshire. Mollie gave birth to a second son, whom they named Leigh. The house was filled with the sounds of another infant voice, and Bierce was finding fatherhood irksome. The conception and birth of a baby was something he preferred to blame on the feminine party to it. He and Mrs. Day were no more friendly than on the day they had met. Obviously, in the spring of 1874, additional editorial or writing chores which would take him more frequently to London were just what he needed.

At this time he received an offer to become a sort of public relations man for the remnants of the Second Empire, which consisted mainly of Empress Eugénie and her "court" at Chislehurst, Kent, and the remaining imperial delusions they harbored. Bierce was selected as knight-defender of their vanished realm through the court dentist, a Dr. Evans, on whom the Papal title of the Marquis d'Oily had been conferred and with whom Bierce had hunted on occasion, and James Mortimer, the American-born editor of *Figaro*. Mortimer, who had lived in Paris for twenty years before the empire fell under the march of Prussian jackboots and had been the friend of both Napoleon III and his consort, was their ardent partisan.

After the surrender to Prussia, Empress Eugénie had fled to England. There she was joined by the ailing Napoleon when he was released from captivity by the Germans. And in close pursuit came one of their bitterest enemies, Henri Rochefort, Marquis de Rochefort-Lucay, a journalist, pamphleteer and Communard, who had just escaped from the prison colony on New Caledonia to which Napoleon had dispatched him. The Marxist-minded marquis had devoted most of his career to puncturing Napoleonic pretensions and had published a paper, *La Lanterne*, which, as Bierce said, "made life in the Tuileries exceedingly uncomfortable. His rancor against the Empress was something horrible, and went to the length of denying the legitimacy of the Prince Imperial. His existence was a menace and a terror to the illustrious lady . . ." Now Rochefort was heading for England with every intention of continuing his campaign against Eugénie, in particular, and her consort by way of ricochet.[15]

Fortunately the empress did not flee France empty-handed.

She had funds to spare for a journalistic defense, which she asked Mortimer to arrange. Mortimer heard that Rochefort intended to start publishing *La Lanterne* again, so he decided to forestall him by registering the title *The Lantern* for a satirical magazine to be issued irregularly. It was to be a combination of humor, defense of the vanished realm, and assault on Rochefort. For the editorship, Mortimer proposed Bierce, who had the skill to attract readers who otherwise would be uninterested in imperial propaganda.

Bierce at first objected to editing and writing all the copy for a magazine to be issued at the whim of its owner, but finally "I consented to do all the writing" if his sponsor was "willing to do all the money losing."[16]

Bierce was established in an office at St. Bride Street and Shoe Lane, and produced the first issue on May 18, 1874. Its contents could hardly have been any more appealing to imperialist-minded Britons than it was to the anti-imperialist Rochefort. One of its featured leaders attacked General Sir Garnet Wolseley, who had just returned from a triumphant campaign against the savage Ashanti:

"We feel a comfortable sense of satisfaction in the thought that *The Lantern* will never fail to shed the light of its loyal approval upon any unworthy act by which our country shall secure an adequate and permanent advantage. When the great heart of England is stirred by quick cupidity to profitable crime, far be it from us to lift our palms in deprecation. In the wrangle for existence nations, equally with individuals, work by diverse means to a common end — the spoiling of the weak; and when by whatever outrage we have pushed a feeble competitor to the wall, in Heaven's name let us pin him fast and relieve his pockets of the material good to which, in bestowing it upon him, the bountiful Lord has invited our thieving hand. But these Ashanti women were not worth garroting. Their fal-lals, precious to them, are worthless to us; the entire loot fetched only 11,000 pounds — of which sum the man who brought home the trinkets took a little more than four halves. We submit that with practiced agents in every corner of the world and a watchful government at home this great commercial nation might dispose of its honor to better advantage."[17]

Bierce did not fail to pay his respects to M. Rochefort, who was reported in his frustration to be establishing *La Lanterne* in Belgium.

"M. Rochefort," Bierce advised his readers, "is a gentleman who has lost his standing. There have been greater falls than his. Kings before now have become servitors, honest men bandits, thieves, communists. Insignificant in his fortunes as in his abilities, M. Rochefort, who was never very high, is not now very low — he has avoided the falsehood of extremes: never quite a count, he is now but half a convict. Having missed the eminence that would have given him calumniation, he is also denied the obscurity that would bring misconstruction. He is not even a *misérable*; he is a person. It is curious to note how persistently this man has perverted his gifts. With talents that might have corrupted panegyric, he preferred to refine detraction; fitted to disgrace the *salon*, he has elected to adorn the cell; the qualities that would have endeared him to a blackguard he has wasted upon Pascal Grousset [an associate of Rochefort]."

Bierce added that rumors were circulating that Rochefort was presently in England but heading for Belgium and Switzerland to challenge certain continental detractors to duels. He made it plain that he would be happy to accommodate Rochefort on the dueling ground himself and spare him the expense of travel. His assault on Rochefort ended: "M. Rochefort, we believe, is already suffering from an unhealed wound. It is his mouth."[18]

At the beginning Bierce evidently saw in *The Lantern* an opportunity to make an essay into personal journalism. The magazine would be his podium, to be shared reluctantly from time to time with the empress. Its voice, certainly, was more Biercean than Napoleonic, as when he stated his intentions as editor: "My future program will be calm disapproval of human institutions in general, including all forms of government, most laws and customs, and all contemporary literature." The exaggerated claims of social and economic reformers and philanthropists would be sternly discounted. He also promised "intolerance of intolerance, and war upon every man with a mission, and disesteem for titles of distinction, from Majesty down to Esquire; no earnestness, no indignation, no declamation; human suffering to be contemplated with a merely curious interest, as one looks into an ant-hill." Obviously it was no program to flatter an empress. Yet Eugénie, who had a special edition translated into French, did not disapprove.

The Lantern carried illustrations in six colors, a spectacular advance in publishing technology, and was a beautiful job of printing craftsmanship. "I winced," Bierce said, "when I contemplated its artistic and mechanical excellence, for I knew at what a price that quality had been attained. A gold mine would be required to maintain that journal, and that journal could by no means ever be a gold mine." Years later he still believed "this pioneer in the field of chromatic journalism . . . the finest thing that ever came from a press."[19]

In the second issue — which proved to be the final one — Bierce for the first time published a department under the title of "Prattle," which was to become the heading for hundreds of columns to come, though under different mastheads and halfway across the world. It was a collection of verse, comment and epigrams, "generally ill-humorous," as its author said.

In one scrap of ill-humorous verse he scorched the whole English nation, picturing it as inheriting from Bacon — the culmination of "British intellect and British crime" — a rather paltry estate:

> *To each a pinch of common sense, for seed,*
> *And, to develop it, a pinch of greed.*
> *Each frugal heir, to make the gift suffice,*
> *Buries the talent to manure the vice.*[20]

By now a badly smoldering firebrand, Rochefort departed from England for the more hospitable Belgian shore. In his memoirs he regarded the commotion raised by *Punch* and other "local magazines" — into which derisive category the *Lantern* apparently fell — with a seigneurial contempt. Soon thereafter he was allowed to return to a republican France, where his talent for malediction was showered upon the various governments until the year before the World War started.* That he had a flame-throwing style matching Bierce's in ferocity and precision was evident from the epithets he hurled at various eminent politicians: Jaurès was "a decayed turnip," Briand "a moulting vulture," Fallières "a fat old satyr," Clemenceau "a loathsome leper." One contemporary, repulsed by his claims to being ultra-liberal at the same time he was joining in the persecution of Captain Dreyfus, neatly epitomized him as a "Baudelaire turned politician."

With Rochefort back on the continent, the empress decided there was no need to continue her brief career as a covert magazine publisher. Undoubtedly this was a great disappointment to Bierce. Later he spoke of the venture as a picaresque episode in the life of a New Grub Street hack, but as he admitted in "Working for an Empress" he had "earnestly" advised Mortimer, as Eugénie's agent, "materially to modify" the plan of irregular publication. Bierce wanted the *Lantern* to be issued every month or quarter, but Mortimer was "obdurate," probably because he knew — as Bierce did not — that the journal was designed only to scare off Rochefort.

Imperial gratitude was expressed not only by what Bierce called "a generous *douceur*" but by the presentation of an ivory card case. This was followed by a "command" from Chislehurst that Bierce present himself at court to be thanked in person. He tried to picture himself being ushered into Eugénie's drawing room among her courtiers and bowing low before the ex-sovereign. It couldn't be done. "My republican independence took alarm," he said, "and I had the incivillity to disobey."[21] Another element in his refusal, which he neglected to mention, may have been anger over having been used as a propagandist, then detached from the imperial payroll when he had served his purpose. The fact that he modeled a later journal he edited (the

---

* He died a few months before Bierce disappeared.

Wasp) after the *Lantern* indicated the poignancy of his hopes for the latter.

Returning to the rougher company of the Ludgate Hill station pub, he was rebuked by Sala, probably with tongue in cheek, for affectation in turning down the empress's command and for "conduct unbecoming a colonial." Bierce, indicating the *Lantern* had been dearer to him than he cynically pretended, replied hotly. The two men quarreled, but made it up before Bierce went back home.[22] Later he was able to philosophize that the editorship of the *Lantern* at least gave him the distinction of being "probably the only American journalist who was ever employed by an Empress in so congenial a pursuit as the pursuit of another journalist."

By then he was becoming more than a trifle disillusioned with the London literary world and wondering whether the charms of expatriation might not be wearing off. One reason may have been his experience with London publishers, first the elusive Hotten, then Chatto and Windus, which published *Nuggets and Dust*. The Andrew Chatto of that firm had been Hotten's business manager, and its offices were often filled with the outcries of indignant authors. One tale told of the firm concerned a distinguished novelist who burst into the office and saw one of the partners standing there, but couldn't remember whether it was Chatto or Windus. "Look here," he shouted, "if you are Chatto, damn Windus, and if you are Windus, damn Chatto!"[23]

For his third book, *Cobwebs from an Empty Skull*, Bierce chose a third publisher, Routledge and Sons. It consisted mainly of the sketches he wrote for Hood's *Fun* and Mortimer's *Figaro*, the nature of which was aptly summed up in a sonnet he wrote that year:

> *Fardels of heartache, burdens of old sins,*
> *Luggage sent down from dim ancestral inns.*
> *And bales of fantasy from No Man's Land.*

He was willing to concede that the London journalist was better equipped than his American counterpart. "He rather moves than 'dabbles' in literature, and not uncommonly takes a hand at some of the many forms of art. On the whole, he is a good fellow, too, with a skeptical mind, a cynical tongue, and a warm heart. I found these men agreeable, hospitable, intelligent, amusing. We worked too hard, dined too well, frequented too many clubs, and went to bed too late in the forenoon. We were overmuch addicted to shedding the blood of the grape. In short, we diligently, conscientiously, and with a perverse satisfaction burned the candle of life at both ends and in the middle."[24]

On the other hand, his English friends tended to speak slightingly of America and its intellectual pretensions, as he later told a San Francisco friend. They were difficult to persuade that the United States wasn't a barbaric land populated by Indians and Indian fighters, or that it was developing its own attitudes that were increasingly less Anglo-Saxon. "The good fellows were clever no end but they were one-sided. They had English wit and English humor, but they knew very little of the fast-growing national humor of America."

While he was roistering in London taverns, Mrs. Bierce stayed in their Warwickshire home and tended their two infant sons. Her mother had returned to San Francisco and she was increasingly lonely and homesick. London gaiety reached her only as an echo in whatever account Bierce gave of his activities there. To her it meant Ambrose coming home with an enormous hangover. The few people she liked were Americans who happened to be visiting England, and her fondest memory of the English years was that of toasting crumpets over an open fire with Prentice Mulford.

Late in the spring of 1874 the homesick Mollie took their sons and sailed for America with the announced intention of returning after a few months at her mother's home. She may have frequently been annoyed by her husband's extended wining and dining in London, but there is no indication in the Bierce letters that there was any serious estrangement between them. He wrote Stoddard that he was "lonely . . . without the wife and babies." He had made himself ill from overwork and living "precariously and abominably." When he recovered his health, he said, "I am coming to London till Mrs. Bierce returns, when I shall have a house somewhere in the suburbs." He reassured Stoddard that he wasn't suffering from any serious illness. "It is only a cursed sort of semi-lunacy, I think, from lack of sleep, hard work, and unchristian cooking."[25]

That summer, back in London, he learned from Mollie that she was pregnant again. Furthermore she wanted to have their third child on her native soil. There were grounds for suspicion, which undoubtedly occurred to the eternally suspicious Bierce, that she was using this means to bring him back to her side: she was already six months pregnant when she informed him of the fact. Perhaps by then he was ready to go back home in any case. His sketches were still selling as fast as he could produce them, but a lot of the joy of his English exile had vanished with the death of Tom Hood. With Sala and the others he always had to be on his mettle, matching wits, thrusting and parrying. But even if he was not too reluctant to leave England, he must have been a little irked by the fact that Mollie preferred to have her mother rather than her husband, if forced to make a choice, at her side during childbirth. Another slight rent in the fabric of a marriage of opposites.

He lost no time about sailing for home, however, and disembarked in New York on September 25, 1875.

The returned pilgrim, having foresworn what he had said was his eventual ambition of becoming a portly, red-faced, irascible Tory squire, now would settle down to an even more demanding role: that of America's unappeasable critic, the most vigorous and unrelenting disturber of the peace until H. L. Mencken came along.

six

An Uncommonly Acerb Prattler

H

IS EXPERIMENT in expatriation ended, probably much against his will and adding to his score against the exigencies of marriage and fatherhood, Ambrose Bierce returned to San Francisco and spent the next twenty years as what has been termed "a kind of West Coast Samuel Johnson."[1] The lordly exasperations of the Great Cham himself would not have been wasted on the place, or on the nation whose western citadel it was. America then was experiencing one of the convulsions which broke the surface of what seems in retrospect a placid and peaceful age. The artificial prosperity created by the Civil War had lasted less than a decade; the fatuous expectations that San Francisco was entering upon an era of endless bounty from her mines, ranches and railroads had been replaced by despair and talk of revolution.

All such talk, and even the milder suggestions of social reform, found Bierce a violently unsympathetic listener. The possibility of equalizing the burdens of poverty and the excessive privileges of wealth made him seethe with vituperation. Social reformers, he said, have a knowledge of the realities of life "a little profounder than a horse but not quite so profound as that of a cow." Their movement, growing in numbers and intellectual force, was "born of envy," and envy was the "wrecker of empires and the assassin of civilization"; the true purpose of their activities was "revenge."[2]

In the fall of 1875 San Francisco was full of envy and thoughts of revenge, directed upward from the wooden-frame tenements to the mansions on Nob Hill. The city was experiencing the first really serious siege of bad times in its brief history. Railroad and real estate promoters had claimed that the city's population would pass the million mark by 1880 after the rails of the Central Pacific and Union Pacific were joined in Utah, but there had been no great influx of Easterners and commerce had suffered from the fact that goods formerly brought by ship and transshipped to the interior now went directly by rail. In 1873 a panic had struck the New York Stock Exchange, causing a depression that spread westward until it reached San Francisco in mid-1875. A few days before Bierce returned to the city early in October 1875, William C. Ralston's supposedly impregnable Bank of California closed its doors, upon which Ralston committed suicide and further contributed to the atmosphere of doom. The value of shares in the Comstock Lode mines dropped by forty-two million dollars in one week. Thousands of men were thrown out of work, and thousands of others were ordered to take "voluntary" wage cuts of forty to sixty percent.

The returning Bierce was caught in the bind like everyone else. There were no posts vacant on the city's dailies or weeklies. On October 30, a daughter was born to the Bierces whom they named Helen; he now had a wife and three children to support, and the carefree days of "shedding the blood of the grape" in Fleet Street's taverns must have suddenly seemed part of a distant and golden past. His chief assets were comprised of a wardrobe of Savile Row tailoring that made him the envy of his old friends.

His only recourse was to attach himself to the government payroll again, this time in the United States Mint's assay office. His brother Albert had come out from Indiana several years earlier and was also working at the Mint. Albert remained his only real family tie, an amiable fellow, so easygoing that even Ambrose couldn't pick a quarrel with him, at least not a serious one, until the last months of his life. Mrs. Bierce, meanwhile, found a house for them on Harrison Street a few blocks from her mother's.[3] Mother Day would continue to be an irritating factor in the Bierces' married life, and often enough his brother-in-law came around to add to the domestic tension. Presumably during this period when he was eking out a living at the Mint he also contributed to the local journals as a part-time freelance.[4]

During the next year and a half, while Bierce was more or less exiled from both literature and journalism, San Francisco was undergoing a major social upheaval. Trade unionism and radical reform were taking over. Practically everyone with a wage-earning job was unionized, and the unemployed were gathered under the banners of the Workingmen's Party, which proposed that the 116,000 Chinese, largely imported to build the railroads, be run out of the country because they were willing to work harder for less than Caucasians, and that capitalistic institutions be destroyed. One of the most eloquent and artful agitators ever to rise from an American soapbox had taken over leadership of the party. He was Denis Kearney, a young Irish drayman who had educated himself at the Lyceum of Self-Culture. Every Sunday thousands gathered in the sandlots adjoining City Hall to hear Kearney exhort them to "lynch and burn out the thieving millionaires, the hell-born, the hell-bound villains, the bloated bondholders," by which he meant such exemplars of free enterprise as George Hearst, Collis P. Huntington, Leland Stanford, Charles Crocker and all the others who had enriched themselves in the mines and on the railroads. Early in 1877 Kearney began leading marches, with himself picturesque and flamboyant on horseback, up to the mansions on Nob Hill to shout under the windows of the nabobs, "Judge Lynch wil decide the fate of capitalism!"

The nabobs got the message. A Businessmen's Vigilance Committee, recalling an earlier solution to lawlessness, was organized and formed the "Pickhandle Brigade" to confront Kearney and his draymen, longshoremen, steamfitters, coal heavers and hod carriers if their militance took a violent turn. Charles Crocker, the railroad magnate, kept a rack of Springfields in his library and threatened to shoot Kearney if he ever set foot on the Crocker threshold.

Inflamed by his own demagoguery, Kearney himself probably saved Nob Hill from the torch and battering ram by going a little too far in his prescriptions for social and economic ills. Every loyal member of the Workingmen's Party was urged to arm himself with a rifle. The state legislature was to be reorganized by hanging most of its members from the lamp posts. Bundles of dynamite were to be gathered and stored against the day when they woud be dropped on Chinatown from balloons. "Disloyal" — by which Kearney meant fainthearted — members of the Workingmen's Party were to be executed by their brothers.

It was obvious to the men of power and wealth, huddling in worried councils in the libraries of their mansions, that San Francisco might fall to the same fate as had Paris a few years earlier, when the Communards threw up their barricades and took over much of the city.

Kearney began to lose much of his following through his constant appeals to the torch, rope and dynamite as correctives for social injustice. Two of the leading newspapers, the *Call* and the *Chronicle*, which had sympathized with Kearney and his party as a matter of practicality, began to back away from him. The Workingmen's Party itself was soon to split over how far to go, by means of physical violence, in seeking compliance with its demands. A slow rise in employment also tended to negate Kearney's efforts; he had not managed to rally his following quickly enough to take violent action, had spent too much time and energy in delivering fiery orations from the saddle while the Pickhandle Brigade was being formed and other countermeasures were being taken.*

Indirectly Kearney and his marching mobs — the sight of

---

* Kearney, disgusted with his followers' lack of spirit, went East in 1878 to attempt organization of a national party. When that failed, he became associated with the Greenback Labor Party. His own party merged with the Socialist Labor Party. The Exclusion Act of 1882, which shut off immigration from China, also cost him much of his following. At the end of his career Kearney became involved in a scandal over his dissipation and misuse of party funds.

which aroused Bierce, in his modest home, almost as much as the wealthy men on the hilltops — provided the means for Bierce's return to a kind of employment more suited to him than assaying chunks of mineral. A prominent citizen named Colonel Frank Pixley, who had once been United States District Attorney and was politically ambitious, decided to establish a weekly titled the *Argonaut*. Its aim was to blot out Kearney and keep the Irish-Americans, who formed much of his support, in a less volatile state. The masthead of the first issue on March 25, 1877, listed Pixley and Fred Somers, a professional journalist, as co-editors, with Ambrose Bierce as associate editor. In practice Bierce was the editor, since both Pixley and Somers had other interests that required their constant attention.

Bierce not only assembled the material that went into the *Argonaut*'s columns but wrote editorials and revived his "Prattle" column, which offered searing comment on the local and national scene in the manner of his "Town Crier" page in the *News-Letter*. Pixley depended upon Bierce to make the *Argonaut* a hard-hitting conservative journal that might provide him with a springboard to the governor's mansion in Sacramento or a seat in the United States Senate. And Bierce signified his intention of living up to the mandate in his first editorial. His purpose, he announced, was to "purify journalism in this town by instructing such writers as it is worth while to instruct, and assassinating those that it is not." No empty threat, it was whispered, since Bierce always kept an army Colt .45 as close to hand as his inkpot.

From the beginning it was not an easy association. Bierce had jumped at the chance to return to weekly journalism, but did not propose to let Pixley or anyone else choose his targets for him. Frequent commands to "let the Irish have it" met with little response from Bierce. In addition to his native independence, he was liberal and tolerant in matters of race and nationality. Without condescension he wrote at various times in defense of Jews and Negroes, even more strongly for the Chinese, against whom local prejudice was focused, and he had nothing against the Irish, providing they did not gather in mobs and start plucking bricks and paving stones. The evil and stupidity done by man, he was convinced, had nothing to do with the color of his skin or the place of his ancestral origin. "I am for preserving the ancient, primitive distinction between right and wrong," was his creed. "The virtues of Socrates, the wisdom of Aristotle, the example of Marcus Aurelius, the selflessness of Jesus Christ, engage my admiration and rebuke my life. I lift reverent eyes to the shining summits of truth . . . I strain my senses to catch the law that they deliver." A man with such a credo obviously wasn't going to assail the whole Irish-American community as a pack of priest-ridden, lawless, violence-prone savages.

Besides differing on whether the *Argonaut* should be a literary journal (Bierce's concept) or a vehicle for anti-Irish invective (Pixley's), they were at odds over Pixley's shortcomings as a paymaster. Pixley was a man of substance but he often absented himself on payday, and Bierce, as a friend wrote, "while an excellent debtor, was an abominable creditor. . . . He did not mind owing, because he was sure to pay, sooner or later, but he positively hated anyone who owed him."[5]

In time Pixley became one of Bierce's pet hates, whom he never wearied of attacking until he was safe underground. The matter of Pixley's military title as well as his claims to valiant service on the battlefield were sharply questioned. As Bierce understood it, "During the Civil War he traveled all the way from San Francisco, following the sound of the heaviest firing, until he arrived upon the field just as the battle of Cold Harbor [in 1864] was going against his side.

"The charger that he rode on that memorable occasion did not live to be celebrated in verse and fed on poets, like the one Sheridan rode up the Shenandoah Valley; it had the misfortune to be drowned by plunging off a cape in Labrador. Colonel Pixley was rescued by the crew of a passing iceberg and returned forthwith to the extreme western verge of the continent. Having in mind his gallant ride from Cold Harbor to Labrador, the Humane Society soon afterward presented him with its great gold medal for saving life. And the Peace Society says that nothing ever so advanced its cause as this editor's sight of a battlefield."[6]

It also irked him in later years that Pixley and Somers were given credit for the *Argonaut*'s almost immediate acceptance in an already crowded field of weekly literary journals and monthly periodicals, even though their associate editor assumed the principal editorial tasks during his several years with the *Argonaut*, which undoubtedly would not have long endured merely as the spokesman for Nob Hill's wrath against Kearney and the proletariat south of the slot. Shortly after Pixley's death in 1895, Bierce wrote in his *Examiner* column that his efforts on behalf of the *Argonaut* were being ignored by the local literary historians. "When Fred Somers died the world was copiously informed that he 'made' The Argonaut. Now that Frank Pixley is dead we are told that it was he who 'made' The Argonaut. In the uncertain light of these statements I seem to see myself standing in the literary Pantheon, before the statues of the two great founders, scratching my poor dazed head and vaguely wondering if I am anybody in particular, whither I have strayed and why I am not put out by the janitor."[7]

Actually Bierce's imprint was on every page of the weekly, and much of its back-of-the-book material consisted of poetry and sketches written by him. Somers was only an occasional visitor at the weekly's offices, and Pixley knew so little of literary forms that the story was told of how he dumbfounded a poet who sent a contribution to the *Argonaut*, had it accepted and appeared in Pixley's office to thank him for "publishing my sonnet."

Pixley looked up and in his bewilderment asked, "What's a sonnet?"[8]

Bierce's output, then and for years to come, was tremendous. Much of his satire is as dead now as the targets at which it was directed, yet an amazing amount still sizzles and lends to its hapless subjects a sort of sacrificial immortality. "Thrown off at white heat as so much of it was, it represents the man who wrote it as no carefully considered writing ever represents its author," as the late San Francisco critic Joseph Henry Jackson commented.[9]

Local poets were often roasted to a turn, among them one Hector Stuart, who retorted in a rival column:

When he lived long enough
He belched his last puff,
And burst like a wad of gun-cotton;
Now here he doth lie,
Turned to a dirt pie,
Like all that he scribbled — forgotten.

To which Bierce replied a week later in his "Prattle" column: "Concerning my epitaph by Hector S. Stuart, it is perhaps sufficient to say that I ought to be willing to have my name at the top of it if he is willing to have his at the bottom. As to Mr. Stuart's opinion that my work will soon be forgotten, I can assure him that that view of the matter is less gloomy to me than it ought to be to him. I do not care for fame, and he does; and his only earthly chance of being remembered is through his humble connection with what I write."

At the time it was his view that local poets should be discouraged, if possible, by sternly ignoring them and their effusions. That he himself was a part-time local poet did not dissuade him. Their notorious touchiness, their bickering and endless feuding offended him as might the yapping from a kennel too close to his windows. They would not be stamped out despite his best efforts. "Have they stopped writing?" he complained. "Have they shut down the back windows of their souls and ceased for even a week to pour a deluge of bosh upon the earth? Who began this thing? As the steel-trap said to the fox."[10]

"Bierce certainly knew the technique of verse," Jerome Hart, a member of the *Argonaut* staff, later wrote, "and knowing it was a savage critic of poets — or let us say, poetasters. . . . There were then many writers of verse who felt the urge for print. Most of their work was mediocre, much of it was bad, and some of it was ludicrous. Upon these 'poets' Bierce was wont to pounce like a hawk on a hen. Similarly their squawks resounded throughout the poetic barnyard as the feathers flew. Most of the poor creatures did not deserve such savage treatment."[11] Hart ascribed the harsh treatment of the local minnesingers to Bierce's own bitter disappointment at not being able to create serious verse.

Bierce finally took notice of Kearney and his followers in the summer of 1877, several months after assuming editorship of the *Argonaut*. In his frustration Kearney had declared that "bullets will now replace ballots" and had loosed his more violent supporters on Chinatown. One night in July they looted and burned Chinese shops, terrorized the residents, set fire to the Pacific Mail Company's docks, and ran wild for two days before the police finally managed to bring them under control. The Businessmen's Vigilance Committee sallied forth with their pickhandles, raided Kearney's headquarters and arrested Kearney himself. Kearney was kept in jail for two weeks before the due process of the law was invoked. Meanwhile the rest of the country was enduring a violent and crippling railroad strike, largely directed at Jay Gould, in which Eastern terminals were destroyed and railroad yards wrecked. For months the whole country seemed to be on the verge of anarchy.

"Thousands — tens of thousands of armed men," Bierce wrote, "are drilling all over the United States to overthrow the government. I tell you the good god, Majority, means mischief."

Reform legislation being pushed through the state legislature, which provided for some regulation of the public utilities and a tax on common carriers, did not meet with his approval. The pickhandle was a better answer to the sandlot demagogues. Legislation of that sort, he said, was "a confection of sin in a diction of solecisms." He had no great faith in the ability of a democracy to cope with such social and economic problems except to answer force with force; the average man was, to Bierce, "that immortal ass." Despotism was the only feasible method of ruling the vast and heterogeneous United States; it was even best for the people so ruled. "The despot is powerful for evil, but equally powerful for good." Civilization was largely "the work of despotic rulers."[12]

For the most part, however, the droller aspects of life engaged his attention. The new dance crazes, "affected by the children of the gaslight," caught his censorious eye. One of them, the Glide, with its "confusion of limbs," was commending itself "alike to the lecherous intelligence of the fading rake and the prying mind of the simpleton, alert for lewd emotion."[13] A local female character noted for her eccentric behavior had been found sleeping in a cemetery, and Bierce commented in "Prattle" that "Mary's preference for lodging with dead men is, I confess, indefensible — she may not be demented; she is indisputably unique." He also flicked his whip at the Masons and their "blazonry of meaningless mystery," and advised them, "Attain to the dignity of Most Worshipful Blue Ring-Tailed Turtle Dove and Past Arch Grand Lunatic. What is the good of it all?"

The elaborate hoax, designed to take in rivals as well as the reading public, was the favorite pastime of nineteenth-century journalists. Bierce could not resist joining the game himself, from time to time, and one result of this semiliterary horseplay was a little volume titled *The Dance of Death*. His collaborators were William H. Rulofson, the photographer, and T. A. Harcourt, who had contributed to the *News-Letter* when Bierce was its managing editor. The book professed to be horrified at the libidinous qualities of the waltz. That dance, declared the pseudonymous author William Herman, was nothing but the "open and shameless gratification of sexual desire." But while denouncing the waltz and those who surrendered to its "lascivious" charms, the authors dwelt in voluptuous detail on women "yielding to the clutches of their partners"; the prose was such as to send the whole population out waltzing in the streets.

Bierce and his collaborators were delighted by the stir the book caused. It sold eighteen thousand copies, though distributed only by a local publisher; clergymen squabbled over whether it was a moral tract or a calculated invitation to further displays of immodesty, and the authors were particularly exhilarated when a Methodist church conference endorsed it. Bierce himself helped sales along by denouncing it in his "Prattle" column:

" 'The Dance of Death' is a high-handed outrage, a criminal assault upon public modesty, an indecent exposure of the author's mind! From cover to cover it is one long sustained orgasm of a fevered imagination — a long revel of intoxicated propensities. And this is the book in which local critics find a satisfaction to their minds and hearts! This is the poisoned chalice they are gravely commending to the lips of good women and pure girls! Their asinine praises may perhaps have this good effect: William Herman may be tempted forth, to disclose his disputed identity and father his glory. Then he can be shot."*[14]

Perhaps his share of the profits from the book was considerable enough to persuade him to make the move back to San Rafael, the Marin County resort town where the atmosphere was kinder to his asthma. He and his wife and three children moved into a comfortable house from which he commuted by ferry to the *Argonaut* office in San Francisco. Unfortunately, from his viewpoint, Mrs. Day decided she couldn't be separated by that much distance from her daughter. His mother-in-law moved in with him, and he gained further insight into his father-in-law's preference for living in remote mining camps.

His own mother died in the spring of 1878 but Bierce, the consistently undutiful son, did not return to Indiana for her funeral; nor had he when his father died two years earlier. Tribal feelings were all but extinct in him even then, and years later he told Walter Neale, the man who published his collected works, that he believed that children should be "reared outside the environs of the homes in which they are brought up."

At home Bierce tended to shut himself off from the family, not only his mother-in-law but his wife and children. He was largely an absentee husband and father, so much so that some of his colleagues believed he was separated from Mollie Bierce. Often he spent his nights tippling at the newly established Bohemian Club, of which he was elected secretary. He held his liquor like a gentleman, regarded himself as an authority on wines and a connoisseur of brandy, which he was to define in *The Devil's Dictionary* as "a cordial composed of one part of thunder and lightning, one part remorse, two parts bloody murder, one part death-hell-and-the-grave, and four parts clarified Satan." It may not have been a ringing endorsement of brandy, but his fellows

---

* Shortly thereafter a book titled *The Dance of Life* was published in rebuttal. Some literary historians believe its author, "J. Milton Sloluck," was also Bierce, but he later denied it while admitting to his role in publishing *The Dance of Death*.

at the Bohemian Club testified he was handy at sinking his share of it. Clubmanship, however, wasn't really his style, and the insistent fellowship of the bar and dining rooms must often have irritated him. Nor was he an unqualified success as secretary of the Bohemians. When the emperor of Brazil came to San Francisco on a visit, Bierce was requested by the board to extend him an invitation to dine with the members. "Idiotic syco-phancy," snorted Bierce, refusing to issue the invitation which he believed would only exhibit the "flexibility of the republican knee and the arch of the republican back."

Even when he tore himself away from the club and various other watering places that lay in wait between the *Argonaut* office and the ferry which took him to sylvan San Rafael, he would hole up in his study, go for long solitary walks, or take off on hunting trips with the sheriff of Marin County. Sheriff James Tunstead was a huge uneducated fellow with no literary tastes whatsoever, and Bierce apparently found much relief in his uncomplicated backwoods personality. Generally Tunstead sim-ply climbed in a window when he came looking for Bierce. Once he did so while Mrs. Bierce was presiding over a tea party. The sheriff, utterly disconcerted at having blundered into so polite a gathering, "fell over a footstool," as Bierce's young daughter Helen would recall, "and remarked in a voice that sounded like thunder in the High Sierras that it was a warm day," then "in a frantic rush escaped to the great outdoors." Bierce would occasionally take approving note of Sheriff Tun-stead's style on the gallows. "Mr. Tunstead is hanging people so neatly and pleasantly that the fellows who wish to die in that way are flocking into Marin to commit their murders."[15]

In the city itself there was always the current feud, the present object of spleen, to amuse him and the readership of "Prattle." As a commentator on human folly he was undeterred by the contemporary practice of inflicting corporal punishment on offending editors and writers. He even dared to attack actresses and suffragettes, who were notorious for resenting unkind re-marks by resort to the parasol, the hatpin or their fingernails. A sizable row ensued when he covered an opening at the Baldwin Theater in October 1878 and referred to the leading lady, Katie

Mayhew, as "a charming blackguard." Afterward he insisted that it was an entirely playful reference to the way she played her part. However, at the time, her husband, Harry Widmer, who directed the orchestra in the Baldwin's pit, considered the remark a reflection on his wife's character, not on that of the part she played, and came storming up to the *Argonaut* office. Widmer found Bierce in his office, walked up to him and slapped him. The two men grappled, knocking over chairs and tables; then Bierce was slammed into a glass-fronted bookcase, the crash of which brought publisher Pixley and other reinforcements on the run. They arrived just as Bierce was reaching for his .45 caliber revolver with every apparent intention of plugging Widmer. Pixley and the others managed to persuade Bierce not to add homicide to his crimes as a part-time dramatic critic, and Widmer was hastily shown the stairway.

Widmer marched over to the offices of the *Chronicle*, whose proprietor Mike De Young was always receptive to any enemies of Ambrose Bierce, and gave an interview in which he stated that Bierce was a liar, coward, ruffian, etc.[16]

Bierce blazed back in the next issue of the *Argonaut*: "Mr. Henry Widmer has not thought it expedient to act upon my studiously respectful suggestion that he disavow the insulting falsehoods published concerning me in his name. Moreover, I can prove him their author — that he devoted the life which I mercifully spared to systematic defamation of my character and conduct. I, therefore, take this opportunity to remind those who have the misfortune to know him, that he has the distinguished honor to be, not a man of principle, but a ruffian; not a man of truth, but a liar; not a man of courage, but a coward. In order that there may be no mistake as to what member of the canaille I mean, I will state that I refer to Fiddler Widmer, the charming blackguard."[17]

Widmer, having caught sight of that heavy revolver, managed to stay out of Bierce's path and decided against accepting what was in effect a challenge to a duel. Perhaps he was more modern-minded than Bierce, to whom an "affair of honor" was still a commendable ritual for the purging of differences between gentlemen.

Bierce's comments on the political scene also seemed likely to involve him in violent retribution, a possibility which caused him to wear that army Colt on the street as well as to keep it in easy reach at the office. Many of them were in the manner of his note on the death of a prominent Oakland citizen: "The personal property of the late Anthony Chabot, of Oakland, has been ordered sold. This is a noble opportunity to obtain Senator Vrooman." He was equally acerb in commenting on the Presidential qualifications of Rutherford B. Hayes, who had entered the White House in 1877: "There was enough of Lincoln to kill and enough of Grant to kick; but Hayes is only a magic-lantern image without even a surface to be displayed upon. You can not see him, you can not feel him; but you know that he extends in lessening opacity all the way from the dark side of John Sherman to the confines of space."* On the death of Governor George Stoneman, whose readiness to pardon criminals attracted Bierce's disfavor, he would write one of those quatrains which later got him in considerable trouble, as when he was accused of having inspired the assassination of President McKinley. It read:

> Stoneman at last is made to dwell
>   Where pardons do not come;
> O Father, thou dost all things well
>   Though rather late with some.

The fall election of 1879 excited considerable interest because the Workingmen's Party — now minus the services of Denis Kearney — had presented a more reasonable platform than genocide for the Chinese and salutary lynchings for the state legislature and proposed a slate of candidates headed by the Reverand Isaac S. Kalloch. The *Chronicle*, which scented a change in the political wind with the gradual upturn of the economy, campaigned vigorously against the reverend gentleman and dug up an old scandal involving him in an unseemly affair. There was a brawl involving Charles De Young, brother of the *Chronicle's*

---

* Sherman was a United States Senator from Ohio, long a power in the Republican party, and brother of General William T. Sherman, for whose generalship and character Bierce had little respect.

publisher, and Kalloch's son which ended with De Young shot dead. The Reverend Kalloch, nevertheless, won the election, and Bierce, disregarding the marksmanship of the new mayor's son, denounced the reverend mayor as "this fallen gentleman, this moral pirate, this preacher pitchforked into power."

Toward the end of 1879, Bierce's contribution to the *Argonaut's* success was so considerable that it was accounted the foremost weekly periodical in the West. His asthmatic condition worsened, however, and he gave up his editorial duties that summer. From then on he contributed whenever his health permitted. San Rafael had not turned out to be particularly conducive to soothing his bronchial condition. Asthma is now believed to be of psychosomatic origin in many cases. Bierce contracted it before his marriage, of course, but the presence of his mother-in-law in the home may have increased the severity of the attacks to the point where he was unable to work regularly. Doubtless Bierce irritated Mrs. Day, and to a lesser extent his wife, not only by his moodiness, his refusal to be thoroughly domesticated, but by the constant presence of Sheriff Tunstead. Association with Tunstead wasn't likely to improve the family's social position, always of prime importance to Mrs. Day, who had been overjoyed when they were all listed in the *Elite Directory*, then San Francisco's social register. Nor were such villainous squibs as his assault on the dignity of society editors: "Mr. Samuel Smith, who lives in Geyserville, exults in a calf which has no fore-legs, but which 'goes backward and forward with equal facility' on his hind ones. Attach a cork right-hand to this creature, operated by strings connected with its tail, and it would write excellent society personals for the daily newspapers."[18] Or his remark about that guide to gentility, *Godey's Lady's Book*: "It is a publication which from the teens of our grandmothers has poured a thick and slab stream of irreparable bosh into the misunderstanding of genderless gents, lettered wet nurses and misses cherishing a blasted hope apiece."[19] Or the utter cynicism of his comment on recent excavations in the Middle West: "Two male skeletons of the mound builders have been dug up in Kentucky, one lying across the other, and the fingers of each clutching the throat of the other. The skeleton of the woman has not yet been discovered, but it is probably somewhere there about, reposing with tender trust on the breast of a third male."[20]

The rumor sped around, of course, that Pixley had fired his unruly editor-columnist, and later the story became part of the San Francisco literary legend. Evidently it was encouraged by their later feuding in print. Bierce returned to his duties at the *Argonaut* in the fall of 1879, and severed his connection with the journal a few months later on fairly amicable terms with his employer. The cause of that severance had nothing to do with his frequent disagreements with Pixley on matters of editorial policy. Actually Pixley was fairly tolerant of the Bierce temperament. (For example, he had started a campaign to remove General Oliver H. La Grange as head of the United States Mint. This embarrassed Bierce because La Grange was a friend of his and had, in fact, given his brother Albert a job at the Mint, not to mention Bierce himself when he returned from England. Bierce was allowed to state his views, urging La Grange's retention, in a column next to Pixley's editorial hotly demanding La Grange's removal.) What had distracted Bierce from pursuing his journalistic career was some rather exciting news from the Black Hills.

Any mob activity except a wholesome lynching met with his heavy disapproval. This held true for gold rushes. In his opinion the men who stampeded to California in '49 were a pack of idiots; it stood to reason that only a tiny percentage of them could hope to strike it rich, and the rest would only succeed in nourishing the soil with their bones. In 1898 he would issue the sternest of warnings against the "horde of fools" who streamed out of San Francisco in leaky barges and ancient sidewheelers bound for the Klondike.

Meantime in 1879 Bierce himself caught the gold fever. The badlands of Dakota Territory reportedly were bulging with seams and pockets of gold. Weekly journalism was a dull business compared with gold-hunting and he simply couldn't resist the temptation, not to mention the opportunity to emulate his father-in-law by putting a few mountain ranges between himself and the dragon on his hearth.

SEVEN

Interlude in Rockerville

I T HAS BEEN observed that in their treatment of the Western frontier Bret Harte made the prevalent contempt for the law picturesque and Mark Twain found it humorous, but Ambrose Bierce labeled it for what it was — murder, armed robbery, assault with intent to kill. His occasional essays into Western crime were as bluntly stated as a police blotter: no chivalrous gamblers, just cardsharks; no courtly gunfighters, just homicidal psychopaths; no golden-hearted dancehall girls, just pathetic whores; no gallant soldiers or stouthearted pioneers, just men on the government payroll bored by routine and farmers looking for a better piece of land. The Western legend was, to use his favorite word, bosh. He would not assist in its propagation despite all the evidence that even while the West was being won — or lost, depending on your viewpoint — people wanted the process glorified and thereby justified.

Bierce's attitude toward that assiduous legend-making undoubtedly was formed both by his trip across the West at its wildest as a member of General Hazen's expedition just after the Civil War and by his experiences in the Black Hills in 1880.

He caught the gold fever in the fall of 1879 when the government announced that the badlands of Dakota Territory were being reopened to settlers and miners. That section, so far as relations between the government and the Indians were concerned, had a squalid history. Ironclad treaties had granted the Black Hills to the Sioux as a preserve guaranteed them in perpetuity, largely because their eroded soil was believed useless to settlers and the Sioux believed the Hills were the dwelling place of the Great Manitou. Early in the Seventies rumors began circulating that the crumbling hills were veined with gold. In 1874, Custer and the Seventh Cavalry invaded the territory ostensibly to find a suitable place for a military post. The real purpose of the expedition was evidenced by the fact that it was accompanied by a geologist and two gold miners. That summer one of the miners with the Custer column panned gold from French Creek — and the balloon went up. A Chicago newspaper claimed that there was "a belt of gold territory 30 miles wide" in the Black Hills. Just as stampeders piled up by the hundreds in Cheyenne, the government, having opened Pandora's box, hastily tried to slam the lid shut, piously reminding everyone that the Black Hills were sacred to the Sioux and forbidden by treaty to white settlement. Cavalry patrols gently removed gold rushers whenever they invaded the Hills but still there "came new mobilizations of eager adventurers to rave and fret at the cavalrymen they had failed to elude."[1]

In 1875 a treaty commission, apparently living in the past when tribal lands could be bought for a stack of red blankets, tried to purchase the Black Hills preserve from the Sioux for six million dollars. The Sioux replied that their price was a hundred million. From this demand the government recoiled in surprise and moral indignation. No more discussions of so outrageous a price were permitted. Instead Washington announced that the army would withdraw its patrols, which had mainly succeeded in sealing off the Black Hills, and prepared for a bitter resistance from the Sioux when the whites rushed into the territory during the spring of 1876. One result was the massacre of Custer and two squadrons of the Seventh Cavalry. But within a year the army had taken its revenge for the Little Bighorn, and the Black Hills were officially opened up for white settlement.

"About this time," recalled Jerome Hart, a member of the

Argonaut staff,* "Bierce grew much excited over the talk of gold mines in the Black Hills . . . His knowledge of assaying acquired in the United States Mint led to his securing a well-paid position with a mining company in the Black Hills. He resigned from the Argonaut staff . . . There was no quarrel with Pixley or anyone else; his parting was amicable; everybody in the office wished him well and envied him his potential wealth as a gold miner."[2]

The company which engaged Bierce was the Black Hills Placer Mining Company, hastily organized in New York to take advantage of the publicity given the rush to the badlands and incorporated in New York City on December 8, 1879. Its president was General Alexander Shaler; Cornelius Vanderbilt was a member of the board of directors. More important, the company counsel was Sherburne B. Eaton, who had served with Bierce on General Hazen's staff and had been his superior during Bierce's service as a Treasury agent at Selma, Alabama. Eaton was two years older than Bierce, who looked upon him as an *ex officio* older brother. After resigning his Treasury post Eaton had practiced law in Chicago, then moved to New York and attained prominence as a corporation lawyer.

In addition to his experience from his assaying work at the Mint, Bierce had two other qualifications for a post with the new mining company. He was a topographical engineer, and in 1877 A. L. Bancroft and Company of San Francisco had published a map of the Black Hills country "drawn by A. G. Bierce" as part of his surveys for the War Department (actually it is likely that only the Wyoming and Montana section of the map was Bierce's handiwork, since Hazen's expedition hadn't entered the Black Hills territory). Also, Bierce may have picked up a certain amount of information about gold-mining technology from his father-in-law. But his ace-in-the-hole undoubtedly was his old friendship with "Sherb" Eaton.

In the spring of 1880 he was appointed to take charge of the company's operations at Rockerville, near the hell-roaring capital

---

* Bierce regarded him with little respect. He wrote that Hart "learned to write poetry, paint on velvet and smile, and became known as the Magnetic Clam."

of the gold rush, Deadwood, Dakota Territory. Meanwhile, the company was raking in hundreds of thousands of dollars from investors with its glowing prospectus. The company claimed it had bought up fifteen hundred different claims in the Rockerville area, comprising hundreds of acres of creek bottoms, bars and gulches, and that its experts maintained there was two billion dollars' worth of gold ore on the land it had acquired. All that was needed was modern mining methods. A dam would be built on Spring Creek and the water necessary for placer mining would be conveyed eighteen miles down the eroded slopes through tunnels and wooden flumes. Hundreds of laborers were already on the scene digging the tunnels and building trestles for the flumes.

Both in New York and in San Francisco it was believed that a bonanza would soon be uncovered. And Ambrose Bierce, appointed general agent for the company at Rockerville, would enrich himself as well as the company and its stockholders. With this golden aura hovering over him, Bierce wrote Henry Sampson, a journalist friend in London, that the venture would rescue him from the haphazard career of a journalist "for good and all." Sampson, however, had witnessed so many such hopeful flights from journalism that he replied somewhat cynically, "How I envy you when you say that journalism is over with you! But I think I read somewhere once about a dog and his vomit which would doubtless apply in my case if it doesn't in yours."[3]

His euphoric mood undiminished, Bierce departed for the goldfields, traveled by rail and stage, and arrived in Deadwood early in July 1880. Deadwood Gulch, a dead-end canyon notched in the Dakota wilderness, was the frontier boomtown at its worst. Every able-bodied thug, whore, pimp, gambler and sharper in the West had been attracted there. A few years earlier Wild Bill Hickok had carelessly exposed his rear while playing poker in one of the dives and had been shot in the back of the head by a youth who wanted to make a name for himself. Miners' courts and a handful of United States deputy marshals attempted to maintain a measure of law and order, but a man without a gun on his hip felt naked walking down the main street. "Deadwood was then hog-wild," said one pioneer resident; "duels and gun-fights in the streets, and often one had to duck or fall flat on the ground to escape a shower of lead." Bierce must have been confirmed in his low opinion of anarchy as a philosophy for the conduct of human affairs.

He must also have been discouraged when and if someone showed him a copy of the Deadwood *Evening News* of mid-March that year which asserted that the Black Hills Placer Mining Company was "the most gigantic fraud ever perpe-trated."[4]

The affairs of the company, as he soon learned, were in a complete mess. His predecessor was a Captain Ichabone M. West, who had been entrusted with a two-hundred-thousand-dollar draft on the First National Bank of Deadwood, which had mostly evaporated by the time Bierce arrived in Rockerville. Furthermore, on July 1, shortly before Bierce arrived, West had been arrested on charges of embezzling the company's stock from a Mrs. Sophie Hale. Even so West, out on bail, didn't intend to hand over authority to Bierce without a fight. At first the executive committee of the company backed Bierce, ruling that he was in charge of all operations; then it decreed that West would continue in charge of construction operations.

Right from the start his experience as a gold-mine executive must have been disillusioning, but he plunged into the job of getting the company's operations under way. During the four months he spent in the mining camp of Rockerville he succeeded in bringing the flume down from the hills and keeping his work force on the job despite delays in meeting the payroll. Mean-while, West, who had personal friends on the board of directors, kept intriguing against Bierce by mail and trying to have him removed. To offset this constant bushwhacking by his supposed subordinate, who was not only crooked but incompetent, he had to rely on Eaton's influence with the executive committee.

He had envisioned himself overseeing the extraction of a stream of gold from the hillsides and creekbeds; instead he spent a miserable, dangerous summer trying to get the flume built before winter set in and writing letter after letter to Eaton in

New York pleading for more funds, more understanding of the situation.

The danger came from the "road agents" who infested the territory and regularly held up the Deadwood stage on its twice-a-week run to Sidney, near Rockerville. "So intolerable had this practice become," Bierce recalled in the only writing he did on the subject of his experiences as a mine executive, "even iron-clad coaches loopholed for rifles proving a vain device, that the mine owners had adopted the more practicable plan of importing from California a half-dozen of the most famous 'shotgun messengers' of Wells, Fargo & Co. — fearless and trusty fellows with an instinct for killing, a readiness of resource that was an intuition, and a sense of direction that put a shot where it would do the most good more accurately than the most careful aim. Their feats of marksmanship were so incredible that seeing was scarcely believing. In a few weeks these chaps had put the road agents out of business and out of life, for they attacked them wherever found. One sunny Sunday morning two of them strolling down a street of Deadwood recognized five or six of the rascals, ran back to their hotel for their rifles, and returning killed them all!"[5]

As his company's shotgun messenger Bierce hired an efficient man-killer named Boone May, who was the current regional titleholder of fastest gun in the Dakotas and who bore the further distinction of being under indictment for murder. May had trailed a well-known bandit named Frank Towle across the badlands to a place called Robber's Roost; there was a two-thousand-dollar bounty on Towle dead or alive. He captured Towle and brought him to within a few miles of Deadwood, when darkness overtook them and they were forced to camp for the night. May picketed Towle out for the night as he would a horse. Toward dawn Towle made an attempt to escape, was shot, killed and buried by the roadside. May returned to Deadwood the next morning and only then learned the size of the reward on Towle's head. He hurried back to the grave, dug up his victim, cut off his head and brought it to Deadwood as proof in claiming the reward. The gentle folk of Deadwood were repelled by May's brutal sense of practicality, and charged him with murder. It was considered a grievous affront to the bounty hunter's trade that his methods should be questioned.[6]

Someone wrote to the New York headquarters of Bierce's company and complained about his hiring a man under indictment for murder. May, of course, was acquitted of the murder charge but Bierce was still in trouble with some of the more squeamish company officials who, however, failed to flinch when Ichabone West was arrested for swindling a stockholder and, worse yet, was unable to account for a large portion of funds entrusted to him for construction work. "Some of the New York directors of my company having been good enough to signify their disapproval of my action in employing 'such a man' [May]," Bierce recalled later, "I could do no less than make some recognition of their dissent and thenceforth he was borne upon the payrolls as 'Boone May, Murderer.' "[7]

Bierce had good reason for stubbornly protecting May's job as the company's resident gunslinger. One day, accompanied by May and his sidearms, he had drawn thirty thousand dollars from the company's funds in the Deadwood bank, largely to pay off his work force, and set out for Rockerville in a wagon. "Naturally, I had taken the precaution to telegraph my secretary at Rockerville to meet me at Rapid City, then a small town, on another route; the telegram was intended to mislead the 'gentlemen of the road' whom I knew to be watching my movements, and who might possibly have a confederate in the telegraph office. . . .

"I knew the road fairly well, for I had previously traveled it by night, on horseback, my pockets bulging with currency and my free hand holding a cocked revolver the entire distance of fifty miles. To make the journey by wagon with a companion was a luxury. Still, the drizzle of rain was uncomfortable.

"May sat hunched up beside me, a rubber poncho over his shoulders and a Winchester rifle in its leathern case between his knees. I thought him a trifle off his guard, but said nothing. The road, barely visible, was rocky, the wagon rattled, and alongside ran a roaring stream.

"Suddenly we heard through it all the clinking of a horse's shoes directly behind, and simultaneously the short, sharp words of authority: 'Throw up your hands.'

"With an involuntary jerk at the reins I brought my team to its haunches and reached for my revolver. Quite needless: with the quickest movement that I had ever seen in anything but a cat — almost before the words were out of the horseman's mouth — May had thrown himself backward across the back of the seat, face upward, and the muzzle of his rifle was within a yard of the fellow's breast!"

What then? With a tigerish yawn, Bierce added, "What further occurred among the three of us there in the gloom of the forest has, I fancy, never been accurately related." In fact, it was never related at all until Bierce wrote his account years later. The fate of the bandit is left a mystery, with a suggestion that he still lies buried in the "gloom of the forest."[8]

The encounter with an out-and-out bandit must have come as welcome relief that summer as Bierce struggled to obtain the funds from New York to continue operations. The most pathetic letters Bierce ever wrote were addressed to Sherb Eaton, whose suppleness as an operator Bierce should have observed more closely when Eaton was his largely absentee superior in the Treasury agency.* Bierce's faith in Eaton was complete; almost every letter to New York reiterates his belief that his old friend was doing his best to protect him against the home-office intrigues. Yet Eaton must have known that the company treasury had been hollowed out long before Bierce was engaged as general agent at Rockerville. It had been tapped, undoubtedly, at both ends. Ichabone West had diverted much of the money for construction, and insiders in New York, operating more subtly, must have enriched themselves at the source. Despite all the talk of a billion-dollar bonanza, New York investors had become wary of the company early that summer; the several wealthy men on its board wouldn't put up a dime to continue operations and find out whether they had really tapped a mother lode. Eaton, as company counsel, certainly knew the hopelessness of the financial position and should have enlightened Bierce.

Meanwhile, through heroic effort, Bierce had brought the

---

* The correspondence has been largely resurrected in a diligent piece of research by Professor Paul Fatout in his *Ambrose Bierce and the Black Hills*, Norman, Okla., 1956.

flume down from the hills. More than once he had to confront a saloon full of enraged and unpaid laborers and plead with them to be patient and wait for their money.

"Believe in me, Sherb, and sustain me," he wrote Eaton more than once,[9] though that plea should have been addressed by Eaton to Bierce.

The company "sustained" him by sending out its treasurer, Marcus Walker, a niggling and small-minded fellow, to investigate the situation. The investigation, of course, was a flimflam to conceal the simple fact that the company's funds had evaporated. It was obvious from the start that Mr. Walker intended to spend his time peering over Bierce's shoulder rather than into the curious ledgers kept by Ichabone West.

Both Bierce and Walker kept writing to the home office to defend themselves and complain about each other. Walker was particularly offended by the sight of Boone May, with his wolfish grin, sitting around the Rockerville office, cleaning his guns and looking dangerous. Walker claimed in a letter to New York that May was actually Bierce's "guard" and should be fired.

"Mr. Walker," Bierce retorted, "is a little afraid of him, but he is really quite harmless if tenderly handled."

He referred to Walker as a "former counter-jumper," who had received his business training in a grocery or drygoods store.

When Walker kept insisting that May be fired, Bierce declared that his pet gunman was a "messenger in a kind of service in which I have not the time to risk my own life instead of his." The board of directors finally upheld Bierce in that matter.

Walker then recommended to the board that Bierce himself be discharged on the grounds that he was "not a businessman."

All the bickering, taken together with the fact that Bierce finally realized that the company was running out of capital and that his own salary was in arrears, impelled him to write Eaton on September 4, 1880, offering to resign if Eaton believed it would be for the best. "Time presses," he wrote Eaton, "winter approaches and I mean to spend next winter with my family somewhere."[10]

Eaton, however, suggested that he stay on. On September 24,

Bierce again offered his resignation. While waiting for it to be acted on, in early October, he found that the company was simply unwilling or unable to raise the money for the payroll. The Deadwood bank, furthermore, had tied up all the funds there because of the growing legal entanglement over Ichabone West's use of the money placed on deposit. Bierce decided to go to New York and see whether the situation could be resolved. He spent two months in New York while Eaton, Walker and other officials of the company dithered. It finally became apparent that they couldn't raise any more capital and weren't willing to part with any of their own money as a sporting flutter on the possibility that the bonanza promised in their prospectus really existed.

Next year the company admitted it was insolvent and its vast patchwork of claims was broken up and worked by various independents until the Nineties. Nothing like an important strike was ever made in the Rockerville region. The profits in the venture in which Bierce became involved through his friendship with Eaton came out of the stockholders' pockets. Bierce himself evidently received little or nothing for his efforts, except a quick brutal education in the facts of business life.*

For years afterward Bierce was involved in litigation over the Black Hills Placer Mining Company's affairs. As late as 1886 he was being summoned to give depositions in a relatively unimportant suit, filed by the company's attorneys against the First National Bank of Deadwood in Bierce's name, for recovery of three thousand dollars claimed due on a bank draft. Once, indicating his attitude toward the company, he wrote the law firm handling the case, "My experience with the company's officers has not been such that I am willing to take any steps in matters affecting them without some guaranty that my action

---

* And, according to Adolphe Danziger, a future protégé, collaborator and biographer, he conceived a scheme, inspired by his journey to and from Dakota Territory, for a publicity campaign through which the Southern Pacific and Central Pacific could colonize its right of way between Utah and California. In return Bierce would be given the post of publicity director of the Southern Pacific. Collis P. Huntington, head of the Southern Pacific, turned the proposal down, according to Danziger. No proof can be found that Bierce ever made such a proposal.[11]

will be acceptable to them." Undoubtedly many of the remarks he made about lawyers and courts and the legal barricades behind which big business operated owed much to his experience in the aftermath of the Rockerville bonanza that wasn't.

There was nothing for him to do but return to San Francisco and confess himself a failure. The confrontation with Mother Day, who had been sheltering Mollie and his children while he was sojourning in the Black Hills, must have been one of the darker hours of his life. He immediately removed his wife and family from the Day home in San Francisco and took a small house in the Fort Mason district on a hillside overlooking the Bay. And then it was back to writing for a living until the end of his life.

EIGHT *Almighty God Bierce*

WITH HIS TALENTS and versatility
Bierce could undoubtedly have tapped a more profitable vein
than writing paragraphs for the weeklies. Yet he insisted on staying a bitter outsider on the literary scene. "Bitter Bierce" they
had called him in London, and the pose had become the man.
Popular literature, he stated more than once, was beneath him.
The niceness, the sunniness, the glowing optimism required of
the popular writer in the years before realism came into fashion
were, at best, dishonest. He would refer to two of his most noted
contemporaries as "Miss Nancy Howells" and "Miss Nancy
James Jr."

"A popular author," ran one of his epigrams, "is one who
writes what the people think. Genius invites them to think
otherwise."[1]

He was quite confident that he could write the sort of romantic confection, complete with happy ending, that the magazines demanded. "I know how to write a story for magazine
readers for whom literature is too good, but I will not do so, so
long as stealing is more honorable."[2] It was, he believed, merely
a matter of technique (a mistake other equally clever men have
made on the subject). But he rejected that course because it was
incompatible with what he regarded as his literary conscience. He

considered himself a hack but an honest one when he devoted most of his energy to paragraphing for newspapers. As C. Hartley Grattan has observed, Bierce "saw the problem of authorship in his America with clear eyes . . . With almost unequalled fortitude he rejected the easiest way and kept faith with himself. Bierce was an extremely self-conscious man — sometimes too self-conscious. Mark Twain, on the other hand, did not see the difficulties of authorship until after he had gone so far along the road to popular acclaim that he could not retreat. Then and then only did he begin to revolt against the restraints that he had let himself in for. In other words, his case is Bierce's reversed. Bierce saw the inevitable result of making concessions before he was tempted to make any."*

The genial conspiracy of successful writers aimed at proving this was the best of all possible worlds — this America of the Seventies and Eighties when the Indians were subjugated, the defeated South was ransacked, the likes of Gould, Fisk, Sage and Vanderbilt looted the American economy without hindrance, the politics of greed and self-interest were triumphant: the whole process of applying the gilt to the Gilded Age — was something in which he would not join. Hypocrisy was high up on the list of his deadly sins. He would rather remain a disaffected outsider, wearing a tattered cloak of iconoclasm, than join in the pretense that life was beautiful provided you voted the straight ticket, bowed tamely to your betters, went to church on Sundays and didn't beat your wife in public.

Although something of a prude in private life himself, Bierce condemned the prevalent nice-Nellyism in letters which was a passport to material success. "Not Shakespeare, nor Cervantes, nor Goethe, nor Molière, nor — no, not even Rabelais — ever achieved that shining pinnacle of propriety to which the latter-

* Grattan, in his 1929 study *Bitter Bierce*, took a decidedly minority view of the comparative potentials of Twain and Bierce. "It is almost beyond question that Bierce's mind was keener, more disciplined, more penetrating, and in every way of a higher quality. If their cynicisms run parallel it is because both were underfed intellectually and both betray a lack of culture. But the quality of their minds was quite different, and the potentialities of Bierce impress me much more than those of Mark Twain."

day American has aspired, by turning his back upon nature's broad and fruitful levels and his eyes upon the passionate altitudes where, throned upon congenial ice, Miss Nancy sits to censure letters, putting the Muses into petticoats and affixing a figleaf upon Truth. Ours are an age and a country of expurgated editions, emasculated art, and social customs that look over the top of a fan."[3]

The deodorizing of literature had deeper consequences, he believed, than met the eye. "Prudery in letters, if it would but have the goodness not to coexist with prudery in life, might be suffered with easy fortitude . . . but it occurs that a literature rather accurately reflects all the virtues and other vices of its period and country, and its tendencies are but the matchings of thought with action."[4]

Thus Bierce consciously set himself the task of attacking all that was corrupt and vulgar in his times. He was a moralist in the trappings of a satirist. His targets were the intellectually deprived and the morally delinquent, with few exceptions. Among the fools whom he appointed himself to chastize were the provincial patriots, the sentimentalists (not least among them the dog lovers), the members of fraternal lodges, and Philistines of all varieties. He did not suffer fools gladly, but he was gentler with stupidity than with villainy. Among the morally delinquent he included five groups of objectionable characters: the literary and artistic and journalistic; capitalists and labor union organizers; all members of all forms of government; all reformers and members of the clergy; and a loose category including most high-ranking soldiers, educators, scientists and physicians. That left him a very narrow segment of the population of whom he could approve, a fact which did not dismay him in the least.

When he returned to San Francisco, Bierce confidently expected to rejoin the staff of the *Argonaut*, if not as managing editor then as conductor of his "Prattle" column. He had made no secret of the fact he believed that he "made" the *Argonaut*. Yet it had survived for some months while he was in the Black Hills, and his former colleagues, Pixley and Somers, found that their offices were much quieter and more serene without Bierce fulminating, aloud and in print, on the premises; Bierce had attracted readers, but he had also made enemies for the weekly and was rarely respectful of editorial policy. Jerome Hart, a member of the staff, was assigned to inform Bierce that he wasn't wanted back on the *Argonaut*. Bierce, said Hart, was enraged at the news and held Pixley alone responsible for the decision and "never forgave him."[5] From then until Pixley's death Bierce used whatever platform was available to denounce his former employer. "Pixley," he wrote in one of his milder moods, "is as good as it is possible for him to be, has all the dignity he needs in making a back for all the rich to play at leapfrog, and as much amiability as is not incompatible with an assassination of character."

For several months he was forced to piece together a living out of freelancing for various newspapers and magazines. One journal to which he contributed during this lean period was the San Francisco *Call*, despite the fact that he had often denounced its weak-kneed policy on the subject of Denis Kearney and other mob rousers. He had also offended its editor, Loren Pickering, a man who prided himself on a lordly command of the language, by admonishing him in the "Prattle" column a year or two earlier: "Mr. Pickering, I have told you a dozen times that to call rain a 'pluvial dispensation,' is to be a magniloquent idiot, compared with whose style the song of a sturdy jackass in braying his love to a star is chaste and elegant diction." The Bierce perversity, it seems, ended even that tenuous connection. While Bierce was contributing occasional pieces to the *Call*, Pickering in an editorial urged San Francisco employers to pay their employees in currency rather than silver, as had been the custom. Bierce, shortly after the piece appeared, went to the cashier's window at the *Call* to collect his money for an article. The cashier attempted to pay him off in silver. Bierce showed him a clipping of Pickering's editorial. A row ensued, but the cashier finally went to a bank, got the necessary bills and paid Bierce off as he demanded. That ended his freelance contributions to the newspaper.

Even while Bierce was scrounging a living out of writing occasional squibs and sketches, an opportunity was opening up for him. There had been a shakeup on the *Wasp*, the satirical weekly, and the new management was looking for an editor and managing editor. Ostensibly its new owner was Harry Dam, but he was only the figurehead behind which a brilliant schemer named Charles Webb Howard operated. Howard was president of the Spring Valley Water Company. As a public utility supplying water to many of the cities on the Bay, the company had a large advertising budget. Why, Howard wondered, shouldn't that money be funneled into an enterprise from which he would profit? Thus, unknown to anyone but Howard and Dam, the *Wasp* was to serve as Howard's hidden source of income; that tidy phrase "conflict of interest" had not yet been coined and wouldn't have mattered if it had been.

Bierce was engaged to take over the editorship with Edward C. MacFarlane as managing editor. He was promised a free hand and promptly exercised it. His first editorial move was to assign himself to revive the "Prattle" column. He also wrote poetry, sketches, short stories and all the editorials, as well as editing all the other material that went into its columns. Soon after taking over he also began a department called "The Wasp's Book of Wisdom" in which many of his epigrams and aphorisms appeared. The "pared phrase," or one-liner as it is now called, may not be the highest of art forms, but certainly, in Bierce's hands, it was a perfect vehicle for his slashing wit and inveterate misanthropy.

To give a certain form to his pungent observations he immediately began publishing in the "Prattle" column the first definitions of *The Devil's Dictionary*, which were later collected in book form and which still provide happy confirmation for any person in a morose mood. He began his compilation, oddly enough, with the letter "P" and then worked back to the beginning of the alphabet. A few of his choicer observations in the early issues of the *Wasp* under his command:

PICTURE, a representation in two dimensions of something wearisome in three.

PLATITUDE, a moral without a fable.

PLATONIC, a fool's name for the affection between a disability and a frost.

POLITENESS, acceptable hypocrisy.

POSITIVE, mistaken at the top of one's voice.

PRAY, to ask that the laws of the universe be annulled in behalf of an unworthy petitioner.

PREJUDICE, a vagrant opinion without visible means of support.

OPTIMIST, a proponent of the doctrine that black is white.

QUILL, an implement of torture yielded by a goose and wielded by an ass.

RIOT, a popular entertainment given to the police by innocent bystanders.

SAINT, a dead sinner revised and edited.

SIREN, any lady of splendid promise and disappointing performance.

SUCCESS, the one unpardonable sin.

TRICHINOSIS, the pig's reply to pork chops.

VIRTUES, certain abstentions.

YEAR, a period of 365 disappointments.

Less impersonally, he loosed a continuous cannonade on all that displeased him on the San Francisco scene. Local novelists and poets were riddled almost without exception, quite possibly because Bierce was conscious of his own inferiority as a poet and his inability (perhaps traceable to a lack of creative stamina) to write anything longer than a short story. It was to this phase of his criticism that the butterfly-crushed-on-a-wheel metaphor applies the most exactly. Bierce's attitude as a literary critic was that of a police magistrate in night court confronted by an endless parade of the witless and fraudulent. Each work submitted to his examination was arraigned, tried and, in most instances, sentenced to summary execution, with no defense entered and no appeals taken.

While Bierce was carrying on his work of literary hangman with such visible relish and ghoulish glee, Fred Somers, who had

moved over to the *Californian* and was still on friendly terms
with Bierce despite the unfriendly severance from the *Argonaut*,
wrote him that his campaign against the talentless was having
results perhaps not recognized by Bierce. "Now if you had not
drummed and hunted these literary pismires out of their holes,
and bruited them into public sympathy and recognition, we
should have been free of them. Yet you still continue poling at
windmills, setting them up often yourself — and for a wage —
sneering at the industry."[6]

When a German-American novelist overstuffed with gemüt-
lichkeit, Harr Wagner, who was editor of *Vanity Fair*, successor
to the *Golden Era*, published his novel *The Street and the
Flower*, Bierce proceeded to demolish it. The novel concerned a
boy of the streets and the lovely girl who brought him salvation.
Bierce plucked its petals one by one; Wagner never wrote
another book. Of the art critic W. C. Bartlett he wrote: "The
old he-hen who makes the *Bulletin*'s art criticism has been in full
cackle ever since the opening of the Spring exhibition. Everything about the exhibition is, to Mr. Bartlett, great and excellent.
Furthermore he has executed this identical prostration of his
spirit every spring since California art began to defy the law
against indecent exposure." Of a poet who boasted that he
managed to create beautiful verse despite the fact he lived in a
garret and dined off crusts, Bierce remarked:

> His poem X ——— says that he indites
> Upon an empty stomach. Heavenly Powers,
> Feed him throat-full, or what he writes
> Upon his empty stomach empties ours.[7]

A cartoon of Bierce which appeared in the *Wasp* several
years after he left its editorship titled "Ambrose Bierce Literary
Dissector" summed up the creative world's opinion of his attitude. Bierce has a half-naked and struggling artist bound to his
dissecting table and has just stabbed a huge quill into his forehead; above him are pictures of other artists hanging from a

noose, being roasted over a fire, being crucified, jumping off a pierhead.

Just as graphically a San Francisco writer, Charlotte Perkins Gilman, would recall him years later as a wholly destructive and sadistic critic. "He was the Public Executioner and Tormentor, daily exhibiting his skill in grilling helpless victims for the entertainment of the public . . . He was an early master in the art of blackening long-established reputations of the great dead, of such living persons as were unable to hit back effectively, and at his best in scurrilous abuse of hard-working women writers. He never lost an opportunity to refer to the cotton-stuffed bosoms of the women writers."[8]

Although he believed there were limitations to poetic license ("all a matter of taste; even grammar must fall if it impede a thought or sentiment good enough to justify the slaughter") he considered that the critic was licensed for an eternal open season on the game he hunted. He warned that he intended to keep the cudgel in hand as long as he was able to wield it: "Now, mark you, rogues of all degrees and lettered fools with phosphorized teeth in mouths full of moonshine, I am among you to remain. While the public buys my rebuking at twice the price your sycophancy earns — while I keep a conscience uncorrupted by religion, a judgment undimmed by politics and patriotism, a heart untainted by friendships and sentiments unsoured by animosities — while it pleases me to write, there will be personalities in journalism, personalities of condemnation as well as commendation."

More soberly, on another occasion, he attempted to define his philosophy of criticism. "I know a chap whose trade is censure," he wrote in a "Prattle" column; "fools are his theme and satire is his song. Knaves and vulgarians, imposters, sycophants, the variously unworthy and the specifically detestable, no sooner draw his eye than he is on to them with bitter abuse . . .

"Moreover, this fellow's social habits are consistent with his literary; he is imperfectly civil to the rich and distinguished, coldly declines invitations, utters his mind with freedom concerning people's characters, takes an infantile delight in cutting men whose acquaintance he deems no longer desirable, cherishes the most shocking convictions, maintains a private system of morality and is not in sympathy with civilization.

"From the books and proverbs it is clearly deducible that this person ought to be the most miserable of men, tormented by conscience, baffled by secret and overt antagonisms, hunted by the dogs of hate reared in his own kennels, and roosted on by homing curses thicker than blackbirds on a tree. So far as I can see, this wretch is mainly engaged . . . in gratifying his soul with a bird's-eye view of human illfare, happy in the prospect of a green old age and indulging fascinating dreams of a blessed hereafter."[9]

A critic with this formidable equipment, callous to the sensibilities of others, indifferent to the aspirations which produced the intended works of art that fell under his examination, was and must be a sort of social outlaw. Expecting nothing from humanity, it must expect nothing from him except his ruthlessly honest opinions. His only duty was to operate his assayer's scales without weighting them with a prejudicial thumb.

The artistic world and its pretensions was only a narrow sector of the front on which Bierce trained his artillery. He usually referred to Frank Pixley as "Mr. Pigsley of the Hogonaut," and composed the famous epitaph for him: HERE LIES FRANK PIXLEY — AS USUAL. The Reverend Mayor Kalloch was continuously reminded of the fact that gunplay by his son was an important factor in his election. The assassination of President Garfield, whom he had disliked from the days of their service with the Army of the Cumberland when Garfield was General Rosecrans's chief of staff, drew only the elliptical comment in "Prattle" that "A convention of colored editors have gravely resolved never to mention in their papers the name of the aspiring youth who shot President Garfield. Things have come to a pretty pass when a man can't keep his name out of the newspapers without shooting the chief magistrate of his beloved country."[10] When a druggist entered the election for supervisor of the Twelfth Ward, Bierce delivered himself of a bit of verse which ended that budding career, remarking on the fact that the candidate had included a plug for his pharmacy in his campaign advertising:

> *Oh, William, such a thrifty trick,*
>   *Closely on genius verges;*
> *Your candidacy makes men sick*
>   *So to your pill-shop double quick*
> *They fly for pukes and purges.*

And when his suspicious eye was caught by a number of "letters to the editor" on the *Chronicle* editorial page urging that Mike De Young, its publisher, enter the race for United States Senator from California, he decided to squelch any such aspirations. After noting that the letters were probably paid for at the usual space rates, he inquired:

> *What! You a senator? You, Mike De Young?*
> *Still reeking of the gutter whence you sprung?*
> *Sir, if all senators were such as you —*
> *Their hands so slender and so crimson, too,*
> *So black their hearts, so lily-white their livers —*
> *The toga's touch would give a man the shivers.*

Not only those who aspired to political office but those who already held it — more particularly the latter, in fact — were subject to unending correction, exposure and chastisement from the Prattler. In 1881 the state legislature was owned by the railroads, particularly the Southern Pacific and its subsidiary, the Central Pacific, and its phalanx of lobbyists and lawyers. Bierce had already fastened upon Collis P. Huntington, president of the Southern Pacific, as perhaps the number-one villain in California. Long-nosed and long-headed, with the face of a Holbein portrait, Huntington was the brain of the "Octopus," as Californians called it, whose tentacles were entwined around every center of the state's political and economic life. With a pack of trade goods, he had come out West during the gold rush, had prospered as a merchant in Sacramento, then had joined up with Stanford, Hopkins and Crockett to pioneer in Western railroading. He was sometimes called "the Jay Gould of the West Coast," but that didn't quite do justice to his talents; he was an original, not merely a Western duplicate of the robber barons. He was shrewd, vindictive, endlessly resourceful (not, in some respects, too unlike Bierce).

Late in the Seventies he had seen that a public utility, to prosper inordinately, had to keep a firm grip on the levers of political power. Instead of sending a lobbyist to Washington in 1878 to obtain favorable legislation, he went himself with a suitcase in which he had packed more than a set of clean collars and a Bible. Bribery, wholesale and unabashed, was his means of dealing with the gentlemen of the Senate. One of the few indiscretions of his long career was detailing just how he set about this in a series of letters to David D. Colton, financial director of the Central Pacific. When Colton died, his widow complained that the "Big Four" were cheating her out of her late husband's interests and handed over to the New York *Sun* the letters Colton had received from Huntington in Washington. Congress, said Huntington, was "a wild set of demagogues" who would accept a bribe but failed to keep a promise. In another letter he vented his scorn for President Hayes, saying "he was not big enough to veto" a bill Huntington wanted passed.[11] During the subsequent Pacific railway investigation by a Congressional committee, Huntington calmly admitted that he made a practice of "lending" money to any legislator who found the cost of living too high in Washington or any of the state capitals where the Southern Pacific's interests were at stake.

In Sacramento, of course, the sight of a Huntington bagman was as common as the handpainted cuspidors on the legislative floor. Early in 1881 a Democratic-Republican coalition had taken over control of the state legislature, but proved no more impervious to Southern Pacific handouts than the Workingmen's Party members who had preceded it. Since the fusion party had promised to throw the rascals out, presumably including the

Huntington agents with their satchels crammed with ready cash, Bierce erupted in outrage when the legislature adjourned in April: "If nonsense were black, Sacramento would need gas lamps at noonday; if selfishness were audible, the most leathern-lunged orator of the lot would appear a deaf mute flinging silly ideas from his finger tips amid the thunder of innumerable drums. So scurvy a crew I do not remember to have discovered in vermiculose conspiracy outside the carcass of a dead horse — at least not since they adjourned."[12]

When he could spare the time from flaying Henry James and William Dean Howells, "two eminent triflers and cameo-cutters-in-chief to Her Littleness the Bostonese small virgin," and political thimble-riggers, Bierce would have a go at religion and its professional practitioners. San Francisco, early in the Eighties, was afflicted by a parade of evangelists who "saved" the city from sinking into Babylonian depravity on the average of once a month: "a procession of holy idiots," as he called them. And worse:

". . . Thick-necked Moody with Sanky of the nasal name; Hallenbeck, Earle, Knops and all their he-harlotry of horribles. And now this grease-eating and salt-encrusted Harrison from the pork regions of the northeast, thinking holy hog-and-hominy and talking his teeth loose for the dissuasion of sinners from their natural diet of sin."

He wondered whether there was anything that would rid the city of visitations from "these phylloxera of the moral vineyard," and hoped the Devil would "smite them with a tempest of sulphuric acid from his Babcock extinguisher."[13]

A local clergyman who was trying one of his female parishioners* on a charge of heresy predictably called down on himself a shower of flaming rhetoric from the Prattler: "Dim-pinnacled in the intense shame of his theological environment, he sits astride

---

* Sarah Cooper, oddly enough, had been a proofreader at the *Overland Monthly* when it was established under Bret Harte's editorship. When he wrote "The Luck of Roaring Camp" for one of its first issues, she revolted at what she regarded as the immorality of some of its passages and attempted to have it killed through protests to the publisher. They were unavailing.

his evil eminence of personal malignity, breaking the seals that close that pestilence, his mind, and its insupportable rain of red ruin falls alike upon the just and the unjust, the while he cackles with unholy glee till the lute-strings of his larynx are aweary of their work. Look at him — the hideous apparition perched between the world and the light, flinging his ugly shadow athwart the scene to fray the souls of babes and sucklings . . . he shall take himself away from Sarah Cooper's burrow or I, for one, will make him wish he were another and better dog."

For those unoffended by his attacks on the religious establishment, the corrupt politicians and the literary and artistic coteries, he continued to publish sections of *The Devil's Dictionary*, now beginning with "A" and working his way forward to "P."

ALONE, in bad company.

AMBITION, an overmastering desire to be vilified by the living and made ridiculous by friends when dead.

BRIDE, a woman with a fine prospect of happiness behind her.

BRUTE, see husband.

CONSUL, in American politics, a person who having failed to secure an office from the people is given one by the Administration on condition that he leave the country.

EGOIST, a person of low taste, more interested in himself than in me.

FRIENDSHIP, a ship big enough to carry two in fair weather, but only one in foul.

GALLOWS, a stage for the performance of miracle plays.

HANDKERCHIEF, a small square of silk or linen used at funerals to conceal a lack of tears.

HUSBAND, one who, having dined, is charged with the care of the plate.

LITIGANT, a person ready to give up his skin in the hope of retaining his bones.

LOVE, a temporary insanity curable by marriage.

MARRIAGE, a master, a mistress and two slaves, making in all, two.

MERCY, an attribute beloved of offenders.

MISFORTUNE, the kind of fortune that never misses.

MOUTH, in man, the gateway to the soul; in woman, the outlet of the heart.

NEPOTISM, appointing your grandmother to office for the good of the party.

NOVEL, a short story padded.

OPPOSITION, in politics, the party that prevents the government from running amuck by hamstringing it.

His several years as editor of the *Wasp* were comparatively serene, aside from the controversies he stirred up and reveled in. At home, perhaps because his mother-in-law was only a frequent visitor instead of a member of the household, he was fairly at peace so long as Mollie and the children didn't intrude too often on his privacy. He was alternately a severe and a permissive father, did not attempt to instill his sons with a moral code but insisted on good manners. He particularly wanted the boys — both of whom ran wild with the "hill gang" on the heights around Fort Mason and fought with boys from the lower regions of the city — to be self-reliant and skeptical of everything they were taught. Once the older boy, Day, fought back when a teacher tried to punish him. Bierce not only approved, but warned the teacher never to attempt such a thing again.[14]

Another time, when a minister was calling on Mrs. Bierce, the younger boy ran into the house to report, "Daddy, Day just said, 'Damn God.' "

Mrs. Bierce flushed with embarrassment, but Bierce calmly told his younger son, "Go and tell Day that I have repeatedly told him not to say 'Damn God' when he means 'God damn.' "

Both boys, it was said, were clever at writing and drawing, had their father's curly golden hair, looked like angels and (out of Mrs. Bierce's hearing) talked like longshoremen. And both were marked for early, tragic ends. They had inherited their father's intelligence, but not his hard core of character and determination. They were flawed in ways that a more interested, conscientious father might have perceived and done something to correct.

For Bierce, however, paternity was a burden, and when he proclaimed the virtues of parenticide (as in the opening of his short story "An Imperfect Conflagration": "Early one June morning in 1872 I murdered my father — an act which made a deep impression on me at the time . . .") he was not excluding himself from its penalties.

Living his own life, in brief, was more important to Bierce than supervising those for which, legally and morally, he was responsible. Whenever he became bored with the day-to-day work of editing the *Wasp* and fending off would-be contributors, whenever the prospect of going home to the house overlooking the Bay displeased him, he would set out along what San Franciscans called the "cocktail route," beginning at Joe Parker's and the Baldwin Theater bar at Kearney and Bush, imbibing at various places along Kearney to Market, stopping off at the elegant bar of Hacquette's and Hageman's Crystal Palace, and ending up at Market and Powell. Then it was a question of continuing the pub-crawl or adjourning for dinner. In the stream of men coursing from one café and saloon to another, Bierce bore — and boasted of — his reputation as a great shifter of the booze. No one, he claimed, and often proved, could drink him under the table. No one ever saw him staggering or heard him mumbling nonsense.

Along this bibulous route he was often joined by two other part-time men-about-town, Arthur McEwen, the red-bearded wit, and the frolicsome Petey Bigelow, both members of the *Examiner* staff.

It was McEwen who proclaimed that the byline on the "Prattle" column, A. G. Bierce, stood for Almighty God Bierce. The town roared over that, and Bierce was not at all displeased.

Bigelow had been a favorite drinking companion of Bierce's dating back to his first years in San Francisco. As McEwen described that blithe spirit, a journalistic type as outmoded now as the flatbed press, "He is tall, slight, wears a bang, dresses elegantly, and is so frail and pale that once when he had shaved his beard off, a drunken man on Market Street started back at the sight of him and muttered, in startled amazement, 'Good

God, the Holy Grail!' Life to him, on the surface, is one long jest and giggle. Seeing him dancing along the street, flower in button-hole, cane in hand and rigged out in Pool's best — for 'Petey' buys his clothes in London — one would take him for a gay young man of fortune. He is stopped every few yards, for he knows everybody."[15] Once, in the *Examiner* office, he threw down his pen and announced, "There are two things I'm going to do right now — have a glass of beer and go to France." And Petey did just that, returning a year later and sitting down at his desk as though he had taken a trip to the watercooler.

"Thank God," Bierce once said, "Petey has no virtues."

Occasionally one of his roistering companions, who composed a more loosely knit group than the "Gang" he associated with in London's Fleet Street, would fall by the wayside. Jimmy Bowman died in 1882 and was memorialized in the "Prattle" column. Both of his collaborators on *The Dance of Death*, William H. Rulofson and T. A. Harcourt, ended their own lives, indicating that brandy was not the cure-all Bierce professed to believe it was. Rulofson, as Bierce stated in the *Wasp*, "executed a dance of death by stepping off the roof of a building." Harcourt, brooding over his wife's desertion, had been trying to drink himself to death, found it too slow, and threw himself out a window. Bierce's epitaph to Harcourt ended:

> *When like a stormy dawn the crimson broke*
> *From his white lips he smiled and mutely bled,*
> *And, having meanly lived, is grandly dead.*

He played the gracious host when his London friend George Augustus Sala came to town on a visit, but the appearance of another literary Englishman whom the city fawned upon, sunflower and all, Oscar Wilde, was greeted with a blast of invective in the *Wasp*'s columns. Wilde's grandiose manner, and the attention he attracted from the social elect, was, Bierce observed, "twin show to the two-headed calf." Bierce always avoided celebrities, perhaps on the theory that one celebrity does not court another.

Also he hated pushing his way through a throng of another man's admirers — hated crowds of all kinds, in fact. Once, standing on an elevation with a friend, watching a mass of people at a midwinter fair below, he remarked, "Wouldn't it be fun to turn loose a machine gun into that crowd!"[16]

Bierce also felt like cutting loose with a machine gun when he learned that the *Wasp*'s real owner was Charles Webb Howard, and that it was no accident that the weekly's columns were so well larded by advertising from the Spring Valley Water Company. Bierce was outraged; he felt that he had been used as an unwitting shill for a rigged game. If Howard didn't dispose of his interest in the *Wasp* at once, he threatened, he would expose him and the way he had siphoned the water company's funds into his own pockets.

Much to his later regret, Bierce even found a purchaser for the weekly. His nominee was E. C. MacFarlane, who was his managing editor and who obtained the money to buy out Howard from his brother George, who owned sugar plantations in the Hawaiian Islands. George MacFarlane's readiness to supply the money for purchase of a satirical weekly was not entirely motivated by brotherly love. Among mainlanders on the islands there was a strong, well-financed movement to have them annexed by the United States, but even before that could be arranged the planters wanted favorable terms for their sugar exports to be included in the draft of a treaty being negotiated between the United States and the island kingdom. George MacFarlane intended that the *Wasp*, if sting it must, go after the opponents of annexation and meanwhile serve as a propaganda organ for the sugar interests.

In such a cause, Bierce would make a poor crusader. He had a very low opinion of the American missionaries who invaded Hawaii, put Mother Hubbards on the women, and lived to see their sons take over the islands' commercial and agricultural and now its political life. The mainlanders who had insinuated themselves into the islands, he later wrote, were bent on plunder, and "not a man jack of them but if he were a saint in Heaven would strip the bark from the Tree of Life and smuggle it into Hades for fuel."[17]

When Bierce and his wife were invited to attend the coronation ceremonies of a new Hawaiian queen in February 1883, Mrs. Bierce joined the junket from the mainland, but Bierce snorted, "Why should I bother to see a negress [sic] crowned queen of the Fly-Speck Islands?" The remark stemmed more from his disgust with the Hawaiian situation than any latent racial prejudice.

Around the time that MacFarlane took over as publisher of the *Wasp* he was also forced to assume Bierce's editorial duties. Once again the Bierces fled San Francisco, ostensibly to find a better climate for Ambrose's wheezing bronchia, this time to the foothill town of Auburn. According to Carey McWilliams's family-authorized biography, there was an additional but not unfamiliar motive: to get away from his mother-in-law and brother-in-law. There had recently been a serious domestic disturbance. His brother-in-law, James Day, had been involved in a love affair with the daughter of an elderly clergyman who had been friendly with both the Bierces and the Days. In the humiliating aftermath, the old minister had killed himself. Bierce apparently was determined that his brother-in-law would have nothing more to do with his branch of the family. He was outraged, not by his brother-in-law's misconduct, but by the fact that he had taken advantage of the clergyman's friendship. For all Bierce's professed cynicism, he was lavishly sentimental on the subject of friendship, and the betrayal of a friend was the greatest crime on the books. Time and again this trait, combined with naïveté, would overthrow his better judgment and place him in a false position.

As with the MacFarlanes. Having forced the withdrawal of the previous owner, he now learned that his own nominee was only a puppet himself. MacFarlane's brother, from his plantation house on the islands, began demanding that the *Wasp* come out in favor of the new treaty the planters were demanding. To comply with his brother's demands, Edward MacFarlane had to reverse the *Wasp*'s editorial stand and its party allegiance in the midst of a national election.

All this Mike De Young was only too glad to point up in the editorial columns of his *Chronicle*. He also charged that Adolph Spreckels, the kingpin of the sugar magnates, was the prime mover behind the MacFarlane brothers and the real owner of the *Wasp*. Spreckels was so outraged at the accusation that his money was invested in such a journal that he cornered De Young in his office and caned him.

No doubt Bierce was ready to reach for his own cane as it became apparent that there was some truth in De Young's charges. He did not, however, resign. Perhaps MacFarlane's pleas of friendship kept him at the task of writing the "Prattle" column from his foothills retreat. There was also the fact that he would have a hard time getting another job, since his strictures on journalism, "conducted by rogues and dunces for dunces and rogues," and more personal attacks on the newspaper business had closed most doors to him.

The discomfiting situation was resolved late in 1885 when MacFarlane sold out to Colonel J. P. Jackson, publisher of the *Evening Post*. The old management bowed out with an editorial probably composed by Bierce: "We retire with an unweakened conviction of the rascality of the Railroad Gang, the Water Company, the Chronicle newspaper, and the whole saints'-calendar of disreputables, detestables, insupportables and moral canaille." It trusted that the new management would extend an amnesty to "mere fools and blockheads, thrifty sky-pilots, sons o' light, literary imposters, aspiring vulgarians hanging onto society by their teeth, inflated patriots, offensive partisans, sentimentalists, quack philanthropers, talking teetotallers and other vine-pests, cobble-trotting whiskey soldiers and peacocking gregarians generally, muckers and the whole lovely lot of potential rogues in the stony soil of whose natures the seeds of crime lie ungerminated by the sun of opportunity . . ."[18] It was a fairly definitive list of those who aroused Bierce's wrath.

At the age of forty-three Bierce once again was unemployed and hard-pressed to pay his bills. He moved his family to higher ground, at St. Helena at the north end of the Napa Valley, while he spent most of his time seven miles away at Angwin's Camp on Howell's Mountain, up among the pines, where his asthma might be soothed. It was wine country, and that too was a comfort to Bierce. Hospitality was always available to Bierce at Jacob Schramm's winery, where many a bottle of Schramsberger coursed down his appreciative throat.

Weekends he usually spent with the family in their cottage, where his daughter Helen remembered him as a mostly silent and brooding figure around whom the household tiptoed. He worked on stories and sketches for which there was no discernible market at the moment. As Helen Bierce recalled, "he worked all night and slept half the day" and "brooded by himself most of the time, sitting motionless and wordless by the library fire." Occasionally he would take Helen or one of the boys along while he went hunting for arrowheads and pine cones, both of which were gathered into huge collections.[19] Although he professed an intense dislike of dogs ("smilers and defilers, reekers and leakers"), he loved birds and made pets of creatures other people gave a wide berth. Up in the pine-terraced high country, it seemed, he was as happy as it was possible for him to be.

One factor, undoubtedly, was his ability to keep most of the people around St. Helena, both the year-arounders and the summer visitors, from intruding on his privacy. He even resented it when the local paper noted that he was staying in the vicinity. Being a near-hermit seemed to suit him best.

One intruder he did not resent at his cabin on the mountainside at Angwin's was the flamboyant, tomboyish yet exuberantly feminine Lillie Coit, ex-mascot of Fire Company No. 5 and self-appointed shocker of Nob Hill society. Now separated from her husband, Lillie was spending much of her time on her estate near St. Helena. Neither then nor later, from all the evidence, was Bierce a womanizer. He was too inhibited, aside from an occasional goatish remark in his role as a literary entertainer, for sexual adventure; he loved Mollie for all their disagreements — most of them traceable to her mother's influence or presence — and was probably incapable of being disloyal to her.

He and the blonde, robustly formed Lillie were simply kindred spirits. She would drive a coach and four down the roads of the Napa Valley as though pursued by a Sioux war party. Even more scandalous was her custom of entertaining large house parties — without a female among them. Often she would appear at Bierce's cabin door dressed in short skirts and hunting boots and go off on hiking and hunting trips with him. The brash and emancipated female, as a type, drew some of his most corrosive comments, but not Lillie Coit, who was about as emancipated as you could get without being run in for disorderly conduct. "Lil," he once said, "is a real woman."

The year or so he spent on Howell's Mountain, in exile from San Francisco and journalism, concerned as he must have been over his finances, was the last brief period of personal and emotional tranquillity he was to know until he disappeared down a Mexican road.

> Billy [Hearst] is the prodigal calf for
> whom the *son* was uselessly sacrificed.
>
> —Ambrose Bierce

NINE   *A Hearstling Is Born*

J UST ABOUT the time Bierce was wondering whether he would ever find steady employment for his "satirical whip," there was a fortuitous change of ownership in the San Francisco *Examiner*. In 1880 the newspaper had been purchased by George Hearst, a rough-mannered Missourian and former hardrock miner who had chipped off a share of the Comstock Lode and would shortly acquire even vaster wealth in the Homestake Mine in South Dakota. Hearst had succumbed to the political disease and yearned for the Democratic nomination to the United States Senate. The *Examiner* was a faltering Democratic organ. It served, however, to help boost him into the Senate six years later.

About the time the elder Hearst was achieving his Senatorial ambition his prankish only son, Willliam Randolph, was departing from Harvard without honors. A misunderstanding over his presentation of chamberpots to various members of the faculty was understood to be the reason for his severance. From Harvard dropout to newspaper publisher seemed to the twenty-three-year-old Hearst a logical move up the ladder of ready-made success. In brief, he wanted the *Examiner* for his own, along with a pipeline to his father's millions, and with the help of his mother, Phoebe Apperson Hearst, a genteel former schoolmarm, he achieved his purpose.[1]

Young Hearst wrote his father that he intended to remake the San Francisco *Examiner*, with Pulitzer's New York *World* as his model, into a newspaper that would make the whole Pacific Coast sit up and take notice. "We must be alarmingly enterprising, and we must be startlingly original. We must be honest and fearless. We must have greater variety than we have ever had. . . . There are some things that I intend to do new and striking which will constitute a revolution in the sleepy journalism of the Pacific slope and will focus the eyes of all that section on the *Examiner*."[2]

One measure toward arousing what one of his editors later called the "gee-whiz emotion" was the employment of the kind of reporters and writers who were adept at stirring up controversy, making readers open up their morning paper with anticipation, whipping up exposés and crusades. Certainly there was no one more expert at getting under people's skins than Ambrose Bierce.

Hearst took over the *Examiner* on March 4, 1887. Before the month was out he had appeared on Bierce's doorstep. Bierce had taken an apartment for the winter in Oakland while his family stayed in the cottage in St. Helena (just how he was able to support two households is a matter for conjecture, since there is no record of his having written anything for publication for months). Thanks to Bierce himself, the encounter became one of the classic anecdotes in American journalism — one of the few in which William Randolph Hearst appeared in the guise of a humble petitioner. They must have made a curious pair: the professional cynic and the gangling, rather naïve young man whom Bierce would describe as "the prodigal calf for whom the *son* was uselessly sacrificed," who was only half Bierce's age, and who looked more like the *Examiner*'s chief copyboy than its publisher.

One day late in March, as Bierce later related, he was lounging around his Oakland apartment when someone tapped gently, hesitantly on his door. "I found a young man, the youngest man, it seemed to me, that I had ever confronted. His appearance, his attitude, his manner, his entire personality suggested extreme diffidence. I did not ask him in, install him in my better chair (I had two) and inquire how we could serve each other. If my memory is not at fault I merely said, 'Well' and awaited the result.

" 'I am from the San Francisco *Examiner*,' he explained in a voice like the fragrance of violets made audible, and backed a little away.

" 'Oh,' I said, 'you come from Mr. Hearst.' Then that unearthly child lifted its blue eyes and cooed: 'I am Mr. Hearst.' "³

It was probably the last time anyone would ever think of William Randolph Hearst as an unearthly child; Bierce himself would watch with something like apprehension as those cornflower-blue eyes hardened, that diffident manner changed for a more commanding air, and that piping voice began trading in European castles and American newspaper properties with an authority never quite equaled. That afternoon, however, young Mr. Hearst was bent only on bargaining for the services of a paragrapher whose slings and arrows had been showered on San Francisco intermittently for almost twenty years. He had always admired the "Prattle" columns and wanted Bierce to revive them for the Sunday *Examiner*.

Bierce was in no position to haggle with the strange young man who was offering to employ him. He did insist on two conditions for reviving the "Prattle" column. It was to appear on the editorial page, and it was to be published as written. If he did any other writing for the *Examiner*, he was to be paid space rates. His starting salary, as he later told an associate, was a far from munificent thirty-five dollars a week.

He went to work immediately, producing his first column for the issue of Sunday, March 27. And the association, incongruous as it seems to anyone considering what the Hearst papers eventually stood for, was to continue until Bierce decided to retire. Until then Bierce's work had reached a comparatively small number of readers in the San Francisco weeklies; now it would attain an ever-growing readership as the *Examiner* became the Coast's leading newspaper. As a pilot-model for all the other Hearst products, the *Examiner* was exclamatory, sensational, hardly the vehicle for a writer who prided himself on polishing each phrase until it shone with the refracted light of its creator's intellect; yet it made room, not only for the scoop-chasing star-reporter and the sledge-hammer editorials inveighing against corruption (spelled Southern Pacific), but for solider writing. Hearst undoubtedly had an eye for talent and a willingness to nurture it. He would engage Stephen Crane to cover the war in Cuba, Jack London as war correspondent with the Japanese army in Korea, would even serialize a Henry James novel under flamboyant and highly misleading headlines.

Practically all Bierce's best work, in fact, was produced while he was on the Hearst payroll (though not always for publication in the Hearst papers or magazines). The job gave him a base from which to operate, a salary that continued, and was increased by methods verging on blackmail, as long as he wanted it, and an employer who was startlingly indulgent with the whims and tantrums of his resident genius. Aside from the time it took to turn out two columns of copy a week for the "Prattle" column, Bierce had the opportunity to work on his own stuff without worrying about the bills. If he was a bargain for Hearst — particularly after, as that young man shrewdly foresaw, his columns appealed as much to daily newspaper readers as to the more sophisticated types who bought weekly or monthly literary journals — the job on the *Examiner* was an even greater bargain for Bierce.

Although hardly the most gregarious of men and displaying a tendency to hold himself aloof from the vulgarities of daily journalism, Bierce must have enjoyed himself in the jovial atmosphere of the *Examiner* offices at 10 Montgomery Street. It was an old building with a rickety single-web press, but modernized to the extent that it boasted two separate telephone lines. The atmosphere was half pirate ship with the Jolly Roger being hoisted on the halyard, half that of a circus brave with hoopla but only a jump ahead of the sheriff (the elder Hearst). In an early issue most of the front page was given over to headlines shrieking:

HUNGRY, FRANTIC FLAMES
Leaping Higher, Higher, Higher,
with Desperate Desire

over the story of a fire which destroyed a hotel in Monterey.[4] Bierce was also pleased by its choice of principal villains on the local scene: Mike De Young of the *Chronicle* and Collis P. Huntington of the Southern Pacific. Several of its staff were favorably known to Bierce as roistering companions on the "cocktail route," which he could once again afford to travel, particularly Arthur McEwen, who was firing editorial broadsides next to the "Prattle" column, and the elegant, dashing Petey Bigelow. Others were bright young people hired away from other papers: Andy Lawrence; Cozy Noble; Blinker Murphy; Annie Laurie, who was credited with inventing the sob story; Jimmy Swinnerton, the cartoonist; and Sam Chamberlain, the mastermind of the sensational journalism Hearst was perfecting for San Francisco. In a few years Hearst assembled one of the great staffs in American newspaper history, one to rank with Pulitzer's *World* before the First World War and James Gordon Bennett, Jr.'s New York *Herald* when Stanley went looking for Livingston.

The *Examiner*, proclaiming itself "monarch of the dailies," began hitting out in all directions, including at least one which must have alarmed Senator Hearst. It helped to defeat a proposed city charter which would have distributed more political power to Chris Buckley, the Democratic boss who had been instrumental in the senior Hearst's election. The *Examiner* also began its long campaign against the stranglehold exercised by the Southern Pacific, with passengers, shippers and farmers all groaning under its exorbitant rates and casual service. In this cause Bierce helped out with satiric shafts aimed at the railroad's cavalier attitude toward its own train schedules. Southern Pacific trains were usually so late, Bierce wrote, that "the passenger is exposed to the perils of senility." On another occasion he noted that "The Overland [one of the railroad's much-advertised "crack" trains] arrived at midnight last night, more than nine hours late, and twenty passengers descended from the snow-covered cars. All were frozen and half-starved, but thankful they had escaped with their lives." He always referred to one of Huntington's partners as £eland $tanford.[5]

Later Bierce would write that he had joined Hearst because of "the easy nature of the service" he was expected to perform — no editorial chores such as had accompanied his previous work on the weeklies — and because "I persuaded myself that I could do more good by addressing those who had the greatest need of me — the millions of readers to whom Mr. Hearst was a misleading light." But that was after he was disillusioned by glimpses of Hearst's vaulting ambition, his attempt to use his newspapers as a springboard to the White House. For the style of the youthful Hearst, concerned only with putting out the liveliest newspaper on the continent, he had a certain reluctant admiration. When one of his editors was offered a bribe by an official of the Spring Valley Water Company, the editor kicked the man out of his office. When Hearst heard about it, he told the editor, "You're a fool! Why didn't you take the money and keep up the fight just the same? He would never have dared to say a word about it." There was a certain unconventionality about Hearst in his business methods that Bierce also found attractive. Once he heard that Hearst had learned that one of his executives in the business management had been caught with his hand in the till, that Hearst knew about it and did nothing. Bierce asked him why he didn't take action against the man. Hearst's straight-faced reply: "I have a new understanding with him. He is to steal only small sums hereafter; the largest are to come to me."[6]

The building on Montgomery Street possessed a fascination for Bierce that he had never found on the premises of any other place he was employed. Hearst tolerated anything and anyone so long as they added to the excitement. One of his top lieutenants was Sam Chamberlain, an erratic genius imported from New York's Park Row, where his sobriquet was "Sam the Elegant, Sam the Drunken." Chamberlain, who had acquired the manner and dress of an English duke, had been the right-hand man of James Gordon Bennett, Jr., when he established the Paris edition of the New York *Herald*. The two men had quarreled while cruising in the Mediterranean on Bennett's yacht, and the unpredictable publisher had severed their relationship by marooning Chamberlain on a rock in the sea. Later Chamberlain established the Paris *Matin*. Shortly after taking over the San Francisco

Examiner, Hearst met Chamberlain in a New York bar and hired him on the spot as ringmaster, or managing editor, of his own journalistic circus. Chamberlain and Bierce became close friends and would remain so to the end of Bierce's career as a Hearst writer.

Between them Hearst and Chamberlain spurred their staff on to so many exploits which had more to do with attracting attention than soberly covering the news that Jerome Hart wrote in the *Argonaut*, "*Examiner* men go up in balloons . . . *Examiner* men jump off ferryboats to test the crews. *Examiner* young men swim to save fishermen marooned on rocks. In brief, *Examiner* men are doing many things these days, and some fine and brave things. I am inclined to believe that many of their exploits are performed more for the love of adventure than for the love of advertising."[7]

Bierce, of course, was not called upon to perform such feats of derring-do in pursuit of a headline. His hacking at the totems of what Mencken would later call the "booboisie," his sustained attacks on established wealth, authority and privilege delighted Hearst and helped to expand the *Examiner*'s readership from a meager twenty-three thousand to twice that figure. Even such revered figures as Hubert H. Bancroft with his assembly-line methods of rewriting American history, the heavyweight champion John L. Sullivan, Thomas A. Edison and the late Charles Dickens (most of whose characters, wrote the fastidious Bierce, "would, I think, have been improved by a more frequent change of underwear") were subjected to his acid bath. And politicians trembled every time their names appeared in "Prattle."

Of one overly talkative statesman, he wrote, "Senator Ingalls is said to suffer an affection of the roof of his mouth. Possibly; he certainly has a loose plank in the floor of it."[8] Another senator specialized in speeches in which, tossing his hoary locks, he spoke as "from one in the shadows of the other world." He dropped that pose after Bierce commented in verse on his otherworldliness:

> *Step lightly, stranger, o'er this holy place,*
> *Nor push this sacred monument aside,*

Left by his fellow-citizens to grace
The only spot where Vrooman never died.

Frequently he would drop the foils and pick up the bludgeon, as when he took after the secretary of the San Francisco police chief, who was suspected of using his position wrongly: "This hardy and impenitent malefactor — this money-changer in the temple of justice — this infinite rogue and unthinkable villain, of whose service Satan is ashamed and, blushing blackly, deepens the gloom of hell — this brilliant malversationalist — this boundless and incalculable scamp, enamored of his own versatility of unworth, invests the moral atmosphere with an audible odor that screams along all the visible ramifications of his influence. . . ."[9]

One Senator Frye was labeled "that slavering sentimentaler," Mike De Young was "Sir Simian," and Anthony Comstock, who was trying so hard to purify American morals, was "that notorious morality sharp."

Often enough Bierce's ministrations so aroused their subjects that the Hearst libel lawyers had to be called into consultation. Hearst, however, would not hear of suggestions that Bierce be advised to draw a little less blood on all but his most libel-proof victims. The product of the celebrated California vintner Arpad Haraszthy apparently offended the Bierce palate during one of his wine-tasting sessions. "The wine of Arpad Haraszthy," commented Bierce in a "Prattle" column, "has a bouquet all its own. It tickles and titillates the palate. It gurgles as it slips down the alimentary canal. It warms the cockles of the heart, and it burns the sensitive lining of the stomach."

The outraged Haraszthy consulted his lawyers, who consulted Hearst's lawyers, who reported to Hearst's editors that Bierce should run a retraction. Equally outraged, Bierce complied to the letter. In his next "Prattle" column, this item appeared: "The wine of Arpad Haraszthy does not have a bouquet all its own. It does not tickle and titillate the palate. It does not gurgle as it slips down the alimentary canal. It does not warm the cockles of the heart, and it does not burn the sensitive lining of the stomach."[10]

Bierce lashed out so furiously — often so indiscriminately — at everything that disgusted and repelled him about his time that Franklin K. Lane, later a Secretary of the Interior, regarded him as an outlaw from the human species. Bierce was "a hideous monster," Lane wrote, "so like a mixture of dragon, lizard, bird and snake as to be unnameable."[11]

Bierce himself later had misgivings about the hasty judgments and intemperate verdicts he rendered during his years as the Prattler. When he heard that his protégé, the poet George Sterling, was going through the old *Examiner* files and reading his "Prattle" columns of the late Eighties and the Nineties, he claimed that he "shuddered" at the thought of those old grievances being exhumed, that he would never be able to reread them himself. "There is so much in it [the column] to deplore — so much that is not wise — so much that was the expression of a mood or a whim — so much that was not altogether sincere — so many half truths, and so forth. . . ."[12] It was the closest he ever came to confessing that in his role as an entertainer — or, as his enemies alleged, a performer in a sadistic ritual which gave a certain obscene pleasure to those who paid their nickel for the Sunday *Examiner* — he was often carried away. The role of the merciless critic, of the professional cynic, the hired moralist may have come naturally to him, but he was also conscious in retrospect that there had been something slightly meretricious in his performance. If the public hadn't been amused by his talent for corrosive comment, uncovered by a shrewd editor shortly after he came to San Francisco and began turning out bits and pieces for the weeklies, his work might well have taken a different turn. As a professional writer, however, he had to go with the market. There was no call for the products of Bierce the poet, or Bierce the essayist, but he could earn a living as Bierce the controversial journalist.

In the main, he was satisfied that his long-running commentary on the low state of the public morality, which extended almost from the end of the Civil War to the years just before World War I, was justified. His aim, he said, was to point up constantly that the human condition was imperiled not by false principles but by the individual whose conduct made him an enemy of society. There were plenty of men available to attack so amorphous an objective as wrong thinking, but only one Bierce with the courage to assail the wrongdoer by name, in print and in defiance of the libel laws. "I care nothing for principles — they are lumber and rubbish," he wrote. "What concerns our happiness and welfare, as affectable by our fellow men, is conduct. 'Principles, not men,' is a rogue's cry; rascality's counsel to stupidity, the noise of the duper duping on his dupe. He shouts it most loudly and with the keenest sense of its advantage who most desires inattention to his own conduct, or to that forecast of it, his character. As to sin, that has an abundance of expounders and is already universally known to be wicked. What more can be said about it, and why go on repeating that? The thing is a trifle word worn, whereas the sinner cometh up as a flower every day, fresh, ingenuous and inviting. Sin is not at all dangerous to society; what does all the mischief is the sinner. Crime has no arms to thrust into the public treasury and the private; no hands with which to cut a throat; no tongue to wreck a reputation withal. I would no more attack it than I would attack an isosceles triangle, or Hume's 'phantasm floating in a void.' My chosen enemy must have something that has a skin for my switch, a head for my cudgel — something that can smart and ache. I have no quarrel with abstractions; so far as I know they are all good citizens."[13]

Yet this determination to pursue the scoundrel rather than inveigh against the times which produced him often led Bierce to overload his blunderbuss. Righteous indignation can touch off larger explosions than may be warranted, with damage done not only to its object but to the institutions designed to protect society from that object. A case in point was his lengthy campaign in verse and prose against a wealthy citizen named Robert Morrow, whose trial came to his attention during his first year as an *Examiner* columnist. Morrow was charged with jury tampering. Bierce naturally ranged wider and declared that Morrow, aside from his attempt to bribe a jury, was "not above robbing the poorest widow in the land."

Bierce was so harsh in his comments on the case that Morrow's attorney moved for a change of venue on the grounds that his client couldn't receive a fair trial in an atmosphere made prejudicial by Bierce's fulminations. The lawyer quoted verse from the "Prattle" column of the previous Sunday:

> The devil felt a sudden thrill
> Of course to defy God's will.
>
> Then Morrow spoke: "As sure as fate
> Their witnesses I'll indicate
>
> Or if that prove expensive sport,
> I'll — whispering — fix the court."
>
> Sing, Muse, the subsequent events,
> Arraignment, trial and defense.
>
> Alas! their footing simply fell
> And all were tumbled into hell.[14]

The judge glowered at the insinuation that the court as well as the jury might be fixed, and lost no time about granting a change of venue. It was more of a tribute to Bierce's influence on public opinion than to his wisdom as a self-constituted court.

During that first year with Hearst, Bierce evidently began seriously considering use of the Civil War as a background to what became the artistic pinnacle of his work. A quarter of a century had passed since Shiloh and the long winter's day of battle on the banks of Stones River. In middle age those events which had scarred his youth both physically and psychologically came into a clear and significant focus. He was unable to attend the reunion of the Ninth Indiana Volunteer Infantry, his old regiment, but wrote in response to the invitation that he "entertained the tenderest regard" for its survivors — a sentiment which had not been evident to many of his old comrades when he was regarded as an aloof, hard-eyed officer commissioned from the ranks.

The invitation caused him to reflect in the "Prattle" column that "To this day I cannot look over a landscape without noting the advantages of the ground for attack or defense . . . I never hear a rifle-shot without a thrill in my veins." Even by then the courthouse squares of America were notable for the collection of G.A.R. veterans who bored the hell out of two generations of American youth with their war reminiscences. Bierce had a certain amount of that "ol' sojer" nostalgia coursing through him, but he would release it in artistic form rather than straining it through a quid of chewing tobacco.

The first result of his middle-aged rumination over the war of a quarter-century before was a short story, "One of the Missing," which the *Examiner* published on March 11, 1888, and for which, one may be sure, young Mr. Hearst paid at space rates since it appeared outside Bierce's two allotted columns of "Prattle." "One of the Missing" contained many of the ingredients of Bierce's subsequent *Tales of Soldiers and Civilians*, first published in 1891: coincidence, precision in timing and background, a sense of foreboding and horror compressed into a few pages, and the transfiguring effect of fear on the bravest of individuals.

The principal character is Private Jerome Searing, a scout for the Federal army during its advance on Kenesaw Mountain, "an incomparable marksman, young, hardy, intelligent and insensible to fear." Completing his reconnaissance, he is convinced that the Confederates have withdrawn from the vicinity. To make sure, however, he climbs into a granary for a better look around. He then sights the tail end of the enemy's rearguard, and cocks his rifle to snipe at it.

Then Bierce brought into play one of his favorite themes, the iron rule of destiny. "It was decreed from the beginning of time that Private Searing was not to murder anybody that morning, nor was the Confederate retreat to be announced by him. For countless ages events had been so matching themselves together in that wondrous mosaic to some parts of which, dimly discernible, we give the name of history, that the acts which he had in will would have marred the harmony of the pattern."

Before Private Searing could fire, through a coincidence Bierce insisted was not freakish (or fortuitous for the storyteller), "a Confederate captain of artillery, having nothing better to do while awaiting his turn to pull out and be off, amused himself by sighting a field piece obliquely to his right at what he took to be some Federal officers on the crest of a hill, and discharged it. The shot flew high of its mark."

The shell strikes the granary, causing it to collapse on the scout hiding inside. Private Searing is trapped in its fallen timbers. This happens at 6:18 A.M., as Bierce notes. Searing is horrified to observe that his rifle is wedged in the debris so it is pointing at his head. Then the rats come out, staring at him in red-eyed anticipation. (The idea of animals gnawing at dead humans was also an obsession of Bierce's, probably dating back to the wild pigs which had rooted around the corpses after the battle of Buffalo Mountain in West Virginia.) The rats terrify Searing; "the man of courage, the formidable enemy, the strong, resolute warrior . . . screamed with fear." In a few minutes he is reduced from brave soldier to terrified boy. He manipulates his rifle so the debris will press against the trigger. "There was no explosion; the rifle had been discharged as it dropped from his hand when the building fell. But Jerome Searing was dead."

A line of skirmishers comes up from the Federal position. It is commanded by the dead private's brother. The lieutenant finds the dead man but does not recognize the face. "Its face is yellowish white; the cheeks are fallen in, the temples sunken, too, with sharp ridges about them, making the forehead forbiddingly narrow; the upper lip, slightly lifted, shows the white teeth, rigidly clenched. 'Dead a week,' said the officer curtly, moving on and absently pulling out his watch as if to verify his estimate of time. Six o'clock and forty minutes."

This was to be typical of Bierce's war stories: no gallant charges, no guidons flying or trumpets blowing, none of the usual muralistic trappings of war literature. The horror of death in war was its loneliness. His scenes were usually isolated from the main action, the roar of battle; probably this was a reflection of his own experiences as a lone scout or a topographical engineer reconnoitering the country through which his regiment was to advance. His characters — none of them "heroes" in the usual sense — were always removed from the comfort of other humans, cut off from the herd, meeting death as he insisted it must always be met — alone. Death was the trap at the end of the path down which Bierce led his readers, and he would make them realize that all the religions in the world, all the philosophers and comforters, could not spring its jaws.

From then on Bierce worked away at his war stories when time permitted. Most of them appeared in the *Examiner* or in the literary periodical the *Wave*, which was edited by a young friend of his, John O'Hara Cosgrave. He made it clear he was not writing for posterity or in the belief that fiction had any great literary merit. In one of his "Prattle" columns about this time, he remarked of fiction that "In its youth it is vigorous, in its age decrepit, in its grave detested. In short, fiction is not literature."[15]

Even so, he must have wondered whether his stories weren't a little too good for the *Examiner*, and whether he wasn't wasting his time working for the willful young Mr. Hearst, whom he now described, on closer acquaintance, as a fellow of dubious means bent toward a possibly sinister end. William Randolph Hearst couldn't help the way he looked, but Bierce was repelled by his "long horse face, close-set eyes and a peculiar restrained smile with a manner that was a combination of Harvard and a faro-bank lookout."

While Bierce was making himself famous in San Francisco as the city's sardonic Sunday visitor, his family life was disintegrating. In the past few years he had become a Sunday visitor, at best, to his own family. He would drop by the small white house on Main Street in St. Helena on his way up to the mountaintop which he called his "breathing place." By then his children had entered their teens and Mrs. Bierce was of an age to begin questioning whether the role of Patient Griselda really suited her. His published comments on women, marriage and family responsibilities could hardly have been a source of comfort. The epigrams and aphorisms which titillated his readers must have seemed to be personal affronts, since Bierce never bothered with any disclaimers that Mrs. Bierce was excepted from their stinging indictments. "A sweetheart is a bottle of wine; a wife is a wine bottle. . . . A bad marriage is like an electric thrilling-machine: it makes you dance, but you can't let go. . . . Of two kinds of temporary insanity, one ends in suicide, the other in marriage."[16]

If he had descended from his lordly view that women were a distinctly inferior half of the species — "Women and foxes, being weak, are distinguished by superior tact"— he might have observed that the domestic fabric was growing desperately frayed, that his absenteeism as husband and father was destroying his family. Undoubtedly, in his self-centered way, Bierce wanted things exactly as they were. He wanted to live his own life, but he also wanted to be secure in the knowledge that the door to a loving and welcoming home was always open to him. The one-sidedness of such an arrangement did not disturb a sense of justice that was unusually keen in other matters. "What a woman most admires in a man is distinction among men," he wrote. "What a man admires in a woman is devotion to himself."

As for the children, and their upbringing, that was Mollie Bierce's business, provided that she didn't share it with her mother or brother. The paternal influence on a child, he seemed to believe, was of little consequence. And apparently he saw nothing contradictory in his belief that women were weak and inferior and his willingness to place them in complete and independent charge of raising children, surely one of humanity's more difficult responsibilities.

In 1888, it became apparent that his blueprint for marriage, which was merely an extension of his earliest beliefs that the family was a miserable institution ruled by two unwilling tyrants, simply wouldn't work even under the authoritarian rights granted the Victorian father. That spring he paid a visit to St. Helena to be informed that his eldest son, Day, only fifteen years old, was determined to strike out on his own.

Day was an exceedingly handsome boy, with his father's golden hair and blue eyes and strikingly Byronic features of his own. Unfortunately he had also inherited his father's headstrong quality. Added to it, undoubtedly, was a resentment of his father's prolonged absences. Townspeople, as much impressed by the boy's assurance, perhaps, as the talent for writing and drawing he had displayed, were certain that he was a genius who would outdo his father.

Day announced that he was leaving home to take up a newspaper career. Bierce himself had left home at the same age to work in a saloon, but naturally that had little bearing on what he wanted for his son. He insisted that Day should finish his education before venturing into the newspaper business. Probably he hoped that in a few years Day would lift his aim to something better than journalism. Newspapers turned out an occasional success — most writers of that period, in fact, had served their apprenticeships in the city room — but produced many more human wrecks, alcoholics, suicides, Skid Road candidates. An alarming percentage of newspapermen, as Bierce observed, cracked up before they were forty. Perhaps, too, he sensed that the high-strung Day had exactly the kind of temperament that made a brilliant reporter at twenty, a frustrated boozer at thirty.

Day refused to listen to either his angry father or his tearful mother. One night he packed up and disappeared. Mrs. Bierce urged that the boy be pursued and brought back home, but Bierce decided against such measures. A few weeks or months on his own might make Day decide to come home on his own, more appreciative of parental shelter. A short time later the Bierces learned that Day had turned up on the staff of the Red Bluff *Sentinel* in northern California. When Mrs. Bierce learned of his whereabouts, she sent him money, which he disdainfully returned.

Day's rebellion must have come as a shock to Bierce, but not so great a one as the discovery that Mollie herself had secretly arrived at the conclusion that Ambrose might be right about marriage producing, as he once said, "dead-sea fruits" which "grow no riper and sweeter with time." Often she must have thought back to the days before her marriage when she had been gay, popular, sought after. She must also have wondered whether she would have married Ambrose knowing that behind the handsome facade, the magnetism which transfixed so many other females, the brilliance of intellect, was a moody, inward-looking, seclusive man; that his bitterness was no pose; that his suspicion of human motives, his disgust at the commonplace social trans-actions that make life more endurable for most people would extend to those he supposedly loved. She still loved him, but could not escape the realization that her happiness was not high on the list of his priorities. There was also, no doubt, the inimical influence of her mother, whose constant refrain was that Mollie could have done so much better in marriage.

His daughter Helen believed that it was Bierce's narrow view of womanhood that caused the trouble. She wrote in a magazine article many years later that she heard him express admiration for only three women in his lifetime. One was the Empress Eugénie, whom he had never met; another was the novelist Gertrude Atherton, despite the fact that she laughed off his amorous inclinations; and the third was the English novelist George Eliot, who was utterly unattractive, with a long equine face, but a "fascinating" and "charming" woman once she began to talk.

"I believe," Helen Bierce wrote, "it was his lack of understand-ing, of sympathy, of appreciation for women that caused the trouble. He was the soul of sincerity in all he wrote, but I feel somehow that with women it was different. He expected too little of them mentally. He had the ancients' view of them as chattels. . . ."[17]

During his absences from St. Helena — it is doubtful whether he spent more than thirty days annually under his own roof during that period — his own chattel Mollie met a wealthy, charming and persuasive Dane who was spending his summers in the mountain resort. When the Danish gentleman wasn't around in person, he wooed her with ardent letters. Her womanly confidence was restored by the flirtation. She could no more discourage her admirer than she could tell her husband about his attentions. Perhaps she feared that Ambrose, with his .45 army Colt always within easy reach, would take direct and fatal action.

Helen Bierce later recorded that, according to the stories she heard, her mother "turned an unheeding ear to the words of her

admirer, and he wooed her in vain with ardent love-letters."
That, Helen said, was only half the truth. Her mother was
fascinated by the importunate Dane. "It was a decorous and
discreet fascination, but — she had certainly not sent him back
to Denmark."[18]

Whatever attraction existed in the Dane for Mollie Bierce
would probably have withered without Bierce ever learning of it
except that one day he found one of the letters and was outraged,
unappeasable. "There was a big scene," as Helen Bierce remembered. So greatly was his pride affronted that he packed up and
left, never to return or forgive.[19] He demanded perfection in the
person permitted to love him, if not in himself. He was enough
of a proper Victorian, in that sense, to believe that a husband
had every right to neglect his wife, and that his wife had no right
to protest. It was unthinkable that anyone who professed to love
him and whom he undoubtedly loved in his own prickly fashion
should entertain the admiration of another man. Rather than
live in a house with a leaky roof he would pull its timbers down
around his ears and take grim satisfaction in the crash.

"Do not permit a woman to ask forgiveness," one of his
epigrams counseled, "for that is only the first step. The second is
justification of herself by accusation of you."[20]

Mrs. Bierce, by way of reply, might have quoted him: "A
virtuous woman is the most loyal of mortals; she is faithful to
that which is neither pleased nor profited by her fidelity."

She was "heart-broken," her daughter later wrote. "She did not
see the other man again, and she swore to me that it had not
been a real romance, but Father would not listen — it was
enough that she had permitted some love-letters to be written to
her."[21]

A greater tragedy was in the making for the Bierce family a
hundred miles to the north, where Day Bierce was a fledgling
reporter and a fiercely romantic adolescent who had stepped into
a man's world with a swagger to equal his father's — and a
temper, a sensitivity also to match.

Day had been working as a reporter on the Red Bluff *Sentinel* for several months when he met a girl his own age at a lodge picnic he was covering. Her name was Eva Adkins, she was comely and flirtatious, and she worked in a cannery. Day fell in love with her and moved into the boarding home kept by her mother, whose second husband was a drunken layabout named Barney, in the nearby town of Chico. From the first, apparently, Eva had encouraged Day only because she was attracted to his best friend, a handsome fellow named Neil Hubbs.

Although both were only sixteen, Day insisted that Eva marry him. As she later was quoted in the Chico *Enterprise,* "I told him to wait one year and if I loved him then I would tell him, but he must not hold me as engaged.

"One night I told him that I thought more of Hubbs than of him. He drew his revolver and threatened to kill me. I begged for my life on the plea that I was too young to die. He said I could live if I would promise to let our engagement stand one year. When his pistol was in his pocket I told him something might happen in about three months, but would say nothing more just then."[22]

Her mother later said Eva "lured him on" as a cover for her romance with Neil Hubbs. The situation grew so tense that Day and Eva's stepfather got into a row and the latter had Day arrested on a charge of assault. The charge was dropped on July 19, 1889, however, when both Eva and her mother testified that Barney had swung the first blow.

Immediately after he was acquitted Day told his friends that he was going to take out a marriage license and marry Eva on July 22. Apparently the fact that she testified on his behalf against her stepfather encouraged him to believe that she really loved him and had been using Neil Hubbs only to make him jealous.

Instead, on July 20, she and Hubbs slipped out of town and were married in nearby French Camp.

The shock of that news drove young Bierce wild. It was hardly cushioned by the headline the local *Enterprise* ran over the story of the elopement: "Course of True Love Runs Amuck!" The story identified him as "the son of the famous satirical writer on

the San Francisco *Examiner*," but did not mention the fact
that — like father, like son — Day Bierce went around with a
gun on his hip.

He was still living at Mrs. Barney's lodging house four days
after the elopement when Eva and her bridegroom returned
from their brief honeymoon.

Hubbs apparently had been warned that his former best friend
might be gunning for him. He also had armed himself. When he
and Eva appeared in Mrs. Barney's living room, Day came in and
spoke to them briefly, almost cordially, then disappeared into his
bedroom. Hubbs didn't like the glint in the boy's eyes, however,
and drew his revolver, keeping it at his side.

Suddenly Day flung open the door, and this time he had, as
gunfight aficionados phrased it, "come out smoking."

They fired almost simultaneously. Day's first shot plunged into
Hubbs. He then turned his gun on Eva and fired again; the shot
went through her ear and grazed her skull.

Hubbs had stumbled out the door, trailing blood, but came
back into the living room when he heard the last shot. Mortally
wounded, Hubbs somehow managed to knock Day down, then
carry Eva out of the living room.

His father's newspaper quoted Day as crying, "My God, Neil,
what have I done? Just put a cartridge in your revolver and kill
me, kill me. I'm not fit to live."

Hubbs refused to do him the favor, and a moment later young
Bierce went back to his bedroom, saturated a piece of cloth with
chloroform and placed it over his face as he lay on the bed, then
fired his revolver into his right temple.

For several hours after both young men were removed to the
hospital they lingered on. Day kept murmuring, "Send for my
father . . . send for my father . . ." Early the next morning
they died within a few minutes of each other.

Later that morning Ambrose Bierce, accompanied by his friend
from Oakland, Charlie Kaufman, came up from San Francisco
and, "sadly broken," according to the Chico newspaper, stared
down at his oldest son's body lying on a marble slab in the
undertaker's.[23]

"You are a noble soul, Day," he is supposed to have said. "You did just right."[24]

He spoke of his dead son as having had the potentiality of "another Chatterton." Later in the day he took the boy's body to St. Helena. He was closeted with Mollie for about an hour, but there was no reconciliation. She afterward said that, seeing his face, with grief and rage hardening on it like a mask, she now realized that he would not come back to her. For several weeks he carried around with him the ivory-handled revolver with which Day had shot his rival.

No "Prattle" columns appeared on the Sunday *Examiner*'s editorial page for a month. Then it was rage, the most powerful of his motive forces, that drove Bierce back to his writing desk. The stunning grief over Day's death was purged in an instant when he read a piece in the *Argonaut* written by one of his favorite whipping boys, Frank Pixley, for whom he had composed the premature epitaph. San Francisco journalism suffered few inhibitions, but even Bierce-haters thought Pixley went too far when he wrote:

"If it be true, as alleged, that the jibes and jeers of the local press so worked upon the *weak* mind of a young man, maddened by passion and crazed by jealousy over an *unworthy* woman, that he should have resorted to murder and suicide to terminate his unpleasant and ridiculous predicament, may not the incident teach a *moral lesson* to those writers who indulge in such cruel and inhuman satire? [The italics are Mr. Pixley's] . . . Does there not rest upon his father the shadow of a haunting fear lest he may have transmitted to a sensitive and tender soul an inheritance which resulted in crime and death, while he was cultivating the gift of wounding natures just as sensitive and tender, who had not the courage to end them in murder and self-destruction, but were driven to hide their sorrows in secret? Perhaps this man with the burning pen will recall the names of those whom he has held up to ridicule and shame; the men and women whom he has tortured and humiliated . . . Upon his tomb may be carved the inscription: 'He quarreled with God, and found nothing in His creations worthy of the commendations of Ambrose Bierce.' "[25]

Bierce bestirred himself from grief to produce a "Prattle" column and reply to Pixley: ". . . You and your kind will have to cultivate fortitude in the future, as in the past; for assuredly I love you as little as ever. Perhaps it is because I am a trifle dazed that I can discern no connection between my mischance and your solemn 'Why persecutest thou me?' You must permit me to think the question incompetent and immaterial — the mere trick of a passing rascal swift to steal advantage from opportunity." Bierce added the opinion that "it is only in your own undisguised character of sycophant and slanderer for hire that you shine above."

It was not one of his best efforts, understandably, but it served to return him to the arena and his old role as lion against the Christians.

Perhaps it was just as well that he never heard of Eva Adkins's comment on the station platform as she watched the body of her husband carried away by one train, Day Bierce's on another.

"Now ain't that queer? One goes one way and one goes another, but here I am!" she remarked to a reporter.[26]

How Bierce would have relished it had she been referring to someone other than the first-born son for whom he had hoped so much.

TEN

"Nothing Matters"

T HE EGOCENTRICITY of the artist helped
Bierce survive the blows inflicted by his son's suicide and the
breakup with his wife. There is no doubt that even his armor of
self-centeredness was shattered by the fate of the elder son he
loved neither too wisely nor too well, or that he had justified
forebodings over what would happen to his younger son Leigh,
whose impulses were less violent but equally self-destructive. As
far as Mollie was concerned, he said on several occasions later
in life that she was the only woman he had ever loved. He must
have known that she wanted a reconciliation, but his pride
wouldn't permit him to accept it. Even though he acquired a
certain local fame as a womanizer — though just how serious his
affairs were cannot be determined, certainly not from the boastful
hints dropped by him — it was evident that he was exceedingly
cautious about getting too deeply involved with another woman.
He was determined, above everything else, not to let life wound
him again if he could help it. Thus he boiled his new philosophy
down to two words: "Nothing matters."

Tragedy, in fact, appeared to have benefited his work, drove
him to creativity as an anodyne. The years following 1889 saw
him at the crest of productivity, during which he turned out his
most memorable work. His mood was darker and more despondent, but he made it operate in his favor.

Certainly his paragraphing in the *Examiner* did not appear to suffer from his personal sorrows. He became embroiled in a feud-by-correspondence with a young navy officer named H. Prescott Belknap who, being offended by something Bierce wrote, challenged the commentator to a duel. Bierce duly reported to his readers that a "chivalrous patriotette" was complaining in the receptive columns of the *Argonaut* that "I will not join it, a minor, in committing a felony on the 'field of honor.'" It was Bierce's opinion that "a feeding bottle of gore" was "exciting it [Belknap] like the dickens." A week later Bierce reported that he had received another letter from Belknap informing him that the young naval officer was "walking the streets of San Francisco, where I do not live, armed with a horsewhip for me." Bierce added:

"Mr. Belknap threatens that unless I come up to be horsewhipped he will tell the public of my disobliging disposition. I shall have to give him the trouble of doing so, for I really do not wish to be horsewhipped if I have to pay the railway fare to enjoy that blessing. The expense of the performance ought, I think, to be assumed by the chief performer. I am still persuaded that Mr. Belknap is a girl."[1]

The publication of Tolstoi's *The Kreutzer Sonata* provided him with the opportunity to vent his spleen on the always-tempting subject of marriage. The novel had been prohibited from circulating through the United States mail and had aroused the liveliest literary controversy of 1890. It was the story of a man who married late and raged with jealousy when his young bride fell in love with a musician; the protagonist resolves the triangle by killing his wife. There were certain parallels between Tolstoi's novel and Bierce's life, on which the latter, of course, did not elaborate. Bierce defended the book and said it should be circulated because it would help teach girls that "marriage, like wealth, offers no hope of lasting happiness." It would also serve to expose the fact that married people were "all members of a dishonest conspiracy" who secretly "chafe and groan under the weight and heat of their chains." Marriage promised privileges which were "deemed incalculably precious" but had no means of "confirming and enforcing" them.[2]

Since public life still had not reformed itself, despite his unending admonitions, Bierce made his whip whistle over those he considered unregenerate malefactors. He was in favor of "war, famine, pestilence, anything that will stop people from cheating and confine that practice to contractors and statesmen."[3] The only remedy he saw for widespread evildoing and mischief-making was "enough of fining, imprisoning, flogging and hanging."[4]

The increasing strength of the movement for equal rights for women also attracted his alarmed attention. Women, he insisted, had no qualifications for equality, suffrage or even serious consideration. They were inferior both physically and intellectually. A woman, he warned, "does not 'leap to correct conclusions'; her saltatory feats commonly land her in a bog, with results distinctly disastrous. To put the matter with entire lucidity, woman hasn't any thinker."[5]

He sent up epigrams on the subject like a shower of rockets; hardly a "Prattle" column early in the Nineties did not contain some jibe or slander against the feminist movement. "When God makes a beautiful woman, the devil opens a new register. . . . If women did the writing of the world, instead of the talking, men would be regarded as the superior sex in beauty, grace and goodness. . . . Empty wine-bottles have a bad opinion of women. . . . To woman a general truth has neither value nor interest unless she can make a particular application of it. And we say women are not practical! . . . The enlargement of woman's opportunities has benefited individual women. It has not benefited the sex as a whole, and has distinctly damaged the race. The mind that cannot discern a score of great and irreparable general evils distinctly traceable to 'emacipation of women' is as impregnable to the light as a toad in a rock."[6]

He would condemn women to a universal and permanent purdah. Personally as well as intellectually, his friends said, his attitude toward them was "Mohammedan." From this time until the end of his life there was always at least one woman hovering around him in the guise of helper, protégée, worshiper, hand-maiden. For all his professed contempt for their sex, for all the ignominy of being labeled a member of "Bierce's harem," they would surround him with their ministrations. Women seemingly are as attracted to misogynists like Bierce or Shaw, provided they are notorious enough, as men are to the man-eating Delilah or Lilith type. Bierce apparently believed that there was safety in numbers; the great danger was to allow one female to become an obsession. "Girls is pizen," he remarked in a letter, "but not necessarily fatal. I've taken 'em in large doses all my life and suffered pangs enough to equip a number of small Hells, but never has one of them paralyzed the inner working man."[7]

It did not take him long to be spoiled by the nimbus of admirers which surrounded him. One of the most candid and detailed portraits of Bierce in action, more or less romantically, was provided by the young novelist Gertrude Atherton, several of whose novels (*Black Oxen*, particularly) were to shock the First World War generation. She was a handsome, venturesome young woman, blonde and saucy, with a striking profile. Like many other young writers in the Bay cities she had sent some of her work to him for criticism and approval. At the time he was living in a hotel at Sunol Glen at a height soothing to his asthma. "Wherever Bierce happened to be staying," Mrs. Atherton noted, "was a shrine to which pilgrims wended their way to offer up incense and sit at the feet of the Master." He invited her to come up and spend a day with him. Somewhat to her own surprise she accepted, "although I had refused to be taken to see George Meredith!" Admittedly she was "consumed by curiosity" about the man whom she believed to be "wasted" on San Francisco because it was "too small a field for his genius."

Nevertheless she did not intend to be patronized or overawed. At Sunol Glen she presented herself to a strikingly handsome middle-aged man, "bristling mustache, beetling brows over frowning eyes, good features and beautiful hands," but "his appearance did not appeal to me, for he looked too much like my father — what my mother would have called a typical Yank."[8]

She let him know immediately, she recalled, that "I had no intention of falling down and worshipping him. What was on his own mind I never knew. I had on a very becoming blue frock, and presumably he thought I was vain and spoilt and a member of the idle rich who wrote merely to amuse herself."

Sam Chamberlain, the elegant and charming managing editor of the *Examiner,* was also visiting Bierce and joined them for luncheon. "But he disappeared when the meal was over — and Bierce led me to his bedroom! He looked cynical and somewhat amused."

There was only one chair in his room, which Mrs. Atherton occupied while Bierce sprawled on the bed "with a muttered apology."

Whatever Bierce may have had in mind when he invited the comely young woman up to the mountain hamlet was banished when she displayed the temerity to differ with him, quite positively, on "every conceivable subject." Evidently Bierce wasn't accustomed to having his opinions derided and laughed at; Bierce the lady killer gave way, at the first sign of opposition, to Bierce the intellectual tyrant. "It was the most disagreeable afternoon I ever spent. We quarreled incessantly . . . He tore my books to rags. I had promise, but I had written nothing as yet worthy of serious consideration. This might be true, but I wasn't going to admit it to him, and I retaliated by criticizing his own work. His stories might be models of craftsmanship and style, and he had mastered the technique of horror, but they were so devoid of humanity that they fell short of true art, and would never make any but a limited appeal."[9]

With heavy irony, reinforced perhaps by concealed rage at how an anticipated easy conquest was turning out, he "congratulated me upon the mature judgment which no doubt had made me in high demand as a critic." Novels, he said, "were not worth writing anyway"; only the short story could be a work of art.

(This campaign against the novel as an art form, a form to which he could not or would not lend his talents, thus making his opinions on the subject rather suspect, was more formally and definitively stated on paper. He insisted with that wrongheadedness to which he succumbed on frequent occasion that the novel was only a padded-out short story. It was "a species of composition bearing the same relation to literature that the panorama

Ambrose Bierce
as an artist sketched him in maturity

A bivouac of Bierce's Civil War regiment, the Ninth Indiana
Volunteer Infantry, the home of his heart in youth and old age

Brown Brothers

Downtown San Francisco
in the years when Bierce traveled its famous
"Cocktail Route"

William Randolph Hearst
Bierce's long-suffering employer, in 1904, shortly
after Bierce's poem helped crush his political
ambitions *Brown Brothers*

bears to art. As it is too long to be read at a sitting the impressions made by its successive parts are successively effaced, as in the panorama. Unity, totality of effect, is impossible; for besides the few pages last read all that is carried in mind is the mere plot of what has gone on before. To the romance the novel is what photography is to the painting. Its distinguishing principle, probability, corresponds to the literal actuality of the photograph and puts it distinctly in the category of reporting . . . The art of writing novels, such as it was, is long dead everywhere except in Russia, where it is new. Peace to its ashes — some of which have a large sale.")

The spirited young woman would not be put in her place. " 'The trouble with you,' I said crudely, 'is that you cannot write novels yourself. All short-story writers are jealous of novelists. They all try to write novels and few of them succeed. Any clever cultivated mind, with a modicum of talent, can manage the short story, even with no authentic gift for fiction — as you yourself have proved. But it takes a very special endowment and an abundant imagination to sustain the creative faculty throughout a story of novel length. *To hold it up.* Only a born novelist carries on without falling down over and over, stumbling along from one high spot to another.' "

They "almost spat at each other," she said, until she realized there was no train until 6 P.M. and she was sentenced to stay in his company for several more hours.

"Finally," she recalled, "I thought I would change my tactics. After all the poor man was ill, and embittered through many misfortunes. He had lost his great opportunity when family obligations forced him to leave London. He was condemned to second-rate hotels in order to support an estranged wife and two children on his salary. . . . So I relented, told him I was sorry I had been so quarrelsome, for no one admired him more than I did. He was a great man and I was willing to admit it."

That confession melted the Bierce arrogance but did not dissipate his raging sense of frustration. "He almost flew at me. He was not great. He wouldn't be called great. He was a failure, a mere hack. He got so red I feared he would have an attack of asthma. He gave me some twenty reasons why he wasn't great, but I have forgotten all of them. I still think him one of the greatest short-story writers that ever lived."

By train time they were on more amiable terms and Bierce walked his visitor over to the station. "He became almost charming. He thanked me for coming to see him and apologized for being so cantankerous, said that he had found an irresistible pleasure in arguing with me, and that I was a blue and gold edition of all the poets!!!"

The train was late, so they strolled around the station. "It grew darker. We were in the shadows between the station and the malodorous grunting pigsty when he suddenly seized me in his arms and tried to kiss me.

"In a flash I knew how to hurt him. Not by struggling and calling him names. I threw back my head — well out of his reach — and laughed gayly. 'The great Bierce!' I cried. 'Master of style! The god on Olympus at whose feet pilgrims come to worship — trying to kiss a woman by a pigsty.' "

A few minutes later the train arrived and Bierce "rushed me to it and almost flung me aboard." He told her, "I never want to see you again! You're the most detestable little vixen I ever met in my life, and I've had a horrible day."

Mrs. Atherton believed that "women had spoiled him and no doubt he thought himself irresistible." Writing about the incident forty years later, she was still able to gloat that "my barb had gone in to the hilt" and that the professional woman-hater had been given his comeuppance.[10] A woman less self-centered and more compassionate might have reflected that he was a pitiable case of a man embittered by frustrations of the most peculiarly Victorian kind.

A more worshipful and compliant group of protégés gathered around Bierce after the publication of *Tales of Soldiers and Civilians*. It was a collection of his horror tales, military and civilian, which had been mostly published in the *Examiner*. One of the more recent additions to the collection was "The Affair at Coulter's Notch," which appeared in the *Examiner* several months before Bierce compiled the volume. Once again he was not ashamed to make use of coincidence, gratuitous or otherwise, to heighten the effect of horror; the story in fact would have been pointless without the coincidence.

Captain Coulter was the commander of a Federal battery which was ordered into an exposed position to lay its guns on the enemy's rearguard. The Confederate artillery was emplaced around a plantation house. Coulter's guns rained shells on the enemy position; the Confederates were driven away, and that evening the Union brigade pursuing them took over the partly wrecked house as its headquarters. A short time later his commanding officer found Captain Coulter in the cellar, his face powder-blackened and unrecognizable, a dead woman and her child clasped to him.

"What are you doing here, my man?"

"This house belongs to me, sir."

"To you? Ah, I see. And these?"

"My wife and child. I am Captain Coulter."

The collection, published when Bierce was forty-nine, included some of his most celebrated tales: "A Horseman in the Sky," "An Occurrence at Owl Creek Bridge," "Chickamauga," "Killed at Resaca" and "An Affair of Outposts," among the military stories; "A Watcher by the Dead," "The Damned Thing," "An Inhabitant of Carcosa," "Haita the Shepherd," "A Holy Terror" and "The Man and the Snake," among the civilian.

It was undoubtedly of psychological significance that in many of his stories the principal character unwittingly or coincidentally killed someone he loved, his wife, child, brother or father. That, of course, was the carefully contrived climax of his stories. A modern writer would avoid coincidence with a shudder and concentrate on the psychology of a man killing a complete stranger; his emotions resulting from that act would be the crucial part of the story.

There was a certain staginess — though a commendable curtness — about the shock of his endings. In "Killed at Resaca," for instance, the narrator gives a spoiled beauty a letter she had written a young lieutenant killed in action. She recoils at the sight of the blood on the letter.

"Madam, pardon me, but that is the blood of the truest and bravest heart that ever beat."

"Uh! I cannot bear the sight of blood! How did he die?"

"He was bitten by a snake."

In "An Affair of Outposts," the main character is a man who rushed off to join the colors because of his wife's unfaithfulness. He is killed, with a heavily ironic touch, while rescuing the man who had seduced his wife.

Then and later Bierce was unsuccessful in attracting the attention of the major book publishers. For the tastes of what later and most inaccurately became known as the "Gay Nineties," his tales seemed too grim and pessimistic. *Tales of Soldiers and Civilians* was brought out under the imprint of a San Francisco merchant and friend of his, and was prefaced by Bierce's statement: "Denied existence by the chief publishing houses of this country, this book owes itself to Mr. E. L. G. Steele, of this city. In attesting Mr. Steele's faith in his judgment and his friend, it will serve the author's main and best ambition."

On the whole it was well received. It was praised in newspapers and magazines throughout the country, particularly by the eminent Percival Pollard, of Baltimore, who was to become his close friend. Even the local reviewers refrained from retaliating in kind for Bierce's harsh published opinions of his contemporaries. Andrew Chatto, his former English publisher, read it and proposed an English edition, which appeared under the title *In the Midst of Life*. The English critics were even more appreciative than the American.

One thing that critics usually brought up was a comparison of his work to Edgar Allan Poe's. This, significantly perhaps, outraged him. It was not that he downrated Poe, but he resented the implication that he was not an original, that he could be classified with anyone else. Regarding one critic who evaluated *Tales of Soldiers and Civilians* as the work of a man who emulated Poe in subject if not style he wrote, "If he had lived in Poe's time how he would have sneered at that writer's attempts to emulate Walpole! And had he been a contemporary of Walpole that ambitious person would have incurred a stinging rap on the head for aspiring to displace the immortal Gormley Hobb."

His red-bearded friend Arthur McEwen, who had praised the volume in a review for the Oakland *Review*, later told of having breakfast with Bierce shortly after it was published. Bierce wanted McEwen's opinion on how it would sell.

"I won't be surprised," McEwen replied, "if it makes a world hit or falls as dead as a landed salmon." He then ventured on his reasons for believing it had a fifty-fifty chance of failing. "You haven't, in all you write, a trace of what we call sympathy. The pretty girl never appears."

"Darn the pretty girl," Bierce snorted.

"That's what is the matter with you," McEwen advised him.[11]

Another thing wrong with Bierce, so far as the requirements for success in his time were concerned, was that he refused to obey the realistic dictates of the doyen of American literature, William Dean Howells, who insisted on the iron rule of probability in any storytelling. Bierce, of course, was a master of the improbable, if not the impossible; of the outré. And the outré was out so far as the Howells establishment was concerned. To which Bierce would reply, "Fiction has nothing to say to probability; the capable writer gives it not a moment's attention, except to make what is related *seem* probable in the reading — *seem* true. Suppose he relates the impossible; what then? Why, he has but passed over the line into the realm of romance, the kingdom of Scott, Defoe, Hawthorne, Beckford and the authors of the *Arabian Nights* — the land of the poets, the home of all that is lasting and good in the literature of the imagination."[12]

On the Pacific Coast, whatever his standing with the Eastern Brahmins of literature, he was regarded as the supreme arbiter of letters. "Seriously," wrote Joseph Lewis French, "I doubt if ever there has been in all the history of letters a more complete dominion."[13] James Rorty called him "the literary leviathan of the Pacific Coast." Another termed him the "Rhadamanthus of Pacific letters," and others openly addressed him as "Master." Even Gertrude Atherton made up with him and began corresponding with him again. "He took a great interest in my work and gave me much valuable advice, for which I have always been grateful. . . . I must have had a hundred of those letters, all expressed in a prose that made every sentence a treasure. And models of calligraphy; save my grandfather's, I have never seen a more beautiful handwritting. But, alas, they perished in the fire of '96. Someone stole a copy of *Soldiers and Civilians* he gave me, and the only memento I have of him is a photograph — autographed on the back!"[14]

Despite this assumption of local literary supremacy, Bierce stayed on at the *Examiner*. It now paid him a hundred dollars a week, after a series of raises occasioned by his threats to resign for various reasons. Perhaps it was the permissiveness of the atmosphere created by Hearst that, more than anything else, held him to the "Prattle" column and the invigorating ambience of the Hearst editorial rooms. Gertrude Atherton, who became a part-time columnist on the *Examiner* thanks to Bierce's introduction of her to Sam Chamberlain, wrote of Hearst and his hirelings, "Poor man, he prided himself on having the most brilliant editorial staff in the United States, but he paid high for the privilege: every one of them was a periodical or steady drinker, and there was a memorable occasion when all of them were down at Los Gatos taking — or pretending to take — the Keeley cure, and he had to get out the paper himself with the aid of the printers. He used to say that no one had ever suffered more from the drink habit than he, although he never drank, himself." Sam Chamberlain would get drunk and turn up in a favorite bar in Antwerp, Belgium. McEwen was also a far-ranging tosspot. Bierce himself was among the "steady" drinkers who could be relied on to meet deadlines and not wander farther than Point Mugu.

It was his intemperate prose and verse, and his touchiness about the way they were converted into cold type, that caused frequent disagreements between Bierce and the "front office." William Randolph Hearst appeased the star of his aggregation in every possible way, as Bierce more than once admitted.[15]

A typographical error or a minor excision in his copy, however, would sometimes send Bierce into a rage and he would stomp away from the *Examiner* building trailing a shower of sparks. Perhaps such incidents were stage-managed by the leading player; even if he wasn't coaxed back by a raise — a hundred a week was then a munificent salary in the newspaper business — there would come one of those flattering, self-abasing letters from young Hearst, such as the one which read:

"Write about anything if you will only write. I only hope you will write 'Prattle' until you can persuade me to relinquish it. Don't for heaven's sake stop 'Prattle.' I shall think myself a terrible 'hoodoo' if immediately on my return *The Examiner* should lose what is to me its very best feature. I hope you will continue. I don't want to have to stop my subscription to my own paper for lack of interest in the damned old sheet. Shall I appoint myself a committee of one to come up and persuade you?"[16]

More than once Hearst had to play Barbarossa to Bierce's Pope, go up to Sunol Glen and appease the prima donna in person.

When Arthur McEwen quit in a rage because Hearst presumed to offer a suggestion on whom to fire his editorial broadsides, he wanted Bierce to join him on the staff of *Arthur McEwen's Letter,* a weekly designed to make California too hot for scoundrels of all degrees. Bierce declined. McEwen thereupon warned him that he would be roasted in the *Letter* along with all the Hearsts and Hearstlings. Undismayed, Bierce wrote a calm appraisal of the *Letter's* first issue: "Mr. McEwen's paper appeared yesterday, and if the remains of some of the persons 'distantly alluded to' found it agreeable reading they are dowered with a breadth and catholicity of acceptance that would be the making of a foraging pig. It is easy to find fault — I find that the 'Letter' covers an insufficient range and variety of topics: I want more scoundrels brought on with several kinds of sauce. That doubtless will be done in good time, for Mr. McEwen is already of middle age, and at the rate of one or two a week would not live to finish his work. They breed like rabbits — the good, good unworthies — like rabbits of Australia. They must be taken by the dozens, or through intervention of death many will escape the grill by falling into the fire." He ended by saying McEwen's integrity was unquestioned and "He has never parted with himself, and if ever sold — as most of us have been — was unaware of the transaction and unprofited by it."

Either piqued by Bierce's refusal to join his crusade or suspecting a premeditated jab in Bierce's remark about his having been "sold" without knowing about it — thereby convicting him of that most ignoble of intellectual crimes, naïveté — McEwen roared out in his next issue that Bierce was attacking him on orders from Hearst, a ridiculous charge on the face of it, and added: "Ambrose Bierce is a polecat that stinks for the hire of a dissolute master."

A friend asked Bierce how he was going to answer the polecat charge. Bierce said he wasn't, that "the red-headed devil tells the truth." Finally, however, he did fire a salvo in McEwen's direction. By insisting that Hearst was ordering him to attack his old friend, Bierce wrote in his "Prattle" column, "Mr. McEwen was obviously only gratifying his ever-famishing vanity, whose giant appetite can, fortunately, be relieved, though not glutted, out of his own mouth, as a fish-hawk feeds her young. I must inform him that my allusion to his sale was in no way suggested by the proprietor of this paper, nor by anybody. The proprietor of this paper, in truth, has not since last summer spoken or written to me of Mr. McEwen's works and ways, nor of Mr. McEwen — an abstention of which I appreciate the delicacy, if such it is, for it was during last summer that Mr. McEwen's name began to be a word at which those must blush whose memories of his honorable past forbade them to laugh. It is really too bad to dispel the fairy illusion of a dreamer inebriated with a sense of his own identity, but my criticisms of him were made, not with a desire to please anybody but myself, but with at least a reasonable expectation of displeasing *him*. That forecast appears to have been a fairly good one, and I'm rather proud of it."[17]

It was entirely in keeping with the opéra bouffe aspects of journalistic life in Montgomery Street that McEwen went broke in three months, was rehired by Hearst, and quit again when the latter sent him a telegram of instructions which McEwen declared was "equally ungrateful and stupid."

If he refused to fly off the handle at the unjust aspersions of "Red" McEwen, an incident, with a parlor house as the farcical background, in which Bierce was innocently and outrageously involved took the best efforts of the editorial brains of the *Examiner* to conclude without bloodshed.

Bierce had always campaigned against prostitution and even referred to the pathetic creatures engaged or entrapped in the business in terms of which pioneer sociologists could not approve. Thus the town rocked with laughter when two prominent citizens in their cups went to a bordello, one of them introducing the other as "Ambrose Bierce." They then proceeded to break furniture and otherwise disturb the tranquillity of the establishment. The police were called, and one of the inmates of the house mentioned to a police reporter that one of the arrested men was Ambrose Bierce. The opposition papers gave jubilant play to stories under headlines such as "AMBROSE BIERCE" WRECKS BAWDY HOUSE. Bierce's sense of humor failed to meet the test. Just as he was about to set out to flog the two culprits and whichever members of the rival newspaper staffs he considered guilty of helping circulate the canard, he was cornered and cooled down by Sam Chamberlain and a covey of editors.[18]

His stated philosophy might have been "Nothing matters," but one exception to that rule was his reputation.

ELEVEN

"Dear Master"

FAIRLY OR NOT, the leader of a literary group, his quality as an adviser and inspirer, may be judged by the talents he has encouraged. It is a judgment of sorts that the names of those Bierce encouraged may be recognized today only by a specialist in the field of San Francisco's frequent and turbulent literary revivals. They included George Sterling, Edwin Markham, Emma Dawson, W. C. Morrow, Herman Scheffauer, Adolphe Danziger, Gertrude Atherton, Walter Blackburn Harte, Carroll Carrington, Kitty and Julie Miles, Agnes and Margaret MacKenzie, Blanche Partington, Margaret Schenck, Alice Rix, Eva Crawford, Mabel Wood, Flora Shearer, C. W. Doyle, Nellie Vore.

Of these only Gertrude Atherton and Edwin Markham ("The Man with the Hoe") would be familiar to even the widely read. The list, which is by no means definitive, is also remarkable for the number of females on it; this despite his well-advertised aversion to women with their intellect showing — for women of all kinds, for that matter. (His favorite toast, after all, was "Here's to woman. Would that we could fall into her arms without falling into her hands.") Regarding one young woman whose cleverness and perception appalled him, he suggested that her male relatives "as a measure of precaution against so monstrous a perversion of natural order . . . have her eyes put out."[1] The only female writer he was heard to speak of with professional respect was Agnes Repplier, the essayist, who, as he gruffly put it, "had a bushel of brains between her ears."[2]

Yet he encouraged a whole twittering covey of female tyros, many of them young and good looking. It was one way of enjoying the society of women, despite his perverse denunciations of their sex. Then, too, it provided an appropriate background to what was becoming his favorite role: Man of Letters. His performance in that part so impressed Percival Pollard that the eminent critic proclaimed that Bierce — not Howells or Twain — was "the only American, living in America, who was completely a man of letters, in the finest sense of that term." Again, crossgrained fellow that he was, Bierce tended to contradict himself. The professional literary man, he maintained, was a microbe ("microcephalus bibliopomps") which should be isolated and stamped out. Nothing written in America, he was fond of saying, was worth a damn. As a coat of arms for American letters he proposed a shield displaying an illiterate ruffian rampant on a field of dead (foreign) authors, with a scroll beneath it containing the motto "To hell with literature."

In his relations with young writers, despite all this, he was infinitely patient and painstaking. Apparently he read every manuscript hopefully presented to him, and pointed out what was good and bad in it. For the apprentice writer, in fact, he demonstrated a tenderness quite invisible in his relations with other people; all his spleen was reserved for those who had it made, Howells and James, Thomas Bailey Aldrich ("colorless jellyfish of literature"), George Washington Cable ("that dear little man"), James Whitcomb Riley, with his celebrations of the joy of barefoot boyhood in Indiana, so different from Bierce's recollections, and Ella Wheeler Wilcox ("mounted on a corn-fed Pegasus"), Elbert Hubbard and all others who prospered at purveying optimism, sweetness and light were endlessly castigated. Bret Harte, who had expatriated himself to England and was reported to have taken up wearing a monocle and an English accent, was "a lazy scamp." Twain he largely ignored. If there was the faintest tint of hope on the horizon, it was with the rising generation. Even the young and promising Hamlin Garland was "one of the curled darlings of the circulating library set."

In his essay "To Train a Writer," he set down some of the principles which guided him as a preceptor. "I have had some small experience in teaching English composition," he said, "and some of my pupils are good enough to permit me to be rather proud of them." He believed it took about five years to train a writer. The first two years would be spent in reading and taking notes. "If I caught him reading a newly published book, save by way of penance, it would go hard with him. Of our modern education he should have enough to read the ancients . . .

"But chiefly this fortunate youth" — Bierce did not undervalue the benefits of his patronage — "should learn to take comprehensive views, hold large convictions and make wide generalizations . . . And it would be needful that he know and have an ever-present consciousness that this is a world of fools and rogues, blind with superstition, tormented with envy, consumed with vanity, selfish, false, cruel, cursed with illusions — frothing mad! . . . He must be a sinner and in turn a saint, a hero, a wretch."

If he was endlessly patient in "training" writers who applied to him for help, he was also a jealous and possessive taskmaster. He expected them to be docile. He intended that they shape themselves and their work on the only acceptable model: Ambrose Bierce. Eventually — and this was not only the traditional ingratitude of the artistic type, the natural tendency of maturity to smash the idol of its youth — almost all of them turned against him, those whom he hadn't already banished to the outer darkness.

One such acolyte, Joseph Lewis French, would recall a score of years after his own apprenticeship, "No man's reputation as a writer was quite made in those days (on the Pacific Coast) until Bierce had pronounced on him. We were his slaves and obedient to his will, and right royally he cracked the whip over us. He even went so far as to pass judgment on the private affairs of the devotees of his circle which finally led to estrangements . . . His disciples gradually fell away as the message became more insistent. That was the fault of Bierce; he did not know when to stop and soothe with humanity the wounds his biting sarcasm made."[3]

The course of his relationship with a neophyte almost invariably was one of discovery and mutual delight at first; then a year or two of slavish devotion on the part of the pupil; then discomfiting revelations that Bierce demanded much in return for his efforts; and finally disillusionment on both sides. One critic of Bierce's life and work, C. Hartley Grattan, has written of Bierce the literary mentor: "[His] influence was narrowing and hardening. His great contribution to his disciples was a worship of clarity in thought and expression. But it seems quite correct to say that he was not the sort of man to exercise determining power over beginning writers. His sympathies were not wide enough. He found it difficult to tolerate anything that diverged far from his own standards of excellence. He acquired greater tolerance when he grew older. His ability to take dictatorship seriously was greatly assisted by the fact that he had an absolute, and consequently unwholesome, belief in his own powers of discerning the right. What he thought was right, and any dissent from his position was not only heresy but treason. If an erstwhile disciple became so willful as to assert his independence he was showered with horrid invective and shoved down to the lower rings of hell."[4]

Among those who addressed him as "Dear Master" — and on occasion in less flattering ways — was Dr. Adolphe Danziger. An immigrant from Germany, Dr. Danziger was variously a dentist, a lawyer, a poet and translator, and for a short time the rabbi of the Congregation Bikur Cholin in San Jose. Twenty-odd years younger than Bierce, a dapper and enterprising fellow who dressed picturesquely in a black slouch hat, a flowing silk tie, a fur coat, with fawn-colored spats and whangee cane, Danziger aspired to become Bierce's collaborator, not merely his protégé. He affected a worshipful attitude after they were introduced by Bierce's friend Petey Bigelow, the *Examiner*'s star reporter, but soon made it clear that he wanted partnership more than patronage.

Danziger, in fact, trailed Bierce up to his retreat on Howell's Mountain and took a cottage nearby. They were constant companions, as Danziger later told it, although "the fenceless harem of his feminine worshippers frequently annoyed me . . . But they adored him and came to bestow their affections upon him without his permission. When I looked at him with 'brown envious eyes,' as he phrased it, he grinned, as the fox did when the raven dropped the baby rabbit." Bierce admirers were "grass widows and women married to poets — who, Bierce said, were sexless and their wives therefore free as air. There were gushing girls who had come to see the great man; there were women who wrote like men, and sometimes men who could not write at all but came with their pretty wives. When Bierce got bored he would lecture them so impressively that the poor creatures sobbed hysterically and blindly stumbled down the road to the omnibus. Peculiarly enough, after such fiascos Bierce would ask me to accompany him up the mountain to look for obsidian arrows."

Bierce, as Danziger recalled, "often assured me that he was never on intimate terms with another man's wife . . . He believed in property, and a married woman was her husband's property. But as he once 'permitted' a married woman to kiss him in my presence, I asked him later how he reconciled his principles with his practice. 'She's a *femme seule* — married to a poet,' he answered."

Bierce was temporarily so charmed by Danziger that he leaped to the literary dentist's defense when Danziger was attacked as "seven hundred and fifty kinds of a scoundrel" by Jacob Voorsanger in the *Jewish Times and Observer*. In his "Prattle" column Bierce retorted that "All the Voorsangers of all the synagogues might play at leap-frog in the shadow of Danziger's mind."[5]

Some of this enchantment, no doubt, was owed to the fact that the bustling Danziger was arranging to have a volume of Bierce's poetry published. Bierce liked the taste of acclaim he had received after publication of *Tales of Soldiers and Civilians*, and hoped that it might be repeated. He kept disclaiming any pretense to being a serious poet; invective set to verse, as he realized, does not aspire to the higher creative realms, but that did not paralyze his pen. "I am not a poet," as he put it, "but an abuser — that makes all the difference . . . so I'm entitled to credit for what little gold there may be in the mud I throw. But if I professed gold-throwing, the mud which I would surely mix with the missiles would count against me." When the great poets admonish "Look on my works, ye mighty, and despair!" — said Bierce — "I, considering myself specially addressed, despair."[6] And that, for Don Ambrosio, was wallowing in humility.

But he wasn't so overcome with self-abnegation that he would keep his versifying from publication. Early in 1892 he was proposing a collection of his rhymed invective in a volume to be titled *Black Beetles in Amber,* a title which a friend of his said should have been changed to *Red Peppers in Vinegar.* Danziger claimed that, major publishers showing no interest in the project, he went to Bierce's employer's mother, Phoebe Apperson Hearst, with the suggestion that she sponsor publication of the volume. That gentle lady replied, according to Danziger, "It is not advisable to put a curse in covers, Doctor."

The enterprising Danziger therefore proposed that they establish the Western Authors Publishing Company, and issue the volume themselves. They would take into partnership Joaquin Miller and W. C. Morrow, the short-story writer, and as Bierce enthusiastically stated, would thereby claim the profits themselves instead of yielding them up to the established publishers who "drank wine from authors' skulls while authors are busy writing applications for admittance to the Poor House." An odder combination of businessmen — Bierce the perennially broke, Danziger the schemer and dreamer, Joaquin Miller whose only commercial talent was a genius for self-advertisement — can hardly be imagined. The result of it all was publication of *Black Beetles in Amber,* which went over its budget and caused a last-minute scurrying for funds. It created something of a local stir because of the many local personalities imbedded in Bierce's congealed contempt. It also became a collector's item among connoisseurs of invective. A sampling of the embalmed "beetles":

> *Dr. Jewell speaks of Balaam*
> *And his vices, to assail 'em.*
> *Ancient enmities how cruel! —*
> *Balaam cudgeled once a Jewell.*

> *Beneath his coat of dirt great Neilson loves*
> *   To hide the avenging rope.*
> *He handles all he touches without gloves*
> *   Excepting soap.*

He also paid his respects to Andrew Carnegie under the title "An Impostor":

> *Must you, Carnegie, evermore explain*
> *Your worth, and all the reasons give again*
> *Why black and red are similarly white*
> *And you and God identically right?*

And the celebrated after-dinner speaker and legal knight-errant on behalf of the Vanderbilt interests:

> *Stranger, uncover; here you have in view*
> *The monument of Chauncey M. Depew,*
> *Eater and orator, the whole world round*
> *In feats of tongue and tooth alike renowned.*
> *Dining his way to eminence, he rowed*
> *With knife and fork up waterways that flowed*
> *From lakes of favor — pulled with all his force*
> *And found each river sweeter than its source.*

Also revolving on the roasting spit were the Reverend Stebbins, "There were no better preachering beneath/ The sun if you'd naught there behind your teeth"; Leland Stanford, who "thought it odd/ That he should go to meet his God"; and William Greer Harrison, a San Francisco broker who dabbled in literature, "Who loved to loll on the Parnassian Mount/ His pen to suck and all his thumbs to count."

The last-named Mr. Harrison was so annoyed at being impaled on Bierce's pen that he responded in terms that fellow victims could only applaud (some, of course, in discreet silence). "The decay of a brilliant mind is under all circumstances a pitiable sight, even where the decay has been self-wrought. Twenty years ago Ambrose Bierce held our small world at his feet. Then his satire had the keenness of a stiletto. Then San Francisco laughed with him . . . Today the world laughs at Ambrose Bierce as they would laugh at any other man who uses a bludgeon believing he is playing with the foil . . . Once Ambrose Bierce was original, now he is content to plagiarize from himself, and quotes Ambrose Bierce as his sole authority. . . . What is Bierce? A critic who cannot criticize, an author who cannot write . . . Ambrose Bierce is the most complete literary failure of the century. He entered the lists splendidly armoured. He had brains, he had education, he had wit, humor, and knew their most dexterous use, but he prostituted them all to a malicious desire to stab . . . But his supremacy is gone, and he is only a sign-post, marking the wreck of an utterly wasted life, and the grave of a literary bully . . ."[7]

Unimpressed by Harrison's dissection of his literary corpse — the autopsy was plainly premature — Bierce merely belabored Harrison, not as the critic of a critic, but as a poet. "Mr. William Greer Harrison is a poet — he will tell you so himself. In his attempt to illustrate the spirit of ancient Celtic poetry, Mr. Harrison has a simple and easy way of creating an ancient Celtic soul under the rotting ribs of his bald and bilious English; he sticks in a few bizarre names . . . and there you are. Celticated to the Queen's taste . . . Mr. Harrison's spirit flies with a free wing, scorning the barriers erected for restraint of flapping mediocrity . . . It is hardly fair of him to spring upon us his private system of prosody without warning and let us wreck our ears in feats of impossible scansion." In all, Bierce found Harrison's poetry as "rhythmic as the throb and gurgle of a roadside pump replenishing a horse-trough."

In other quarters *Black Beetles in Amber* was received with kindlier attention. John O'Hara Cosgrave, editor of the *Wave*, then the most literary of San Francisco's periodicals, commented, "Never has anyone written such scathing satire. He exhausts the possibilities of vituperation, and does it in verse that has the crystalline polish of Pope's . . . The form and style of these verses is so polished, so graceful, that they must live, and the day will come when they will form a commentary to the history of the State." Arthur McEwen, in his revived *Letter*, declared that Bierce had found "San Francisco a microcosm, and in flaying the fools and pretenders of this town he has flayed the fools and pretenders of the world." To Gertrude Atherton, "Ambrose Bierce sits alone on the top of a mountain and does work which twenty years ago would have given him instant fame. He has the best brutal imagination of any man of the English-speaking race. His sonnets are exquisitely tender and dainty. His fables are the wittiest that have been written in America. The reserve and cynical brutality of his stories produce an impression never attained by the most riotous imagination."

In the backwash of the publication of *Black Beetles*, Bierce and his copublisher had their first falling-out.

Bierce, as Danziger afterward related, was outraged when he learned that most of the copies of *Black Beetles* were being bought — and immediately destroyed — by persons caught in the amber of his poetic wrath. "When the book failed," Danziger said, "he poured the vials of his wrath on my head," and ordered Danziger to sell the remainder at an auction. "I arranged it but had to pay the auctioneer, as the sale did not meet the auction expenses."[8]

Danziger then went to a well-to-do friend of Bierce's and "borrowed" three hundred dollars to save Bierce the humiliation, as he explained it, of being sued for the printer's bill. When Bierce heard about this he exploded again, denounced Danziger and broke his cane over his copublisher's head.

Bierce saved the pieces of the broken cane, as he told his friends, to remind him of "the nature of friendship."[9]

During the summer of 1892, part of which he spent as a guest at his brother Albert's camp on the shore of Lake Temescal,

Bierce met George Sterling, who was to become the St. Peter of his band of disciples. Sterling had been angling for an introduction, he said, ever since hearing Joaquin Miller describe Bierce as "an old soldier, a damn cynic and the former friend [sic] of Empress Eugénie." The first evening of their meeting Bierce and the twenty-two-year-old Sterling slept out under the stars, each wrapped in a blanket, and what Sterling remembered of that sleep-out was that "throughout the night the cynic's eyes under shaggy yellow eyebrows were fixed on the fainter blue of the star Lyra."

Sterling was overwhelmed by the Bierce personality. More than any of the protégés — even the fluttery young poetesses and poets' wives — he was held in thrall by the man he always addressed as "the Master." The relationship turned stormy at times, when Sterling failed to live up to Bierce's artistic and personal standards, but it endured through the years. To Sterling, Bierce was the greatest writer alive. To Bierce, Sterling was, as he frequently proclaimed, the equal of any of the century's poets and the superior of most. The ego of each, requiring more sustenance than most men's, benefited accordingly.

Sterling was a tall, bronzed, handsome fellow with the profile and physique of an ancient Greek. He had come to California two years earlier, the member of an old and respected Sag Harbor, Long Island, family which like Bierce's traced its lineage to Puritan ancestors. His father had been the senior warden of the Episcopal church, but was converted to Catholicism when Sterling was seventeen. Sterling was thereupon deposited in a Catholic college in Maryland with instructions to study for the priesthood. Fortunately he fell in love with poetry rather than the priestly vocation — though he would have made a superbly picturesque bishop provided he survived the lower ranks — and was then dispatched, with paternal disgust, to Oakland. His uncle, Frank C. Havens, was the leading real estate operator in Oakland and provided Sterling with a job in his office. Sterling, however, was no more suited to real estate than the priesthood; the role of a hard-living, Villonesque poet was all that appealed to him.[10]

And Bierce encouraged him, not, until later, realizing the vain, neurotic, wayward quality of the young man's character which also failed to suit him for the disciplines of a career in poetry. He had a way with words, with crafting ornately jeweled images, with creating the glittering metaphor; but content and meaning were something else. He also had a tendency to follow other men's banners — first Bierce's, then Jack London's, then Robinson Jeffers's — with a slavishness that denoted an inner hollowness, a lack of the independence the true artist needs more than anything else.

Bierce encouraged him to break away from the stodgy routine of Uncle Frank's real estate office and the security his rightly concerned family hoped he would find in a steady job; was uproariously delighted when Sterling and a prankish friend hoisted a pirate flag to a church steeple. However, he also warned Sterling — already a fairly heavy drinker and always ready to adopt a romantic pose — that poetry was hard work, that he must stay away from "posturing in cafés" and avoid the spurious delights of the Bohemian life. Bierce had had his own whirl in Bohemia, London variety, but he now defined that realm as "a taproom of a wayside inn on the road from Boeotia to Philistia." The frenetic buzzing and self-dramatizing of the Bohemians, he told Sterling, was more harmful to the embryonic writer or artist than bad liquor or coldhearted landlords. He also advised Sterling that he must not sap his creative energy by taking up lost or humanitarian causes. Socialists and anarchists were then exceedingly active in San Francisco and Oakland, and Bierce feared — rightly as it turned out — that Sterling would catch the virus.

Social reformers, Bierce said, were "missionaries who, in their zeal to lay about them, do not scruple to seize any weapon that they can lay their hands on; they would grab a crucifix to beat a dog. The dog is well beaten, no doubt ... but note the condition of the crucifix." There was no doubt of his detestation of Marxism in all its variations. Once after taking the negative side of a debate with Morris Hillquit over whether socialism would work in America, he bought the Socialist dialectician a drink in a nearby bar, smiled wolfishly and told him, "You have a lovely long neck, Mr. Hillquit, and some day I hope to be one of those who will put a rope around it."

The story told by Upton Sinclair that Bierce turned against socialism after he lost a girl to a Socialist named Lawrence Gronlund — a story often retold — was sheer nonsense. He had detested all radicals ever since the early Seventies when he observed how close San Francisco came to anarchy with Denis Kearney whipping up class and racial hatreds. He was as violently opposed to predatory capitalism as he was to any form of Marxism; a Huntington or a Rockefeller would bring down upon himself diatribes equally as searing, and oftener repeated, than any social or political reformer.

A Marxist critic in writing Sterling's obituary commented that "Sterling discovered socialism, which was excellent. Simultaneously, however, he was discovered by Ambrose Bierce, which was almost fatal."[11] Sterling, in fact, did not "discover" socialism until after Bierce left San Francisco. Nor was Bierce's influence "almost fatal." He did not suggest Sterling's choice of subjects or his rhetorical treatment of them, but served as his editor and tutor, reading every line Sterling wrote, publishing much of it in his "Prattle" column and trying to find other means of publication. In one manuscript Sterling submitted for Bierce's approval, the latter, Carey McWilliams has found, made twenty-two suggestions for changes in words and sentence structure, all of which Sterling accepted.

Bierce thought so highly of the young man that when his son Leigh, at nineteen, insisted it was time he struck out on his own, Bierce arranged that he share an apartment in the Blake Block with Sterling and Roosevelt Johnson.[12] Leigh was, like his dead brother, a handsome replica of the elder Bierce, but less aggressive, hot-tempered and independent than Day. "The very image," Dr. Danziger noted, "of what his father must have been at the same age." Physically, perhaps, but Leigh Bierce showed no great promise of talent or enterprise. He wanted to become a newspaperman also, and early showed tendencies toward dissipation which alarmed his father. Bierce apparently kept a close watch on him. When he heard that Leigh had become involved with a girl "unquestionably unworthy of marital alliance," as Danziger put it, Bierce immediately descended on the apartment he was sharing with Sterling and Johnson.

Both Sterling and Danziger claimed to have been witnesses to the showdown. Sterling recorded that after Bierce closeted himself with his son, Leigh came out weeping and said, "My father is a greater man than Christ! He has suffered more than Christ!" Leigh agreed to see no more of the girl.[13]

Danziger cast himself in the role of eavesdropper and claimed that he overheard what Bierce told his son.

Bierce asked the name of the girl Leigh intended to marry. When Leigh gave it, Bierce told him, "You compel me to make a confession of the real cause why your mother and I live apart . . . Years ago I had relations with a woman. A child was born. Your mother learned the truth and I have been doing penance ever since."

Leigh, according to Danziger, asked what that had to do with his own romance.

"Nothing much," Danziger quotes Bierce as calmly replying, "except that the girl you love is the child of that woman."

Danziger then pictured Bierce as emerging from that conference with "the yawn of a tiger," laughing over having conned his son out of an unsuitable marriage with what he called "a bit of skillful inveracity."[14] The most that can be said for Danziger's account is that it is questionable whether Bierce was ever that brutal in his personal, particularly his paternal, relations, or that dishonest. It would have been in character for him to rage and bully, but he had an obsession about telling the truth that doesn't match up with any quoted sophistry about "skillful inveracity." Danziger also reported that he once came across Leigh "reeling out of one of the lowest dives in San Francisco. I took him with me; and although I offered him every possible aid, he would not accept. 'I want to go to hell,' he said alarmingly."

Whatever the exact circumstances, it was obvious that Bierce was headed for a second parental failure; Leigh's tragedy merely took more time to develop than Day's.

He simply was unable to devote the time and patience to his

children that he could spare for his swarm of strivers and neophytes. It didn't seem to occur to him that he had never attached himself to any "Master"; that anyone who needed as much help as many of them clamored for probably couldn't be helped. A case in point was Herman Scheffauer, a darkly handsome young Bavarian immigrant, an architect by profession, a poet by avocation. In worshipfulness he equaled Sterling and the poetesses, addressed Bierce as "Thor" and "Magister," and later credited Bierce with having "bewitched me against many threatening dangers of sentimentality and absurdity which frequently steal upon the young American writer." Later Bierce would berate Scheffauer for his "intolerable conceit" as he admonished Sterling for his irresponsibility.

While the honeymoon phase of protégé and patron was still in effect, Scheffauer wrote a long poem titled "The Sea of Serenity," which reminded Bierce of Edgar Allan Poe. (Yet when Scheffauer inscribed a book to Bierce as "the twin of Dean Swift," Bierce as always flew into a rage at the indignity of being compared to anyone else.) Bierce proposed that the poem be used as the basis of a hoax in the "Prattle" column, and Scheffauer agreed. Bierce published it with a foreword stating that it was a long-lost fragment of Poe's work which had been sent him by a Poe descendant in Southern California. The hoax ended in a dismaying fizzle. Although he had hoped to stir up a controversy over its authorship, he found that his readers didn't give a damn who wrote it. Nobody wrote in to praise or complain. Next week Bierce confessed in his column that the poem was written by Scheffauer, whose "modesty alone was responsible" for the prankish attempt to pass off the work on the defenseless Poe.

In 1892 Adolphe Danziger realized his ambition to see his name coupled with Bierce's on a title page. Predictably the collaboration landed them both in a prolonged and acrimonious dispute over financial and artistic matters. At the beginning of the venture Danziger stood high on the list of Bierce favorites, "a tremendous scholar, a prose writer of distinction in many languages, a gentleman . . . clean in heart and life," as one reference to him in "Prattle" read.[15]

Danziger had translated and brought to his mentor a long story published in a German magazine. It was titled *The Monk of Berchtesgaden* and was written by a Professor Richard Voss, who adapted it from a medieval manuscript acquired from a Franciscan monastery in Bavaria. In brief it was the Teutonic version of *The Scarlet Letter*, the story of a monk who fell in love with a hangman's daughter, went mad with jealousy and finally killed her. On another level it was a psychological study of the religious mind torn between sexual desire and avowed duties. This, naturally, was a subject Bierce found congenial.

Danziger was fearful that its publication in the United States would bring down the wrath of the Catholic Church, but as he nobly put it, "My literary life stood above personal considerations." His translation did need polishing, however, and for that purpose he took it to Bierce. As Bierce explained in the preface to a subsequent edition: "As Dr. Danziger had at that time a most imperfect acquaintance with the English language, he asked me to rewrite his version of Herr Voss's work for publication in this country. In reading it I was struck by what seemed to me certain possibilities of amplification, and I agreed to do the work if given a free hand by both author and translator."

One "amplification" Bierce may have made was in an early passage when the monk, Ambrosius, is sent from Passau to the monastery at Berchtesgaden. The young monk, about to complete his novitiate, is overwhelmed by the grandeur of the mountains which surround the monastery (the same mountains, incidentally, which produced so many murderous fantasies for the late Adolf Hitler in his Berchtesgaden retreat). His feeling of exaltation, the awe of a lowlander catching his first sight of mountains, was a fairly close transliteration of Bierce's own experience as a youthful soldier marching into the Appalachians of West Virginia.

In his rewrite Bierce also pointed up and dramatized the role of sexuality in religious fervor, an observation which undoubtedly stemmed from his unwilling attendance at backwoods revival meetings when a boy. Image after image in the story, which Bierce retitled *The Monk and the Hangman's Daughter*, superimposes sexual over religious ecstasy. In some ways it anticipated Freud. The reigning pashas of American literature dismissed Bierce as an archconversative, antihuman, antiliberal, yet his work on *The Monk* indicated that he was several steps ahead of the procession in that respect.

When the rewrite job was done, Bierce took it to his friend Cozy Noble, then Sunday editor of the *Examiner*. Appalled at what he considered to be an essay in anti-Catholicism, Noble refused to publish the story. Bierce, as Danziger told it, waited until Noble went on his vacation, then submitted *The Monk* to Petey Bigelow, who was substituting for Noble and who immediately agreed to publish it. When the first installment appeared under the byline "G. A. Danziger and Ambrose Bierce," Noble rushed back to San Francisco to order it stopped. Publisher Hearst, however, had read the first installment, liked it, and ordered it to run as scheduled.

A minor Chicago publisher teetering on the brink of bankruptcy, F. J. Schulte Company, proposed to bring the story out in book form. Schulte insisted that Bierce's name should appear first on the title page, since it was the better known and his contribution as rewrite man was more important than Danziger's as translator. Danziger balked, declaring that "my name is very dear to me." Quite reasonably Bierce replied, "We are not actresses to quarrel whose name shall appear in larger letters on the billboards. We are artists, creators. In the end the publisher merely makes his demand as a merchant. He believes that my name will bring more money. Why quarrel with good fortune?"[*][16]

---

* Publishers, he wrote in a "Prattle" column, were "connected by narrative with Ali Baba." He was annoyed because Schulte brought out a first printing of only six thousand copies and wasn't lavish in his advertising. "What, then, is a publisher?" he continued. "He is a person who buys of a small class of fools something which he sells to a large class of fools."[17]

Danziger finally yielded, but the two men were soon embroiled in a lively feud. Bierce claimed that Danziger was trying to snatch the larger share of proceeds from the book. He was also irked about this time by Danziger's borrowing money from a friend of his, leading to the caning episode. Furthermore Danziger was going around town proclaiming himself the sole author of *The Monk and the Hangman's Daughter.*

Worse yet, Bierce, who didn't mind patronizing but couldn't bear being patronized even by the most august personages, was exceedingly annoyed when he learned that the promotion-minded Danziger had sent a copy of *Black Beetles in Amber* to Prime Minister Gladstone. Danziger undoubtedly had heard the story of how Gladstone had praised Bierce's earlier work published in England, and thought he could extract a few lines of praise to help promote the sale of the volume. The first Bierce learned of what had been done was when he received a letter from the Prime Minister thanking Bierce for sending the book.

Bierce haughtily wrote Gladstone that "it seems to me a serious impertinence in anyone to ask your attention to my work," and that he had had nothing to do with the presentation copy. He followed this up with a blast at Danziger in his "Prattle" column. The Gladstone incident, he ruminated, "illustrates one of the countless disadvantages of a literary relation with an outmate of a detaining pound for wild asses. If a writer desires to be made seventeen kinds of a holy show let him associate himself with a king of conceit who is loud and proud of the connection. If ever again I choose a partner it will be some high soul who will blush for me as deeply as I blush for myself."[18]

Several weeks later he followed that up with a more definitive analysis of the Danziger character, which apparently was prompted by the rumors Danziger was circulating that he was being swindled out of his share of the proceeds from their collaboration. "It cannot make any material difference whether I swindled him or he swindled me; commercial usage and the proprieties of business were sufficiently observed if some one was swindled. Nor with reference to 'The Monk and the Hangman's

Daughter' is it important whether he or I had the larger hand in spoiling the work of a better man than either . . . For the nourishment of his insatiable inner dog, Dr. Danziger would steal any bone of recognition that he could not get by cheating . . ."[19]

He then took up the controversy over Danziger's career as a rabbi in San Jose, in which previously Bierce had defended him against the charges of Dr. Voorsanger in the *Jewish Times and Observer*, and retracted his former defense of Danziger as a clergyman. "As a matter of fact, the wretch is a 'minister' in the same way that Jonah, after being spewed ashore, was a part of the whale. I never was ashamed of being an infidel until Dr. Danziger assured me that he was one. For ten minutes I was an easy prey to any strolling exhorter that might have passed that way, cadging for souls.

"In Dr. Danziger is a dual individuality like that of a two-headed calf; the natures of saint and sinner are so intimately interblended as to make him preeminently a man of parts. He is a layman for lying and a minister for fighting. He carries his sacerdotal character in his hip-pocket and pulls it only when his face is slapped. He carries a pistol there, too, but when invited to pull that he says it is the proudest moment of his life, but family reasons, largely hereditary, compel him to decline. But, Lord, Lord, you should have heard this holy man of God swear when tapped upon the nimbus! And dance! why not a curly worldling in San Francisco's entire 400 ever footed it so neatly! O, a fine and serious minister he! — isn't he, Dr. Voorsanger? By the way, Voorsanger — shake."[20]

Several weeks later Bierce took up the knout again over the matter of who did what in producing *The Monk and the Hangman's Daughter:* "I wrote every word of [it] as published. Until Dr. Danziger saw that it was a creditable book he never, so far as I know, professed to have done more than translate the German story by Dr. Voss upon which it was founded. I have never seen that story and do not read German; what changes he may have made I do not know, nor care. If there was as little of Dr. Voss in his version as there is of him in mine, I am unable to conjecture what the original yarn was like. It was for lying about that and other matters that I punished him; and apparently he is not yet reformed."[21]

The controversy, except for the more violent aspects of it, was of little interest to anyone but Bierce and his collaborator, a fact which seems to have escaped them. It displayed Bierce's technical mastery in adapting a Gothic romance, but, as he freely admitted, the plot and characters were developed by other hands. Perhaps also it directed his attention to the German masters of the supernatural, and the Frankenstein-type of monster which appears in both German and English literature.

One of his better efforts along this line, "Moxon's Master," owed something to this tradition. Certainly Bierce himself was conscious of his great predecessors in that genre and demonstrated that he had studied them with care. Of members of the literary "patrol" who seemed to regard his stories of the supernatural as something unliterary and therefore unworthy, he commented, "Tapping, as they do, two of the three great mother-lodes of human interest, these tales are a constant phenomenon — of the most permanent, because the most fascinating, element in letters. Great Scott! has the patrol never heard of *The Thousand and One Nights,* of *The Three Spaniards,* of Horace Walpole, of Monk Lewis, of DeQuincey, of Maturin, Ingemann, Blicher, Balzac, Hoffman, Fitz James O'Brien?"*

The breach between Bierce and Danziger, for all the recrimination they loosed upon each other, eventually was healed. Danziger claimed it was Bierce who, in his gruff fashion, made the first move toward reconciliation when he sent Danziger a note reading, "If you don't come up to Angwin's, I'll come down and shoot you." Danziger wasn't quite sure whether he meant that literally, but went up to the mountain retreat and "spent a couple of weeks most delightfully with Bierce." If Danziger is to be believed, it was one of the few instances in which Bierce managed to forgive anyone without putting him through the wringer.

---

* Fitz James O'Brien was a highly promising young Irish-American writer who was killed in action during the Civil War.

Anti-Semitism was not only socially acceptable and morally respectable in the Nineties but almost a fashionable parlor game in the years when the Jewish immigration became a floodtide. Bierce himself, fiercely intolerant on so many subjects, may seem to have been inevitably anti-Semitic. Certainly he did not hesitate to dislike and oppose anyone just because he belonged to a minority. But attacking anyone solely on the ground of his color, race or creed seemed too cheap and easy a target for one who regarded himself as an intellectual sportsman. Bierce preferred to take on a majority, the larger and more vociferous the better. If he frequently assailed Protestants, it was only because there were more of them, not because he looked any kindlier on Catholic doctrine.

The charge of anti-Semitism was leveled at him, however, during the David Lezinsky affair. It was an ironic tribute to whatever genius he possessed that he is the only poet ever accused of having instigated the assassination of a President, although perhaps not the only critic ever charged with having caused the death of a poet.

The poet was David Lesser Lezinsky. Bierce had nothing against him but artistic incompetence, a crime of sufficient severity to summon up his most scalding invective. Every occasion on which Lezinsky placed his work on public display Bierce was waiting to pounce. Early in 1893 a relative of Lezinsky's accused him of being anti-Semitic. Danziger, the former rabbi, told the accuser that Bierce "didn't like any religionists" but that Lezinsky's faith "had nothing whatever to do with Bierce's condemnation of his poetry."[22] Other Lezinsky partisans also charged Bierce with being too harsh, one of them writing a letter which Bierce published in the "Prattle" column:

"Your reputation as a critic has suffered severely by the brutal attack which you made recently upon David Lezinsky. Mr. Lezinsky is a rising young man of great genius and his literary work has met with the approval of abler thinkers . . . Perhaps, however, even these lines are wasted upon you, and you will still continue to deride where you cannot equal. In that case I can only say that I have heard that Mr. Ambrose Bierce is more

careful of his skin than he is of his literary reputation, and he will
richly deserve the thrashing which he is destined to receive at the
hands of Mr. Lezinsky."

Bierce's reply to this was milder in tone than usual when his
literary authority was challenged. ". . . I shall continue to deride
until I experience the Lezinsky heavy hand." He then quoted
several verses of Lezinsky's work with the comment that "their
lofty style and noble thoughts are suspiciously suggestive of
plagiarism. They strongly recall Mrs. Plunkett's famous 'Ode to a
Dead Cow.'" And he added:

"Mr. Lezinsky's prose is frequently intelligible and sometimes
grammatical. In any case, I hope he will think it needless to
thrash anybody: I am seldom thrashed by poets without feeling
my position keenly. Still, if he must use his hand either to thrash
me or write verses the public will find me faithful to duty and
ready for the sacrifice. But I fancy he will write verses if he can
catch another dead man to damn with his poetic fire.* Well, it
will make the poor fellow appreciative of Hades."

Dr. Danziger, who frankly pictured himself as something of a
busybody where Bierce's affairs were concerned, claimed that he
looked up Lezinsky. "Instead of finding a cultivated John L.
Sullivan, I found a youth with the face of a bilious Jesus. . . .
He was sad — sad beyond speech that the heathen Bierce would
not let him rise to the literary surface. In a burst of anguish he
told me that he was 'done with this grim world'; and to show me
that he meant what he said, he stretched himself on his lounge
and went to sleep."

When he told Bierce of his visit with Lezinsky, Bierce commented that "the young man was suffering from excess emotion-
alism and should go to some asylum for a long rest."[23]

A few days later Lezinsky committed suicide, and everyone

---

* The lines written by Lezinsky and quoted by Bierce included this stanza:

Your greatness is a growing star
That shoots with comet's flame.
Amid the crash of falling worlds
Will still be seen your name.

Obviously Bierce was willing to rest his case on the quotation.

who had felt the Bierce lash himself or disliked his methods on less personal grounds accordingly blamed him for the young poet's death.

One friend quoted Bierce as saying, "It is perfect rot to say that I am responsible for Lezinsky's death. I have never met him and would have refused to do so had the occasion risen. I never once attacked him personally but only his verse. When he elected to become a poet, he impliedly consented to public criticisms of that which he made public."[24]

Dr. Danziger reported a more callous reaction. "I knew he would," he quoted Bierce as saying. "It is the only decent thing he ever did!"

Ina Coolbrith, the gray-eyed Sappho of Russian Hill, was among those who turned away from Bierce after years of friendship and admiration. There was, in fact, something suspicious about their eagerness to disavow him on the grounds of ruthlessness. In the past he had been equally brutal, or more so. Comparing Lezinsky's offering to the imaginary ode of the ephemeral Mrs. Plunkett was pretty mild stuff for the conductor of "Prattle," which as its title suggested wasn't meant to be a final true bill against those it denounced or criticized. It almost seemed as though some of his friends and associates had been waiting to seize upon such an occasion to justify their rejection of him.

In a letter to a friend, Bierce, apparently stung by some of the defections, wrote that "All my life I have been hated and slandered by all manner of persons except good and intelligent ones; and I don't greatly mind. I knew in the beginning what I had to expect . . . Just run over in your mind the names of men who have told the truth about their unworthy fellows and about human nature . . . They are the bogie-men of history. None of them has escaped vilification . . . When you strike you are struck. The world is a skunk, but it has rights; among them that of retaliation."[25]

It was left to Arthur McEwen, long his comrade in what they regarded as lonely service at a cultural outpost, to offer the definitive rundown on Bierce's failings as man and writer, but at least he waited for a decent period after Lezinsky's suicide to draw up his indictment. Undoubtedly *McEwen's Letter* enjoyed its peak distribution the week Red McEwen took after Bierce with his own bullwhip.

Bierce, he declared, had now been a "promising" talent in San Francisco for a quarter of a century, always seemingly at the point of delivering a masterwork. Publication of his *Tales of Soldiers and Civilians* should have been followed by even stronger work; instead he had served up *Black Beetles in Amber,* a rehash of his newspaper work, and *The Monk and the Hangman's Daughter,* a rewrite job. "The literary world was ready for the performance to begin," but Bierce had been unable to supply it with evidence that he could outwrite "contemporary authors at whom he had been cleverly sneering." McEwen then proceeded to treat his old friend to the same sort of scatter-shot assault that Bierce himself had used so effectively. Some of his more trenchant observations on Bierce included:

"He who had been for half a lifetime knocking over sparrows with an elephant rifle, when admitted to elephant country appeared there with no better weapon than a paragraphic popgun.

"In outliving his wit he is becoming a mere blackguard.

"His vanity is large and sore. Touch that, and he becomes savage and mean.

"The pretense of independence is as gratifying to him as independence itself would be, and the applause of a coterie of lady amateurs and amateur Boswells is a substitute for fame.

"He is most at home when breaking butterflies on the wheel, when torturing poor poetasters and female scribblers of verse, who but for him would remain unheard of.

"He is matchless in his petty trade of village critic and scold . . . what is left is a millionaire's literary lackey, whose soul is cankered with disappointment at his own emptiness, and whose narrow mind is ulcerated with envy of writers who are out of livery."[26]

There was harsh truth in the McEwen indictment. Recognizing him, perhaps, as a man as ruthless with himself as with

Collis P. Huntington *Brown Brothers*
chief of the "railrogues" against whom Bierce crusaded to a
successful end

Leon F. Czolgosz
the assassin of President McKinley whose bullets made a
Bierce prophecy come woefully true

Brown Brothers

Edwin Markham
whose "Man with a Hoe"
infuriated his former patron

Brown Brothers

Ambrose Bierce
poses for his portrait at the age
of 54 with his favorite weapon
in hand, a rolled-up copy of the
San Francisco *Examiner*

others, Bierce did not reply to McEwen's charges of artistic defalcation or the more personal attacks. He did hotly deny in his "Prattle" column that he was Hearst's lackey and did classify McEwen as being "as honest a gentleman as ever garbled letters, falsified telegrams and instigated murder." In the days of personal journalism, that was so mild a response that it almost constituted a plea of guilty as charged.

TWELVE

"How My Fame Rings Out"

WITH THE PUBLICATION of *Can Such Things Be?* in 1893, Bierce became wider known as a literary figure, not as a popular one because he was too uncompromising for popularity but as one around whom a sort of cult was forming. Some years later H. L. Mencken would write that "The reputation of Bierce has always radiated an occult, artificial, drug-store scent." Yet even the Eastern critics had to concede that he had a place in literature, difficult though it might be to define. The poet Edwin Markham, who had been a semiprotégé, reported in the New York *Tribune* that "The man I hear most inquiry about just now is Ambrose Bierce."[1]

Bierce's obsession with the ghastly, the ghostly and the inexplicable, which was given free play in *Can Such Things Be?*, undoubtedly dated back to the dreams which afflicted him in childhood and which he always remembered with an unusual clarity, even a sort of affection. The images of Civil War carnage — wild pigs eating corpses, headless bodies strewn over the battlefields he came across with the blood and smoke still upon them, weird coincidences that could crop up only in that ultimate fantasy of human combat — were catalogued and treasured in his memory. A critic versed in psychoanalytic techniques could probably make a good case for Bierce as being notably

neurotic. His obsession with death might also have been reinforced by his asthmatic condition, his almost constant struggle
for the breath of life. A man who must often have awakened late
in the night, with the breath barely wheezing through clogged
bronchial tubes, would feel the constant presence of death. Yet
there was something almost robust about his enthusiasm — more
that of the connoisseur of horror than the neurotic frightened by
his visions — for the supernatural and the terrible. Clifton Fadiman has written that Bierce's morbidity was too controlled to
suggest any form of mental disturbance, that "It merely expresses
his fury at our placid healthfulness."[2]

Bierce himself had no apologies for scaring the wits out of his
readers. To a correspondent who criticized the gore which
flavored much of his writing, he replied, "If it scares you to read
that one imaginary person killed another, why not take up
knitting?"[3]

His interest in the violence men could inflict upon one another
never slackened, never declined through its essential lack of
variety. He was a murder buff to equal the youngest police
reporter. Visitors to the city were always escorted to the scene of
the latest atrocity. Once during the Nineties he was observed
leading two New York writers to the site of a murder so recent
the blood was still congealed under sawdust sweepings and
complaining that the bloodthirstiness of the citizenry had declined and their inventiveness in butchery had decreased. But it
may have been going too far to say, as Thomas Beer did, "If the
high quality of slaughter had been maintained, Bierce would
never have left San Francisco."[4]

For Bierce death was a joke, murder was high comedy. The
reader had to accept that as his basic premise or quit, appalled at
his misanthropy. His variations on the theme that death was a
farce which only a truly civilized man could appreciate, laugh at
rather than weep over, were endless. Among them were the
accidental return of the protagonist to the grave of someone he
loved and meeting death there himself; dreaming of death and
having the dream turn into reality; grappling with a dead body in
the dark and thus dying from fear; hallucinations of attack by a

dog which lead to death and the discovery of teeth marks on the body; instances of telepathy, haunted houses, ghostly visitations; death from fear by a person who laughed at ghosts until he was induced to believe he had seen one; death from the effects of inherited fear; body-snatching involving a man who turns out to have been buried alive — and this is only a brief rundown. In most of them, fear is the villain, death merely an element in the atmosphere.

Some of his best efforts along these lines were contained in *Can Such Things Be?* One of the most frequently anthologized is "The Death of Halprin Frayser," perhaps because of an element of modernity in its treatment of the Oedipus complex, with its quite typical and marvelously compact opening:

"One dark night in midsummer a man waking from a dreamless sleep in a forest in the Napa Valley lifted his head from the earth, and staring a few minutes into the blackness, said: 'Catherine Larue.' He said nothing more; no reason was known to him why he should have said so much.

"The man was Halprin Frayser. He lived in St. Helena, but where he lives now is uncertain, for he is dead . . ."

Frayser, it develops, was deeply attached to his mother. She had remarried and her second husband had killed her. Frayser, who had disappeared several years before, knew of neither event. He had fallen asleep — and here coincidence intrudes, in fact is the story's motive force — in a country graveyard near a marker bearing the name "Catherine Larue." Just before he is strangled by a lunatic he is confronted by an apparition which he believes is his mother's face but is actually his murderer's. The grave near which he was killed was his mother's; her new married name, unknown to him, was Catherine Larue. One of the detectives investigating his murder complains that "There is some kind of rascally mystery here," and from out of the surrounding fog comes "the sound of a laugh, a low, deliberate, soulless laugh, which had no more of joy than that of a hyena night-prowling in the desert . . ."

A less macabre story in the volume was "Jupiter Doke, Brigadier General," a fable celebrating the idiocy of military legend. It tells the story of how a backwoods politician bumbles his way to glory in the Union Army. The climax to his career is a battle in which a mule stampede routs the Confederates and wins the field for Brigadier Doke, upon which Congress passes a resolution thanking him and his brigade for the "unparalleled feat of attacking — themselves but 2,000 strong — an army of 25,000 men and utterly overthrowing it, killing 5,327, making prisoners of 19,003, of whom more than half were wounded." Undoubtedly the story was based on a similar victory of the vainglorious General Hooker's, in which a stampede also scattered the enemy, during the Chattanooga campaign, in which Bierce participated.

In "Moxon's Master," Bierce seemed to be anticipating the age of cybernetics. It has been oddly neglected by those considering the brief history of science fiction, yet it created a situation which can be considered contemporary by readers of seven decades later. It was also one of the few instances in which Bierce set up shop as a prophet.

The story opens with the narrator and an inventor named Moxon discussing the possibilities of a man-made machine which has the power to think. Moxon believes he has constructed such an automaton. Machines have the ability to think, he contends, because "consciousness is the creature of rhythm." A machine operates rhythmically and inevitably will develop consciousness, then the power of thought.

The narrator argues against Moxon's theory, but is given pause a few minutes later when Moxon goes into the adjoining room, which is his laboratory. He hears sounds of a struggle and arguing voices. When Moxon returns to his guest, he bears a scratch on his cheek. He explains that his mechanical man resented being left alone with nothing to do. Amused by the explanation, the narrator leaves Moxon saying, with tongue in cheek, "I'm going to wish you goodnight; and I'll add the hope that the machine which you inadvertently left in action will have her gloves on the next time you think it needful to stop her."

On leaving Moxon's house, however, the narrator begins thinking over what Moxon has told him and comes to the conclusion that his friend may not have been playing a hoax on him. He returns to Moxon's house, opens the laboratory door despite Moxon's warning that he must never enter without knocking. There he finds Moxon and his creation absorbed in a game of chess. Suddenly Moxon rises from his chair after calling out "Check!"

The gorilla-sized automaton is annoyed, and the buzzing of the mechanism which operates it rises to a clatter that fills the room. It reaches across the tables and clutches Moxon by the throat. During the ensuing struggle, the lights go out. Suddenly there is a flash of flame, by which the narrator catches a glimpse of Moxon lying dead on the floor, "his throat still in the clutch of those iron hands, his head forced backward, his mouth wide open and his tongue thrust out; and — horrible contrast! — upon the painted face of his assassin an expression of tranquil and profound thought, as in the solution of a problem in chess."

Moxon's house catches fire, and the narrator is saved only by the advertent appearance of Moxon's laboratory assistant, who drags him to safety. He recovers consciousness in a hospital three days later, remembering that final scene in the laboratory, but unable to make sure he saw what he believed he saw because the fire has destroyed Moxon's house, its owner and the homicidal automaton.

Several of the stories in *Can Such Things Be?* were in the Western tall-tale category which Mark Twain and Bret Harte had exploited so successfully. "The Famous Gilson Bequest" worked the same vein as Twain's *The Man That Corrupted Hadleyburg*, and conveyed with exactness Bierce's views on the doltishness of human behavior. Gilson is a wretch who has been run out of a number of mining camps for his antisocial activities. Finally he is justly hanged as a horse thief. In his will Gilson leaves his estate to the town's leading citizen, who is also the man chiefly responsible for his trip to the gallows, with the proviso that his heir will receive the estate only if he has cleared Gilson's name of the slanders against it in a stipulated period. The heir works diligently at Gilson's rehabilitation and his own ruin. At the end of the story the heir has bankrupted himself in a successful effort to clear Gilson's name through bribing those the gallows bird has injured — and is left brokenly insisting on Gilson's virtue.

"My Favorite Murder" is also a satirical assault on frontier justice. The joshing begins at once, with the opening sentence, "Having murdered my mother under circumstances of singular atrocity, I was arrested and put upon my trial, which lasted seven years." The narrator evidently has enjoyed a flavorful home life. "Four years after we had set up the road agency an itinerant preacher came along, and having no other way to pay for the night's lodging that we gave him, favored us with an exhortation of such power that, praise be, we were all converted to religion . . . The family then moved to Ghost Rock and opened a dance house. It was called 'The Saints' Rest Hurdy-Gurdy,' and the proceedings each night began with prayer. It was there that my now sainted mother, by her grace in the dance, acquired the sobriquet of 'The Bucking Walrus.' " What the defendant, in his pride of craft, resents is the judge's proclamation that the matricide was the most horrible of crimes. The defendant-narrator then recalls the artistic integrity with which his Uncle William was dispatched. The uncle was bludgeoned, trussed up, put in a sack and butted by a ram who tossed him high in the air until he fell with a broken neck. "Altogether," the story concludes, "I cannot help thinking that in point of artistic atrocity my murder of Uncle William has seldom been excelled."

Two other notable stories in the collection were "A Jug of Sirup" and "The Damned Thing." The latter concerned a man who met death at the hands of an invisible "thing." In "A Jug of Sirup," less typical and more elaborate than most of Bierce's fables, he undertook an examination of the nature of mass hysteria.

As in many of his studies in the supernatural, he provided a setting utterly commonplace peopled by ordinary folk to heighten the phantasmagoric effect when he stirred up his witches' brew.

"A Jug of Sirup" opens with Alvan Creede, the town's banker, returning home to be greeted by his wife at the door. He had been carrying home a jug of sirup, which he put down for only a moment to take his keys out of his pocket. When he bends to pick up the jug, he finds it has disappeared. And it occurs to him that he bought the jug from a storekeeper named Silas Deemer a short time before. But, he suddenly realizes, Silas Deemer has been dead for weeks.

Most reluctantly, the sobersided banker grapples with the conclusion that he has "seen a ghost." His attempts at rationalizing are interrupted when his daughter comes in and says her brother wants to know whether he can have the little jug he had seen his father carrying when he came home. His mystification is only compounded when he reflects that the entire stock of Deemer's store was sold to a competitor.

The story of Alvan Creede's ghostly visitation spreads throughout the town, and next evening a curious and excited crowd gathers outside Deemer's empty store. They seem to catch sight of the late Silas Deemer inside the store working over his account books in a dim ghostly light. Finally they work up the courage to enter the store. In the darkness they knock over boxes and barrels, fly into an unreasoning panic, curse and fight and trample each other in a mass surrender to unreasoning fear. Only Alvan Creede, still skeptical, has the sense to resist the outbreak of hysteria and calmly walks away.

Next day Deemer's empty store looks like a battleground. When the townspeople examine the ledger they had thought Deemer's ghost was working over the night before, they find it opened to the date of his death. And there is no record of the sale of a jug of sirup to Alvan Creede. The reader is left with a mystery, but no explanation.

In "The Damned Thing," the same calm objectivity is displayed, the "facts" recited, the reader encouraged to make up his own mind about them. The man who sees the "thing," however, is permitted to plead his case in scientific terms: "At each end of the solar spectrum the chemist can detect the presence of what are known as 'actinic' rays. They represent colors — integral colors in the composition of light — which we are unable to discern. The human eye is an imperfect instrument; its range is but a few octaves of the real 'chromatic scale.' I am not mad;

there are colors that we cannot see . . . And God help me! the Damned Thing is of such a color!"

The remarkable quality about the stories in *Can Such Things Be?* is the economy with which they are related, the spareness of Bierce's descriptions, the striking ability to introduce the element of horror into a contrastingly commonplace scene. Few of the stories run more than a couple thousand words. As a modern student of Bierce was to remark, his "mastery of pared phrasing was equalled only by Shaw and Wilde" among his contemporaries.[5] But those contemporaries, Bierce believed, stubbornly refused to recognize his talent even after the publication of two volumes of his stories. Or, as he put it:

> *My how my fame rings out in every zone*
> *A thousand critics shouting, "He's unknown!"*[6]

But his fame was growing, and with it came a comparative prosperity. It did not gentle his nature to any noticeable extent. A protégé whose work displeased him received the reproof, "You must have written that for the *Waverly Magazine.* When you were a schoolgirl." The protégé was male.[7] His relative affluence allowed him to take a fairly well-appointed apartment in Berkeley, and with some reluctance he invited his son Leigh to move in with him. He was then in his early fifties and too crusty of temperament to make him suffer the presence of a struggling journalist in his early twenties, even if the latter was his son. Apparently he recognized his failings as a family man, for he wrote a friend, "I feel a profound compassion for any one whom an untoward fate compels to live with *me.* However, such a one is sure to be a good deal alone, which is a mitigation."[8] Not much later his worshipful younger son moved to Southern California and took a job on the staff of the Los Angeles *Record.*

During the several years since they had separated, Bierce saw his wife only once, meeting her accidentally on a mountain road near St. Helena. They talked for only a few minutes before he turned away. Since then, Mollie had moved to Los Angeles with her now aged mother. They lived in the seclusion ordained for

Victorian widows, a classification which included the woman separated from her husband. Her daughter Helen later recorded that Mollie still loved Bierce and regarded him as "her ideal" of what a man should be. This devotion, if it was visible to its object, did not impress Bierce in the least. His marriage was shut away in the past. He even avoided communication with Mollie in the slightest degree by sending the checks for her support through their daughter. They would never meet again.

By 1894 the United States was again floundering in a severe economic depression. An apparent pattern was emerging. About every twenty years, it seemed, there was a panic on Wall Street followed by mass unemployment and industrial shutdowns. Whether or not it had been a matter of cause and effect, there had been a speculators' disaster on the stock market in '93, and now there were hundreds of thousands of jobless and this time — for the first time, in fact — they were in a mood for massive demonstration against the system blamed for producing such cyclical sufferings. And this time, too, there was no outlet for the mass frustrations. In '73 thousands had migrated from the Eastern cities to California and elsewhere on the frontier. Now the frontier was gone, and the children of the pioneers themselves were in the breadlines and soup kitchens. The West itself, once the dreamland of free enterprisers, was clamorous with radical remedies, ranging from free silver to updated versions of Populism. And in the East a new prophet had risen, his doctrines even more suggestive of socialism. The self-appointed General Jacob S. Coxey was prepared to lead an army of the unemployed on Washington with demands that Congress immediately issue five million dollars in greenbacks — a sizable sum then — to provide work for the jobless on nationwide road-building projects.[9]

In Oakland and San Francisco the agitation for economic and social reform attained a feverish pitch in the spring of 1894. The spirit of the late Denis Kearney seemed to have reincarnated itself. One of Kearney's old propagandists, "Humble Carl"

Browne, had become General Coxey's chief adviser; it was his idea that seventeen "brigades" be recruited and converge on Washington from all parts of the country. In Oakland a young printer named Charles Kelly was raising a "brigade" of two thousand men to join the march on Washington and meanwhile to make the privileged classes of the Bay cities aware of the turbulence and discontent below. The fire and police departments, with a regiment of the national guard standing by in reserve, were hard-pressed to preserve order in the streets. One of the malcontents milling in Oakland's streets, as yet unknown to Bierce, was a teen-age juvenile delinquent named Jack London who would ride the boxcars east (as far as Iowa) with Kelly's brigade of Coxey's army.

Secure enough himself for the moment, Bierce was a bemused spectator of these events. He may have been a conservative, but he was not unmoved when considering the sufferings of the unemployed. Although he may not have been aware of it, there was probably some truth in Jack London's later observation (to George Sterling) that if he had been born a generation later he would have been a Socialist himself, and probably not one of the passive variety. In one "Prattle" column he even considered that there was a necessary element of socialism in any modern republican government, but "unfortunately, no people in the world is fit for Socialism."[10]

A few weeks earlier he had gone so far as to advocate a state program of make-work projects — not much different from the Coxey prescription — "under such regulations as would not encourage" the unemployed to "depend upon it" or "cripple private industry." He added:

"So pitiable an object and so dangerous a moral force as a man anxious to find work yet finding no work is something that a community has not the right and should not have the folly to permit."[11]

It was hardly an unregenerate mossback who could advocate in a "Prattle" column that to cushion the American economy against recurrent depressions all private ownership of land be abolished, something like an inheritance tax system be established to keep vast fortunes under control, the various states be compelled to provide work programs during hard times, and the importation of cheap labor be prohibited.[12]

For a time, as he viewed the human suffering caused by the malfunctioning of the capitalistic system, it almost seemed as though Karl Marx had enlisted a new follower.

As the economy slowly regained its strength and the jobless were gradually taken off the streets, he reverted to his former position that anarchism, socialism, unionism, capitalism — all ism's, in fact — were malignant oversimplifications and like all solutions to human problems were riddled with human error. Laissez-faire capitalism seemed the least harmful because it interfered the least with the spectacle which provided him with so much savage amusement.

The trusts which were gaining so firm a control over the economy, and which soon would give rise to the popular governmental pursuit known as trust-busting, were, he held, inevitable. "The entire trend of our modern civilization," he wrote, "is toward combination and aggregation . . . Labor combines into unions, capital into trusts, and each aggregation is powerful in everything except in combating its own methods in the other . . . Governmental ownership and governmental control are what we are coming to . . . and with the industries and trade in fewer hands the task of regulating them will be greatly simplified, for it is easier to manage one defendant in a single jurisdiction than many in a hundred."[13]

The great villain on the American scene, he had come to believe, was the growing power of the American press. In those years of a mass movement toward literacy, of the newspaper unrivaled as a medium of information, as an institution rooted in the life of every American who could read with moving lips the boxcar type of the headlines, a press magnate was indeed a lordly fellow. Hearst himself was then only a slowly lengthening shadow over the land, yet it may have been that shy, enigmatic figure who gave rise to his apprehensions. More than once he started to write a biography of Hearst that would warn against the power one man could attain through ownership of newspapers all speaking in his voice; once he desisted because he didn't want such a book to be published while Hearst's mother, whom he held in great and unusual respect, was alive; but he did leave a testament, to be cited later, outlining his feelings on the subject of William Randolph Hearst.

Newspapers, he warned, "are sycophants to the mob, tyrants to the individual," which had assumed "rights" and privileges to which they weren't entitled for the purpose of controlling public opinion for their own purposes. As such they did compose a separate "estate" which, by controlling all present forms of communication, could become a dictatorial force in itself. "They constitute a menace to organized society — a peril to government of any kind; and if ever in America Anarchy shall beg to introduce his dear friend Despotism we shall have to thank our vaunted 'freedom of the press.' . . . When by virtue of controlling a newspaper a man is permitted to print and circulate thousands of copies of a slander which neither he nor any man would dare to speak before his victim's friends a long step has been taken toward the goal of entire irresponsibility . . . The right to publish news *because* it is news has no basis in law nor in morals."[14]

Once he had purged his mind of the procession of gaunt faces moving down the streets of Oakland and San Francisco in the drifting aimlessness of the unemployed in the spring of 1894, he returned to the subject of socialism. The Marxist remedy for human inequities, which he regarded as inevitable if not ideal, was sentimentality run amok. "The Socialist notion appears to be that the world's wealth is a fixed quantity, and A can acquire only by depriving B. He is fond of figuring the rich as living upon the poor — riding on their backs, as Tolstoi (staggering under the weight of his wife, to whom he had given his vast estate) was pleased to signify the situation. The plain truth of the matter is that the poor live mostly on the rich — entirely unless with their own hands they dig a bare subsistence out of their own farms or gravel claims . . . Yet the Socialist finds a pleasure in directing attention to the brass hoofs of the millionaire executing his joyous jig upon an empty stomach — that of the prostrate pauper — poets, muckrakers, demagogues and other audibles celebrating the performance with howls of sensibility."[15]

All his convictions in regard to socialism as a false doctrine came boiling up during the acrimonious circumstances under which Edwin Markham's "The Man with the Hoe" was published in the Sunday *Examiner*.

The goateed Markham, then an Oakland school principal and quite close to Bierce, had written the poem on being inspired by Millet's painting of the same title. At a New Year's Eve party in Carroll Carrington's apartment — Carrington was a Bierce protégé also — Markham read his tribute to the man who works with his hands as his ancestors have:

> *Bowed by the weight of centuries he leans*
> *Upon his hoe and gazes on the ground,*
> *The emptiness of ages in his face,*
> *And on his back the burden of the world.*
> *Who made him dead to rapture and despair,*
> *A thing that grieves not and that never hopes,*
> *Stolid and stunned, a brother to the ox?*
> *Who loosened and let down this brutal jaw?*
> *Whose was the hand that slanted back this brow?*
> *Whose breath blew out the light within this brain?*

Among Carrington's guests was Bailey Millard, the literary editor of the Sunday *Examiner*. He was so enthusiastic over the verse that he published it two weeks later, upon which Markham was paid a fee of forty dollars. It was one of the best buys a Hearst editor ever made, one of the few poems which became a journalistic sensation. It was reprinted in newspapers throughout the country; lecturers inveighed against it or compared it to the Sermon on the Mount; it was quoted from pulpits as an expression of the Christian spirit, and from sandlot soapboxes as the new gospel of socialism. William Jennings Bryan proclaimed it "a sermon addressed to the human heart," and Collis P. Huntington demanded to know, "Is America going to turn to Socialism over one poem? Markham's Hoe man has a hoe. Let him rejoice. The only man to commiserate is the man who has no hoe; the man who cannot help to enrich the world."*[16]

William Randolph Hearst was delighted with the poem because it expressed the liberal, antitrust sentiments which then graced his editorial pages. The nationwide approval of the poem demonstrated to him that he was in key with public opinion; it also indicated that the road to the White House might be open to a man who could dramatize further the plight of "The Man with the Hoe" and promise betterment of his condition. "Significantly," as his most recent and definitive biographer has written, "thereafter his attacks on the trusts became even more systematic and violent."[18]

For once Bierce, as chief bear baiter of the Hearst circus, found himself unabashedly in agreement with his employer's appointed enemy, Huntington of the Southern Pacific. He detested "The Man with the Hoe," called it "seepage from the barnyard." Bierce was outraged not only because of the poem's theme but because his protégé had been brought to national attention by someone else. He was also bilious over Millard's taking credit for Markham's new fame, and his introduction, which read in part, "Is not here a new and grand voice, deeptoned, sonorous, singing grandly?"[19]

Sonorous, yes, Bierce agreed, but he would differ in column after column about its "grandness." He regarded it as an incendiary piece of work, the literary equivalent of sandlot socialism. "The notion that the sorrows of the poor," he wrote one week after the poem's appearance, "are due to the selfishness of the great is 'natural,' and can be made poetical, but it is silly. As a literary composition it has not the vitality of a sick fish."[20]

---

* One of the many parodies "The Man with the Hoe" inspired was that of a Boston bicycle enthusiast:

> Bowed by the drooping handle-bars he leans
> Upon his bike and gazes at the ground;
> His back is humped and crooked and his face
> Is strained and agonizing in its looks.
> Who made him sit upon a wheel like this?[17]

The San Francisco literary world was delighted by the feuding which "The Man with the Hoe" aroused. Markham himself maintained a dignified and injured silence; he would not reply to the man of whom he had written, "His is a composite mind — a blending of Hafiz the Persian, Swift, Poe, Thoreau, with sometimes a gleam of the Galilean." There was nothing "Galilean" about Bierce's continued fuming over his poem. Bailey Millard later wrote that "When literary California rang with the bugle note of 'The Man with the Hoe,' the literati turned to Bierce as to one who should say whether the poem should be permitted to live or die. Probably for no other reason in the world than that [Markham's work] was tremendously popular Bierce turned down his thumbs."*[21]

If there had been an element of small-mindedness in his condemnation of Markham's poem, however, Bierce atoned for it later. When a poetess named Cora Case claimed that Markham had stolen the verse from her, Bierce immediately assumed the role of defense counsel for the poet. And some years later when Hearst was looking for an editor for his new acquisition, *Cosmopolitan* magazine, Bierce unhesitatingly recommended Markham's artistic defender, Millard, for the post on the curious grounds that "The little fellow is a true aristocrat."

---

* Dr. Danziger quoted Bierce as saying, "His Majesty, King Populus, is an ass," in regard to the public's taste in poetry. "He'd rather eat a mess of thistles than bother about an author, unless he is clothed in glory like our friend Joaquin Miller."

Here Huntington's ashes long have lain
Whose loss was our eternal gain,
For while he exercised all his powers
Whatever he gained, the loss was ours.

—Bierce's epitaph for
Collis P. Huntington

THIRTEEN *Don Ambrosio Crusades
Against the "Railrogues"*

THE LONG CAMPAIGN of William Randolph Hearst and his *Examiner* to curb the power and influence of Collis P. Huntington came to a climax in the winter of 1895–1896. It also provided the opportunity for Ambrose Bierce to display his talents as a crusading journalist, posing him as the champion of the people's rights and the government's treasury against the Octopus. In the role of St. George, Bierce performed with a gusto — and an instinct for his opponent's jugular — that resulted, in great part, in a surprising defeat for one of the robber-baron generation which had never been really challenged since the Civil War.

That winter Huntington and his battery of lawyers and lobbyists had invaded Washington with a bold proposal to place before Congress. The Funding Bill, proposed by Huntington and his associates, would have delayed indefinitely paying off the indebtedness of the Southern Pacific and Central Pacific, estimated at sixty to seventy-five million dollars. Before, during and after the Civil War the railroads had borrowed vast sums from the government which, despite the fortunes made, had never been repaid. The government favored a gradual repayment.

Instead the railroads proposed to turn back part of the land grants given them by the government for their rights of way. Or, as Huntington and Company now proposed in the Funding Bill, since the public seemed to demand more than a token payment, the debt would be refunded and paid off in low-interest bonds maturing in eighty-three years. In effect, the Southern Pacific would be shucking off its debt, as Huntington's opponents pointed out.

Hearst ordered his *Examiner* staff, and that of the New York *Journal*, which he had just acquired as the second link in his chain, to go after Huntington and his allies with every weapon at their disposal. The heaviest caliber in the arsenal was, of course, Ambrose Bierce, who began cannonading early in 1896. He not only attacked Huntington as the chief of the "railrogues," but such backers of his scheme as Sidney Smith, a San Francisco meat packer, who "should have been born a fish and educated as a prune," and Lovell White, a banker, who should have been "soldered up in one of Mr. Sidney Smith's tin cans." Mr. Huntington, he observed, not hesitating to descend to the personal, had a head like a dromedary with "its tandem peaks of cupidity and self-esteem." The Southern Pacific's scheme for dodging its debt was ridiculous because "a corporation which for thirty years has defaulted on the payment of interest and is about to default on payment of principal because it has chosen to steal both principal and interest can [not] henceforth be trusted to pay both." He also raked up the old charges, initiated by Arthur McEwen when he was in charge of the *Examiner*'s editorial page, that several hundred brakemen had lost their lives on the railroad because Huntington refused to install automatic safety devices on his freight cars. Furthermore, he reported that Washington was overrun by lobbyists in Huntington livery, each prepared to bribe any Congressman smart enough to indicate his vote was in doubt over the Funding Bill.

A Hearst "crusade" was always something to marvel at, a combination of charivari and Indian war dance with built-up drum section. Headlines grew taller and blacker. Mass meetings were held almost every night. A petition was circulated against the Funding Bill, for which almost two hundred thousand signatures were obtained.

From New York Hearst sent Bierce a telegram which was considered so important it was published in the *Examiner,* stating "Railroad combination so strong in Washington that seems almost impossible to break them, yet it is certainly the duty of all having interests of coast at heart to make most strenuous efforts. Will you please go to Washington for the *Examiner?*"[1]

Bierce would indeed. He was appointed chief Hearst correspondent and Huntington watcher in Washington, with a staff of his own to command and his dispatches and editorials to be published in both the San Francisco paper and the New York *Journal.* He entrained for Washington and took his son Leigh along with him, the latter to be given a job as a reporter on the New York *Journal* as a bonus.

His arrival in Washington was regarded as so important a factor in the struggle to make Huntington pay up that he was interviewed by a capital newspaper and given the attention ordinarily reserved for high visiting dignitaries. The newspaper justified its full-dress treatment of Bierce on the grounds that "of all the clever talkers and forceful writers with which this country is blessed there are few who can excel the man who was sent here by the San Francisco Examiner to oppose the Funding Bill which gives Huntington & Co. one hundred additional years of credit," and described him as "ordinarily soft of speech and possessed of charming manners."

It quoted him as saying, with a gesture like a cavalryman swinging his sabre, "In California the interest is intense. At a meeting to voice San Francisco's opposition to a measure similar to that now favored by Mr. Huntington . . . there were fully 13,000 persons who could not secure admittance to the big hall. The great majority of those actively concerned folks knew, of their own knowledge, how much of wicked greed was centered in the group of which Collis P. Huntington is now the only surviving figure; they knew how the directors of the Central Pacific Company had transferred to themselves, as directors in a closely related organization [the Southern Pacific], everything that could be regarded as worth having; they knew that this conscienceless gang had entered upon the work of railroad construction and operation as poor men and had somehow or other — the details read like the report of a grand larceny trial — acquired fifteen to twenty million each; they knew that competition in freight-carrying had been and still is systematically and murderously choked out of existence to the end that Huntington and his associates may become more and more wealthy . . .

"One of the surprising features of the campaign is the unwillingness of the average legislator to admit testimony bearing upon the moral phase of the controversy. It ought to be quite plain that those who unrighteously possessed themselves of $60,000,-000 thirty years ago, and who have never given up one cent of either principal or interest, have no claim upon which to base a demand for an extension that would continue the outrageous condition for a hundred years to come . . ."[2]

Bierce was so virulently opposed to the Southern Pacific that he suggested that Congress "foreclose the mortgage" on Huntington and build "a Government railroad from Omaha to San Francisco." It didn't seem to bother him that this could be considered a socialistic measure. His hatred of injustice occasionally was stronger than his loyalty to conservative doctrine.

He had come to Washington not only to head the Hearst bureau, but to carry a banner in the crusade himself. During the early months of 1896 he worked himself to the point of exhaustion, turning out a story a day and often an editorial, directing the efforts of other Hearst reporters to uncover Huntington's activities in the capital, and himself acting as a lobbyist, propagandist and buttonholer of Congressmen who might be persuaded to join the cause. The country at first had been largely indifferent to what had seemed a California problem. The Hearst tom-toms, however, were making it a national issue; there was hardly a section of the country that didn't feel itself similarly in the tentacles of an octopus-like railroad, and the growth of this sentiment would naturally result in pressure on the Congressmen from their constituents, remote though they might be from California. That was the value of the journalistic crusade: it put pressure on Huntington from quarters he expected to be neutral at worst.

The Bierce talent for invective had not evaporated over the years. In one of his first articles he wrote that "Mr. Huntington is not altogether bad. Though severe, he is merciful. He says ugly things of the enemy, but he has the tenderness to be careful that they are mostly lies."

Less than a month after Bierce arrived in the capital at the head of a wrecking crew which included reporters, photographers and the able political cartoonist Homer Davenport, Huntington decided it was time to try buying off the chief gadfly. One day late in February, Huntington met Bierce and some other men on the steps of the Capitol as he left a committee hearing. He asked Bierce what his price was for letting up on himself and the Southern Pacific. At every offer Bierce, flinty-eyed and contemptuous, shook his head.

"Well, name your price." Huntington raised his voice in exasperation. "Every man has his price."

Bierce chose his words carefully, almost as if he realized his reply would be quoted in newspapers around the world. "My price," he said deliberately, "is $75,000,000. If, when you are ready to pay, I happen to be out of town, you may hand it over to my friend, the Treasurer of the United States."[3]

Later Huntington was asked why he had approached Bierce so openly on the Capitol steps. "Oh, I just wanted to see how big he was. I know now." There were no more attempts at bribery.

With heightened malice, Bierce observed every move by the man who thought he could be bought off. When Huntington appeared to testify before a committee, before which he upped his "estimate" of what it had cost to build the Central Pacific from $36,000,000 (as he had testified before the Railroad Commission of 1887) to $122,000,000, Bierce observed that Huntington "took his hands out of his pockets long enough to be sworn in."

When Huntington, as a public-relations gesture, announced

that he was opening up opportunities for employment of women on the Southern Pacific, Bierce wrote, "It is cheering to note that new 'avenues' are being constantly 'opened' to women; Mr. Huntington, for example, employs thirty or forty female 'spotters' to travel over his several railways and afflict dishonest conductors. A noble 'mission,' truly — that of sewing up the holes in Mr. Huntington's pocket to keep other persons' money from flowing down his leg."

As for the "nobility" with which one of Huntington's late colleagues, Senator Leland Stanford, had endowed the university named after him, Bierce considered it "a restitution by Senator Stanford of the money stolen from the people."

Huntington appeared before a Senate committee with the poor-mouthed plea that his companies simply could not bear the burden of repaying their debt to the government on any short-term basis. Bierce was on hand to describe it: "To that august body Huntington expounded himself with considerable prolixity. The Senate Committee listened to his tale of woe with the respect due to his wealth and the sympathy compelled by his reluctance to die and leave it. The sympathy, it may be remarked, is wasted on imaginary disaster. Before this good man shall long be in the New Jerusalem he will undoubtedly find an opportunity to pull up a pack-load of blocks from the golden pavement and retire to Hades to enjoy them like a gentleman."

The mayor of San Francisco, Adolph Sutro, was then under attack from the Huntington interests for joining in the popular fight against the Funding Bill. Bierce advised him that he "may reasonably hope to survive Mr. Huntington, though doubtless Mr. Huntington's rancor, blown about in space as a pestilential vapor, will outlive all things that be. It is his immortal part."

In April 1896, Representative H. Henry Powers of Vermont, not unfriendly to the Huntington camp, a bland and plausible fellow whom Bierce dubbed the "Chairman of the Committee on the Visible Virtues," introduced a bill which would require the Southern Pacific to repay the government loan and accumulated interest through issuance of two percent, long-term bonds. Neither Bierce nor the other Huntington opponents were at all pleased with the bill, but it was a step toward collection of a just debt. It was better than the Funding Bill, and the Hearst papers proclaimed a moral victory.

Bierce, however, continued to pound away at Collis Huntington as "a promoted peasant with a low love of labor and an unslakeable thirst for gain," as "the surviving thirty-six" of "our modern Forty Thieves," as a gold-laden old "pigskin" who "knows neither how to enjoy nor to whom to bequeath" his wealth.

He buckled under the strain of his round-the-clock labors in Washington and went to Gettysburg, where the higher ground and dryer climate was easier on his asthma. For several weeks his condition was so grave that it was feared he might not survive. To the inquiries of anxious friends he later responded with jeering references to the death which was his constant companion. It was his "mechanism of concealment," as Lewis Mumford has written, to pretend that death was a clownish, ineffectual enemy whose worst and most horrifying aspects were merely ridiculous.

He returned to the crusade for a bill that would force Huntington to pay up in the near future, making his headquarters in New York during the fall of 1896. The Powers bill came up at the second session of the 54th Congress in January 1897, and again Bierce was on hand. He must have been taken aback by the counterattack launched by the Huntington faction, when it was asserted that the San Francisco *Examiner*, like many other California journals, had tapped the Southern Pacific treasury for bribe money disguised as advertising appropriations. The fight was getting dirty. Representative Grove L. Johnson, the father of Senator Hiram Johnson, got up on the House floor to denounce William Randolph Hearst in terms that would hardly have been permissible elsewhere:

"We knew he was erotic in his tastes, erratic in his moods, of small understanding and smaller views of men and measures, but we thought 'Our Willie' with his English plaids, his cockney accent, and his middle-parted hair, was honest.

"We knew that he had sought on the banks of the Nile relief from the loathsome disease contracted only by contagion in the haunts of vice, and had rivaled the Khedive in the gorgeousness of his harem in the joy of restored health, but we still believed him honest, though low and depraved.

"We knew he was debarred from society in San Francisco because of his delight in flaunting his wickedness, but we believed him honest, though tattooed with sin."

With ostensibly heavy heart, Representative Johnson then proceeded to expose the fact that Hearst "admitted that he had blackmailed the Southern Pacific Company into a contract whereby they were to pay him $30,000 to let them alone, and that he received $22,000 of his blackmail, and that C. P. Huntington had cut it off as soon as he knew of it, and that he was getting even now on Huntington and the railroad company because he had not received the other $8,000 of his bribe."[4]

On Hearst's behalf, Representative James C. Maguire of San Francisco denied the Johnson charges completely.* The *Examiner* had signed an advertising contract, during the recent World's Fair, for one thousand dollars a month for thirty months while Hearst was in Europe. After twenty-two months "a controversy arose," Maguire explained, because "the *Examiner* had occasion to editorially denounce some scheme in which the company was interested." The Southern Pacific insisted that it desist, but Hearst had replied that no one but himself controlled the editorial content of his paper. Huntington then cut off the advertising contract. Furthermore, using tactics worthy of the opposition, Representative Maguire inserted in the *Congressional Record* the declaration that Representative Johnson, thirty-four years before, had been indicted for forgery in New York.[5]

Bierce refused to believe the blackmail charges against his employer. Hearst was too wealthy to lose his head over a mere eight thousand dollars. Undoubtedly he realized that Hearst was using the Southern Pacific debt issue as an instrument for acquiring political power himself by posing as a public-spirited crusader. During the summer of 1896, William Jennings Bryan

---

* It should be noted that Hearst's most recent biographer, William A. Swanberg, says that the charges regarding his subject's "loathsome disease" were false.

had received the Democratic nomination with his gaudy "cross of gold" metaphor; the political winds were blowing strongly for reform and progressivism, and young Mr. Hearst was nimble enough to be among the first to vault onto the bandwagon (which, however, was overturned by William McKinley). All of Hearst's writers were instructed to get excited over the orotund Bryan. Bierce abstained, couldn't abide the ripeness of the Bryan style and suspected the emptiness of the Bryan content. "Mr. Bryan's creation," he said, "was the unstudied act of his own larynx; it said 'Let there be Bryan' and there was Bryan."

While disagreeing with Hearst over the advisability of boosting Bryan into the White House, he refused to believe that his employer had "blackmailed" the Southern Pacific. If Huntington could prove his accusation, as mouthed by Representative Johnson, Bierce said, he would volunteer to shake hands with Huntington, "which recently I have twice refused when he offered it." He would make one condition, however: "Mr. Huntington is not to object to my glove."[6]

While commuting between Washington and New York, Bierce quarreled with the Hearst management, which was getting top-heavy with overeager editors. There was even an editor-in-charge-of-Bierce. Hearst, looking back on all the controversy in and out of court caused by Bierce's sometimes reckless wit, apparently had decided to try the curb and bit. Willis J. Abbot was hired away from the Chicago Record with editing Bierce as his principal assignment, and soon was to remark that he had "secured very renumerative employment in a lunatic asylum." Hearst himself instructed Abbot to "eliminate everything that I thought would be offensive."

That wasn't part of Bierce's agreement with Hearst. Abbot's authority to wield his copy pencil was soon put to the test. In between harassing Huntington and his allies and other matters of national importance, Bierce had found time to dwell on the recent death of a prominent and much-loved actress. "Always famous for her composed manner," Bierce commented, "she is now quite decomposed."

Abbot slashed away the offending sentence. Bierce flew into a rage and forwarded his resignation to Hearst. And Hearst, as usual, backed down, apologized, said it wouldn't happen again. Bierce grudgingly agreed to withdraw his resignation, "probably," Abbot guessed, under the soothing effects of "an increased salary."[7]

Bierce returned to San Francisco shortly before the offensive Powers bill came up in the House of Representatives, assured that he had done his work well. He was greeted in San Francisco, in fact, as a returning hero. He resumed his "Prattle" column after a year's absence.

He relayed to his readers his regret that he wasn't in Washington to witness the forces of righteousness as they vanquished Huntington and his followers. "I feel rather like a fool sitting here three thousand miles away while my co-workers of last session set their breasts against this giant iniquity. Faith, it were good to be there again in the thick of it."[8]

Some days later he and most of his fellow Californians could jubilate over the bulletin from Washington: the House had killed the Powers bill, 168–102. There were several more years of rearguard action from the Huntington interests, but eventually a more equitable measure was adopted by Congress which forced the Southern Pacific to disgorge in a reasonable period — and at a six percent interest rate. It was finally agreed that the railroads would repay their government loan through refunding with twenty notes, one falling due each six months. Thus the debt was repaid in ten years instead of the eighty-three the Southern Pacific wanted. Even that didn't quite suit Bierce, who said he could applaud the victory only "with difficulty."

Some years later the muckraking era was in full swing. It was an activity which Bierce viewed with distaste, characterized as it was by various ism's he abhorred. Yet he was not visibly offended when one of the chief muckrakers, Charles Edward Russell, claimed him for a pioneer of that journalistic movement. (This was, of course, inexact. The muckrakers specialized in exposure of conditions they regarded as evil; Bierce was not so much the investigative reporter in his crusade against the Southern Pacific as a satirist, gadfly and angry prophet.) Russell, however, wrote in his series on the misdeeds of the railroad barons that Bierce's jeremiad against the Southern Pacific was chiefly responsible for its final humiliation.

"These articles," Russell wrote, "were extraordinary examples of invective and bitter sarcasm. . . . When Mr. Bierce began his campaign, few persons imagined that the bill could be stopped. After a time the skill and steady persistence of the attack began to draw wide attention. With six months of incessant firing, Mr. Bierce had the railroad forces frightened and wavering; and before the end of the year, he had them whipped. The bill was withdrawn and killed, and in 1898 Congress adopted an amendment to the general deficiency bill, providing for the collection of the Pacific Railroad subsidy debt, principal and interest."[9]

Yet there is no statue to Ambrose Bierce in San Francisco, a city well populated with effigies to men who have done less for her.

FOURTEEN

A Less Than Total Patriot

T HERE WAS SOMETHING about the Span-
ish-American War, perhaps the aspect of Uncle Sam as a bully
falling with his youthful power upon the senescent Spanish Empire, which strongly repelled Bierce. He gave a number of reasons
for his distaste for the venture in empire-building which ranged
from the Caribbean to the western Pacific. Perhaps the most
significant though unmentioned one was that his employer was
so hotly for it, and what Hearst wanted, Bierce had become convinced, was likely to be noxious for everyone else. A hint of that
feeling was conveyed in an essay on patriotism, part of which
has been frequently quoted:

"Patriotism deliberately and with folly aforethought subordinates the interests of the whole to the interests of a part . . .
Patriotism is like a dog which, having entered at random one of
a row of kennels, suffers more in combats with the dogs in the
other kennels than it would have done by sleeping in the open
air . . . Patriotism is fierce as a fever, pitiless as the grave, blind
as a stone and irrational as a headless hen."[1]

For several years Bierce had viewed with public disgust William Randolph Hearst's relentless campaign to arrange a war
between the United States and Spain. Six-inch headlines in the
Hearst papers almost daily reminded the country that the Spanish occupation in Cuba was conducting a reign of terror, throw-

ing nuns in prison, roasting priests over slow fires, poisoning wells, and doing its worst to exterminate the Cuban population. Every damp squib of a filibustering expedition to the Cuban coast carried a Hearst "war" correspondent on its roster. The lurid confection of anti-Spanish propaganda in the Hearst shops was unrivaled until World War I, when the Hearst techniques must certainly have been studied with care on both sides of the Western Front. Unrivaled, that is, by all except Hearst's ardent competitor in fomenting hostilities and selling newspapers, Pulitzer's New York World. The Hearst-Pulitzer competition to see whose editors could contribute the most inflammatory "incidents" — most of them imaginary — reached a climax when the Hearst forces fabricated a "Cuban Joan of Arc" named Evangelina Cisneros, rescued her from a Havana jail and the island itself, and then noisily congratulated themselves in the headline "An American Newspaper Accomplishes at a Single Stroke What the Best Efforts of Diplomacy Failed Utterly to Bring About in Many Months."

Three years before Mr. Hearst and his cohorts succeeded in bringing off what would be called "the splendid little war," Bierce served notice that he could not be counted upon to beat the drum for the anticipated war against Spain. "War — Horrid War! —" he wrote in an *Examiner* column on March 17, 1895, "between the United States and Spain has already broken out like a red rash in the newspapers, whose managing commodores are shivering their timbers and blasting their toplights with a truly pelagic volubility and no little *vraisemblance*." It was not that Bierce shrank from any risk involved in confronting Imperial Spain, which was pleading for peace right up to the moment the Senate was journalistically blitzed into passing a war resolution. He was certain that the United States could whip Spain with hardly more than a twitch of its sword arm because "we belong to the race of gluttons and drunkards to whom dominion is given over the abstemious. We can thrash them consummately and every day of the week, but we cannot understand them; and is it not a great golden truth, shining like a star, that what one does not understand one knows to be bad?"[2]

It seemed to Bierce that the United States was dispatching its expeditionary force to succor an inferior people. The rebellious Cubans, he wrote, were "superstitious almost beyond belief and brutal exceedingly," while their Spanish rulers were members of a "highly civilized and chivalrous race." He almost seemed to be saying that Spanish imperialism was tolerable but American was not. The rapidly rising enthusiasm in the United States for liberating Cuba was less a passion for spreading the blessings of democracy than for gobbling up the island possessions still feebly clutched by Spain. "We are at war with Spain today merely in obedience to a suasion that has been gathering force from the beginning of our national existence. The passion for territory once roused rages like a lion; successive conquests only strengthen it. That is the fever that is now burning in the American blood." He observed with sardonic distaste how patriotic fervor was "splendoring the Land of the Comparatively Free."[3]

Once the invasion of Cuba was launched, however, the military buff rose to the surface. Considering himself a strategist at least the equal of General-in-Chief Nelson A. Miles or General William Shafter, the commander of the expeditionary corps, he commented freely on their movements as well as on the tactics of the American admirals charged with smashing the Spanish hulks. All the senior United States officers in his opinion were incompetent. The land campaign which resulted in the capture of Santiago and the surrender of the Spanish army on Cuba struck him as elephantine, unimaginative and falteringly executed. While the nation was exulting over the storybook charge of the Rough Riders over San Juan Hill, which carried Lieutenant Colonel Theodore Roosevelt into the White House, Bierce was picking at such details of the assault as were available and deciding the laurel was being placed on the wrong heads. It was not the overpublicized Rough Riders which deserved the glory, he observed, but the hard-fighting Tenth Cavalry, an all-Negro outfit except for its officers.* He ridiculed the failure of a United States naval bombardment to reduce the ancient fortress of

---

* A view later upheld by military historians with more facts than were then available to Bierce, who did have a keen eye for penetrating the camouflage of official reports and journalistic hero-making.

Morro Castle. He condemned Admiral William Sampson's extreme caution in proceeding to bottle up the long-obsolete Spanish fleet. Compared to the military and naval actions of the Civil War, the campaign seemed to Bierce a piddling affair, "a freak war," and its conduct "should, I think, be regarded rather as a political than a religious duty."

He was particularly outraged by the spectacle of William Jennings Bryan playing at war. Bryan was raising a regiment of Nebraska volunteers, which got no farther than the boondocks of its Florida training camp. The task of reducing the magniloquent Bryan to size — a task finally completed by H. L. Mencken, who studied the Biercean method to good and thorough effect — had been engaging him for some time. Bryan, to Bierce, was simply a potentially dangerous demagogue. He was no more than an immense pair of lungs attached to a vocal apparatus which the Wurlitzers might have envied; the danger was that he might be manipulated by subtler men who would know how to use his magnetism for the populace of the Bible Belt. "A week before the convention of 1896," wrote Bierce, "William J. Bryan had never heard of himself; upon his natural obscurity was imposed the opacity of a Congressional service that effaced him from the memory of even his faithful dog, and made him immune to dunning. Today he is pinnacled upon the summit of the tallest political distinction. . . . To the dizzy elevation of his candidacy he was hoisted out of the shadow by his own tongue, the longest and liveliest in Christendom. Had he held it — which he could not have done with both hands — there had been no Bryan. His creation was the unstudied act of his own larynx . . ."[4]

Now this Mr. Bryan, who professed to love all mankind, was proposing to loose himself upon the Spanish at the head of his own regiment. That outfit, he suggested, should be called the "Nebraska Immunes" because it would never come within sight of any battlefront. He further proposed that the life insurance companies extend special rates to those who volunteered to serve under Bryan, on the actuarial certainty they would never suffer any danger greater than the hoofs of an army mule.

From the sordid spectacle of "the freak war" — which he

predicted, again with accuracy, would culminate in "an exposure of rascality and incompetence" ranging from the tainted-beef scandals to the multiple failures of the military bureaucracy — he turned to his beloved mountains and a resumption of his role as literary taskmaster. He stayed in a hotel at Wright's Station at the crest of the Santa Cruz Mountains, overlooking the Santa Clara Valley, up among the pines and redwoods. To that mountain paradise came a stream of his admirers and protégés. Not all of the former were welcome. A San Francisco woman came up to the mountaintop demanding that he supply her with advice on the proper method of rearing children. He dodged her for hours but finally was cornered. She asked if he could recommend any ancient philosophers to read on the subject.

"Study Herod, Madam," he snapped. "Study Herod."

He became friendly with Josephine Clifford McCrackin, who dated back to the Harte-Twain days and who was living on a small ranch near Wright's Station. Mrs. McCrackin had served as an assistant to Bret Harte when he founded the *Overland Monthly* and had published a book of realistic sketches on the life of an army officer's wife at frontier outposts. Though they were contemporaries, Mrs. McCrackin addressed him as "Dear Grossmeister." Later, when her mountain home was burned to the ground, Bierce found a publisher for a volume of her short stories and wrote the introduction himself.

In the spring of 1899, once again, he fired off a letter of resignation to William Randolph Hearst. The immediate cause of that resignation was his discovery that editors of Hearst papers other than the San Francisco *Examiner*, which picked up his "Prattle" columns as filler for their editorial pages, were slashing at his copy as they saw fit. His arrangement with Hearst himself had always been that there was to be no tampering with his columns. But he assigned a nobler reason for his resignation in a letter to an admirer in Galveston, Texas: he could no longer permit himself to be the pawn of "fools, fakers and freaks" who were "yellowing" journalism to the point where newspapers were becoming indistinguishable from circus posters.[5]

The resignation was rescinded, as always, a few weeks later

when Hearst himself promised to restrain his editors' passion for brevity. By the fall of 1899 Bierce was negotiating with the Hearst management for his return to the East. Much as he loved the northern California mountains, he was restless for a change. One reason may have been his quarrel with Mrs. Una Hume, a charming widow who owned a luxurious ranch home and entertained considerably. Evidently Bierce objected to some of her other guests, commenting that the Hume ranch was a paradise only during "the closed season for snakes." Mrs. Hume refused to get rid of the "snakes" so she would have to do without the formerly smitten company of Ambrose Bierce. Writing to his Galveston correspondent late in November, he reported that he would be moving to Washington, probably for good, "simply a change of duties, excepting that I shall probably do more work for *The Journal* and less for *The Examiner*."[6] Oddly enough he undertook this transfer despite the fact that most of his quarrels over copy-cutting were with the editors of the New York paper, which suggested that his annoyance with Mrs. Hume was considerable.

With Washington as a statelier stage for his role, he would assume the mantle of chief commentator for the Hearst papers on all matters, "the first of the Hearst Philosophers," as Carey McWilliams has aptly defined him, "explaining to the lowly the great mysteries of existence," until Arthur Brisbane came along to replace him by coining the "art of the startling platitude." Platitudinous was not the word for Bierce; he would continue to write with fierce effectiveness in a way that cut against the grain of Hearst policy. Bierce was not only the first of the Hearst Philosophers, but the first and last to express himself freely in the Hearst papers. Even Bierce would admit that the growingly authoritarian Hearst allowed him to speak his mind, and once told Walter Neale, his publisher-biographer, "He [Hearst] did not once direct nor request me to write an opinion that I did not hold, and only two or three times suggested that I refrain from expressing opinions that I did hold."

The San Francisco *Examiner* gave no hint that Bierce's removal to Washington would be a permanent arrangement, but informed its readers: "The 56th Congress seems to be of extraordinary interest. The subjects before it includes such matters as the War in the Philippines, the adjustment of our new Colonial policy, the disposition of Cuban affairs, and the action that Congress may or may not take with reference to the trusts. These are all questions of great national importance. For this reason, *The Examiner* has sent Ambrose Bierce to Washington, where he will remain during the present session."[7]

Thus he was in the press gallery of the United States Senate when Senator Albert Beveridge of Indiana, the handsome and eloquent advocate of American expansion (which had spread to the Philippines, where the natives had ungratefully launched an insurrection that would occupy the attention of the United States army until 1913), called upon the country not to shrink from its colonial duty. "We will not renounce our part in the mission of our race, trustees under God, of the civilization of the world," he told the Senate on January 8, 1900. He further informed his colleagues that God, for the past millennium, had been preparing "the English-speaking and Teutonic peoples" for advancing this mission.

Bierce had come to believe that it might be in the national interest to hold Cuba as a Caribbean outpost and the Philippines as a western Pacific base against the rising ambitions of Imperial Japan, but insisted that it was hypocritical to pretend that in doing so the United States was obeying any heavenly commands. American liberals were trying to rally the nation against succumbing to the imperialistic impulse, but Bierce would not place himself under their standard. "Certainly wherever the silk hat is worn," he wrote the day after Beveridge's speech, "there we have the highest and ripest civilization; and wherever it penetrates a region where it was previously unknown, religion, art, justice and education follow and set up their benign reign."

When Senator Hoar of Massachusetts rose to present the anti-imperialists' position and plead for a withdrawal from the Philippines, Bierce took his accustomed stance in opposition to both sides. The idealists represented by Senator Hoar, he believed, were living in a never-never land. Regarding Hoar's contention that invading the Philippines on the pretext of driving out the Spaniards, then staying on to subjugate the people we were supposed to be trying to liberate was morally wrong, he commented, "I dare say that is the right view to take of it. I am sure that it must be wrong for nations to be wicked. But in the larger politics of this worst of all possible worlds it does seem as if ethical considerations had not more weight and influence than that to which their beauty entitles them. According to the principles so dear to the hearts of the worthy gentlemen who lift protesting hands when the rights of weak nations are invaded by strong ones, not a people on earth today has a right to be there. All have dispossessed some other people."

Several days after listening to the Hoar-Beveridge debate, he summed up his attitude toward colonialism in the title of his article, "The Survival of the Fittest." Darwin was right, after all, he had concluded. There was no point in speaking of morality among nations. "Manifest Destiny," as the imperial-minded called their cause, was simply a polite guise for brute force. Nor was there any sense in resisting the natural law.[8] Thus when the Boer War broke out, Bierce was all for the British in their drawn-out attempt to suppress the Dutch settlers. His articles on the war drew him into a long correspondence with the British Commander General H. H. Kitchener, on the principles of strategy involved in fighting a guerrilla war.

His flirtation with liberal thought in connection with the war against Spain was not long-lived. As the twentieth century began, he seemed to those who were enchanted by the mystique of progress, that great byword of the pre-1914 world, to be retrogressing further into the nineteenth instead of slipping gracefully into the new century.

He strongly advocated a firmer control over the masses: "a vigilant censorship of the press, a firm hand upon the church, keen supervision of public meetings and public amusements, command of the railroads, telegraph and all means of communications." Otherwise anarchy or socialism would take over. Everything, he announced, "foretells the doom of authority." A government such as he recommended admittedly would be termed despotic. The word did not frighten Ambrose Bierce. "It is the despotisms of the world that have been the conservators of civilization." European rulers had grown so slack and permissive, he asserted, that "No heart in Europe can beat tranquilly under clean linen." Russia was an excellent example of what could happen when a strong government lost the will to govern. "In 1863 Alexander II of Russia freed 25,000,000 serfs. In 1879 they had killed him and all joined the conspirators."

Nihilism was so dangerous and infectious a disease, as he saw it, that "mutilation followed by death" was the only way to handle anarchists who committed acts of violence. It was not a philosophy but "a policy of assassination tempered by reflections upon Siberia." Americans who sympathized with the Russian anarchists striving for the Czar's overthrow should know that their feelings were "the offspring of an unholy union between the tongue of a liar and the ear of a dupe."[9]

The underdog had a measure of his sympathy, but was pitiable in his belief that he was sharing in the bounty of civilization. "The cant of civilization fatigues," he wrote with brutal honesty. "Civilization is a fine and beautiful structure. It is as picturesque as a Gothic cathedral. But it is built upon the bones and cemented with the blood of those whose part in all its pomp is that and nothing more. It cannot be reared in the generous tropics, for there the people will not contribute their blood and bones. The proposition that the average American workingman or European peasant is 'better off' than the South Sea Islander, lolling under a palm tree and drunk from over-eating, will not bear a moment's examination. It is we scholars and gentlemen that are better off."[10]

The establishment of the World Court at The Hague, the first session of which was held in the spring of 1899, would never head off international conflicts through arbitration. It would merely result in the "substitution of many burning questions for a smouldering one . . . disputes that have reached a really acute stage are not submitted. The animosities that it has kindled have been much hotter than those it has quenched."[11]

He was even less tolerant on the subject of immigration. Hundreds of thousands were coming to the United States from southern and eastern Europe, but Bierce was all for dousing the torch held aloft by the Statue of Liberty. "It is the immigration of 'the oppressed of all nations' that has made this country one of the worst on the face of the earth. The change from good to bad took place within a generation — so quickly that few of us have had the nimbleness of apprehension to 'get it through our heads.' We go on screaming our eagle in the self-same note of triumph that we were taught at our fathers' knees before the eagle became a buzzard. America is still an 'asylum for the oppressed'; and still, as always and everywhere, the oppressed are unworthy of asylum, avenging upon those who gave them sanctuary the wrongs from which they fled. The saddest thing about oppression is that it makes its victims unfit for anything but to be oppressed . . . In the end they turn out to be fairly energetic oppressors. The gentleman in the cesspool invites compassion, certainly, but we may be very well assured, before undertaking his relief without a pole, that his conception of a prosperous life is merely to have his nose above the surface with another gentleman underfoot."[12]

A Supreme Court decision which bolstered the effect of the Fifth Amendment drew from him a suggestion that the medieval trial by ordeal be revived in its place. "This ancient and efficient safeguard to rascality, the right of a witness to refuse to testify when his testimony would tend to convict him of crime, has been strengthened by a decision of the United States Supreme Court. That will probably add another century or two to its mischievous existence, and possibly prove the first act in such an extension of it that a witness cannot be compelled to testify at all . . . Any pressure short of physical torture or the threat of it, that can be put upon a rogue to make him assist in his own undoing is just and therefore expedient."[13]

America's attempt at achieving an open society, at perfecting its libertarian aspects, would be increasingly antithetical, if not abhorrent, to the man who would soon begin styling himself the "Curmudgeon Philosopher."

Obviously, however, to his new friends in Washington, he compressed his curmudgeonly attitudes into his writing. The hail-fellow of Washington bars, clubs and press galleries, according to all the available testimony, was invariably a pleasant and genial companion. The despair he felt over the past dozen years of his life, during which his son Day had killed himself, he and Mollie had separated, and Leigh was exhibiting all the signs of instability continuing into manhood, he reserved for letters to his intimates in San Francisco. Still more than a year short of his sixtieth birthday, he wrote a woman friend on the Coast, he was "leading a life of mere waiting" for "the end of it all." His only ambition was to "go on with as little friction as possible." Most people he knew probably "would say I'm having a pretty good time, and that's what I usually say myself; but may Heaven punish the malefactor who invented that deadly dull thing, a good time."[14]

Frictionless was probably a good description of his life in Washington. Tranquillity grew out of a stodgy routine, seldom varied from day to day, and coziness was made to serve as a substitute for stronger wine and madder music. Perhaps middle age was beginning to drag him down, and certainly his frequent bouts with asthma didn't make him feel any younger. At any rate the ex-Bohemian trudged his rounds daily like a postman. Up in midmorning, then a stroll from his apartment (part of a larger apartment on Iowa Circle during most of his years in Washington) to the Army and Navy Club, where he picked up his mail. He continued on to the Washington office of the Hearst papers, where he liked to joke with his fellow workers before settling down to write his column, which now bore the title of "The Passing Show." At noon he strolled back to the Army and Navy Club for lunch, often with active or retired officers whom he had known ever since the Civil War. After another session at his desk in the Hearst office, he walked over to one of his two favorite "boozing dens," Coppa's restaurant or Roche's bar, for a few rounds of drinks before dinner. At night he would rarely venture from his apartment. Either he worked on magazine pieces, with a pot of coffee nearby and his pet canary flitting around the room or perched on his head, or he had a few people in for games — usually anagrams at which, naturally, he excelled — and conversation. At some time during the evening, Bierce usually took out his chafing dish and whipped up a Welsh rarebit which connoisseurs praised.

Apparently Bierce had succumbed to the Edwardian craze for "cozy corners," the epitome of bourgeois taste. An interviewer for a Washington newspaper, describing the sitting room of his apartment, wrote that it was draped and carpeted in Turkey red and "contained a Turkish couch piled high with pillows, a table full of interesting books, and a quaint little sideboard filled with a mixture of curious glasses, decanters and a chafing-dish." To his interviewer Bierce swore he would "never publish another book," an oath soon to be broken, of course. He also declared that he had "no faith in his own or anybody's inspiration."[15]

Shortly after he moved to Washington, the bouncy and indefatigable Dr. Adolphe Danziger, who was living on the lower East Side in New York, expressed a yearning for a reconciliation. The rabbi-dentist-writer wrote him that their quarrel over *The Monk and the Hangman's Daughter* and other matters was inconsequential compared to the depth and warmth of their former friendship. To that overture Bierce responded with a cold formality:

"Unless you have made yourself over (there is no change in me) you and I are incompatible inhabitants of different worlds. I bear you no ill-will — have neither time nor taste for animosities — but of all that is regrettable between us no considerable part can, I think, be effaced by saying: 'It is effaced.' . . . If your friendly overture denotes more than a transient feeling, or some scheme of self-interest, it is creditable to you; but that I have no means of knowing . . ."[16]

If Bierce had a weak spot in his emotional armor, as Dr. Danziger evidently realized, it was his surviving son Leigh. So Danziger hustled around to the *Morning Telegraph* in New York — then a racy sheet full of Broadway gossip and sporting news, the latter edited by the old Western gunfighter Bat

Masterson — to get in touch with Leigh Bierce, who was a member of its staff.

Shortly after Bierce came East, he and Leigh had become estranged over the young man's plans for marriage. Leigh, in his middle twenties, was following the Park Row tradition of the hard-drinking newspaperman; he was also a temperamental young man who would knock down a waiter whose manner was not sufficiently respectful. Bierce apparently considered his son too unstable and impulsive to go about choosing a wife for himself with any sense of discretion. Leigh seemed to be proving his father's point when he announced that he was going to marry the pretty but otherwise unsuitable daughter of the woman who operated his boarding house. Always at his worst as a father, Bierce peremptorily forbade the match. His father's disapproval only propelled Leigh into an immediate marriage.

"Why," Bierce was quoted as asking a friend, "should both of my boys have gotten mixed up with trashy women?"[17]

Flora Bierce, his new daughter-in-law, did not deserve to be described as "trashy" even by an irate father-in-law. She simply lacked social graces and distinction. Dr. Danziger, who intended to use the situation as a wedge to regain entry into Bierce's confidence, said she was a "very charming girl," if lacking a finishing-school polish.

Danziger was shrewd enough to realize that Bierce's crotchets were often superficial, often regretted when Bierce had time to think them over. By then, however, Bierce would be too stiff-necked in his pride to make amends. The good doctor accordingly set about arranging a reconciliation between Bierce and his son, who had broken off relations for months following the young man's marriage.

By September of 1900, Bierce, under Danziger's soothing ministrations, had come around to believing everything might work out all right for Leigh and his bride. "Your pleasure in the boy and girl," he wrote Danziger, "is most agreeable to me. Yes, I have hopes of him; he seems to have pulled through a pretty bad bog and got upon rising ground."[18]

That Danziger had already presented his bill as a volunteer

counsellor in domestic relations was apparent in the rest of the letter. Danziger, for one thing, wanted an interview with William Randolph Hearst. Bierce replied that the request was impossible. "He [Hearst] was here a few weeks ago, and we met only accidentally in the street. We are not friends (though not unfriendly) and never communicate except through others. He would give no attention to a note from me, even if I felt at liberty to write one."

Danziger's second proposal was that they collaborate on a dramatization of *The Monk and the Hangman's Daughter.* Bierce, well aware of the pitfalls awaiting the amateur venturing into the theater, at first blew cold on the scheme. "I know nothing of writing for the stage, for which I have an imperfect respect. To write for it one should be in sympathy with it. I don't enter a theater once in two years."

For the writer who sees his work only in print, there is something alluring about the possibility of watching his characters come to life, approximately, behind the footlights. Nor is he immune to its fabled glamour. It didn't take Bierce, despite his professed contempt for the medium, more than a few weeks to find the possibility of dramatizing *The Monk* a fascinating project; besides he'd always had a bumpkin's infatuation with actresses, and there was the additional lure of royalties coming in every time the curtain went up. Soon he was rushing up to New York to interview various leading ladies in hopes that their interest would attract a producer, who would dig up money to pay for the dramatization. Once again Bierce and Danziger began working at cross-purposes. Bierce was trying to arouse the interest of Blanche Bates, a San Francisco-born star, in playing the star-crossed Benedicta; he also invited a writer on the New York *Herald* to try his hand at converting *The Monk* into dramatic form. Meanwhile Danziger was conducting his own talent hunt and had settled on Margaret Anglin as the heroine of their unwritten play. Miss Anglin's stipulation was that the play be written in blank verse, which would be composed by Bierce himself.

After weeks of heady talk on and off Broadway, Bierce became disgusted with the project and the useless publicity it reaped. He had managed to gain admittance to Blanche Bates's dressing room, he wrote, but "saw her only a moment . . . Possibly she thought I only wanted to throw myself at her feet and shower her with diamonds." As for Miss Anglin's proposal, Bierce replied that "I could not think of undertaking it. I try never to write any kind of thing (as literature) in which I should fall much below the best — and plays in blank (verse) are Shakespeare's kind of thing." Miss Anglin would probably make an excellent Benedicta but "she cannot call spirits from the misty sleep nor conjure up a poet."[19] Ten days later, giving up the project altogether, he complained to Danziger in a letter of December 22, 1900, that the brief flirtation with theatrical glory had left him with nothing "excepting an ache — a wine-ache."

Something more dreadful than a head bursting from the aftereffects of wine-bibbing with theatrical entrepreneurs was in the making even as Dr. Danziger read that letter. On Christmas Eve Leigh Bierce, whom his father had visited on amicable terms during his trips to New York, was assigned by the *Morning Telegraph* to accompany its expedition into the slum districts of Manhattan with a wagonload of toys and provisions for the poor. Perhaps what the young reporter saw depressed him; Hell's Kitchen and the Tenderloin, located just south of the old carbarn in which the *Morning Telegraph* was published, were frightful enough outside the holiday season. In any case Leigh seized upon the occasion, as his father had so often in the past.

When the *Morning Telegraph* wagon, decorated with banners proclaiming its noble mission, stopped at a tenement to distribute its sacks of food and toys, Leigh ducked into a nearby saloon. Long before the expedition reached its goal Leigh was uproariously drunk and began giving away the *Morning Telegraph*'s presents to whoever would accept them. It was a scene which might have opened one of his father's little essays into black comedy: madly drunken young man, staggering about in a driving snowstorm, hurling Christmas goodies around outside a saloon while families counting on the provisions promised them waited in vain in their cold tenements.

Leigh came down with a heavy cold as a result of that experience. He stayed on his feet, however, and apparently his employers forgave him for dispensing their charity with such an uneven hand. He continued working at the paper as his health deteriorated. The elder Bierce had survived a dozen such escapades during his days as a young journalist in San Francisco, but his constitution had been hardened by Civil War campaigning and a more rigorous upbringing than Leigh's.

About the same time Dr. Danziger was removed to a New York hospital after having ruptured a throat vessel from coughing, and was in need of money to stay there. Leigh, much sicker than Danziger, was pressed into service by his father to deliver the money to Danziger.

During the first week in March, Leigh's persistent cold turned into pneumonia. His father hurried to New York as soon as he learned that Leigh was in serious condition and had been hospitalized. "I found Leigh a very sick boy — a mere skeleton too," he wrote Danziger on March 16, 1901; "but today he is somewhat better. He will not be out of danger for a week at the best — so of course I am a little 'blue' myself."

Four days later Leigh showed few signs of improvement. "This is supposed to be the critical day with him," Bierce wrote Danziger, "and this morning he shows a slight improvement — enough to justify at least a hope."

Stern-faced and stoic, Bierce stayed at his son's bedside for another eleven days while Leigh unavailingly fought for his life. On March 31, Leigh died at the age of twenty-seven, and his father announced it in telegrams to the family, Dr. Danziger and others in words stripped of feeling: LEIGH PASSED AWAY THIS MORNING.

His daughter Helen attended the funeral, but not Mrs. Bierce, who was compelled to stay in Los Angeles to look after her aged mother. The greatest consolation to Bierce, according to Walter Neale, was the presence of John O'Hara Cosgrave, formerly the editor of the *Wave*, the San Francisco literary journal which had published some of Bierce's best stories. Neale said that he saw Bierce weep three times in speaking of the past: when telling of

Day's death, when telling of Leigh's death, and when recalling Cosgrave's "constant solace" and "attempts to divert him" after Leigh's death.[20]

"I am hit hard," Bierce wrote George Sterling a few days later; "more than you can guess — am a bit broken and gone gray of it all."

A year later he wrote Sterling that he still "counted the days" since Leigh's death.

Until then, his hair had retained the golden sheen, almost of youth, but now (according to Neale) it turned white in a few weeks.

His daughter Helen stayed with him for a while in Washington and acted as his hostess at the Welsh rarebit parties in his Iowa Circle apartment. Other women hovered around, she later recalled, but he told her, using her childhood pet name, "Bibs, there is only one woman I have ever loved, and that woman is your mother." Her father drank a lot in the weeks following Leigh's death, she said, but "I never saw him drunk. He was too fastidious for anything as uncouth as that."[21]

FIFTEEN

The Bullet That Sped East

ONE OF BIERCE'S pet phobias was the personality and political career of President William McKinley. He considered McKinley a lackluster nonentity who had been boosted into the White House by cleverer men, and blamed the President for being so spineless as to allow the jingos, particularly those of the press and most particularly William Randolph Hearst, to goad him into going to war against Spain. Dr. Danziger, who was not unwilling to impute ignoble motives for many of Bierce's actions, claimed that Bierce also had a more personal reason for disliking President McKinley. He quoted Bierce as saying that the President would have found a suitable place for Brevet Major Bierce, thirty-odd years out of uniform, in the War Department "if he had the service of the army at heart." There is no other evidence, however, that Bierce yearned for a desk among the army bureaucrats.

Of his dislike of President McKinley there was no doubt. Early in 1900, as the result of continued feuding over the state election, Governor-elect William Goebel of Kentucky was shot and killed. Bierce commented on that event in a quatrain which may not have bolstered his inconsiderable reputation as a poet but which made larger waves in history than much more elegant verse. What other poet has been blamed for inciting the assassination of a President? The quatrain read:

The bullet that pierced Goebel's breast
Can not be found in all the West;
Good reason, it is speeding here
To stretch McKinley on his bier.

It was published in the New York *Journal* on February 4, 1900, and for all its brutally bad taste it attracted little attention. Perhaps the Hearst editors in New York would have killed it, except that only a few months ago Bierce had quit, then been coaxed back into the Hearst stable over the issue of editorial surgery on his offerings. "The Chief," as Hearst now liked to be called, was in Europe and could not be appealed to.[1]

Month after month that quatrain lay buried in the files like a time bomb.

Meanwhile the Hearst papers were laying down a drumfire barrage against the McKinley Administration. McKinley would obviously be a candidate for reelection in 1904, and that, unfortunately, was the year Hearst himself intended to enter the White House. Among the choicer Hearst editorial attacks on the man who stood in the way of the presidency of William Randolph Hearst were Arthur Brisbane's nomination of McKinley as "the most hated creature on the American continent," and an inflammatory suggestion on the editorial page of the New York *Journal* of April 10, 1901, that "If bad institutions and bad men can be got rid of only by killing, then the killing must be done."

On September 5, 1901, President McKinley, returning from a speechmaking tour of the West, stopped off in Buffalo to address the Pan-American Exposition. The next day he attended a public reception in the Temple of Music at which, massive in his frockcoat, he extended his large soft white hand to hundreds of citizens who lined up to greet him. Among them was a twenty-eight-year-old anarchist named Leon Czolgosz, who appeared in the reception line with his right hand covered by a handkerchief. When his turn came to shake the presidential hand, Czolgosz instead extended the revolver concealed by the handkerchief and fired two bullets into the President before he could be overpowered. Eight days later, on September 14, the President died, to be succeeded by Vice President Theodore Roosevelt.

Political and journalistic enemies immediately joined in raising a clamor that Hearst and his minions — principally Bierce — were responsible for inciting the assassination of the President. It seemed an excellent means of blocking Hearst's political ambitions and reducing the influence of his newspapers. Bierce's quatrain as well as the long series of anti-McKinley editorials and cartoons which had appeared in the Hearst papers were reprinted from coast to coast.

"During all this carnival of sin I lay ill in Washington," Bierce wrote later (he was suffering from a prolonged and almost fatal attack of asthma), "unaware of it." When he recovered, much too late to be effective, he explained that his quatrain on Governor Goebel's assassination had been intended as a warning against the insufficiency of security measures against a presidential assassin. It was a rather feeble excuse.[2] To charge Bierce, however, with intentionally inspiring an anarchist — the breed he hated above all others — to kill the President was ridiculous; as ridiculous as it was ironic.

Meanwhile the issue was being used effectively to quench Hearst's candidacy for governor of New York, a post he coveted as the first and last way station to the White House. President Roosevelt, with Hearst squarely in mind, declared that Czolgosz was probably incited by the "reckless utterances of those who, on the stump and in the public Press, appeal to the dark and evil spirits of malice and greed, envy and sullen hatred." It was widely reported, erroneously, that Czolgosz had a copy of the New York *Journal* in his pocket when he shot President McKinley.* Hearst's life was threatened, and his newspapers were boycotted by libraries, clubs and other organizations across the country.

In describing the public fury at his employer Bierce related

* Under questioning by persons who hoped he would admit his crime had been inspired by the Hearst press, Czolgosz disappointed them terribly by saying he had been inflamed to the point of murder instead by a lecture by Emma Goldman, the anarchist leader.

that his quatrain on Governor Goebel's assassination was "taken as complicity" in the assassination itself. "As such they adorned the editorial columns of the New York *Sun* and blazed upon a billboard in front of Tammany Hall [Hearst was then running as an anti-Tammany Democrat] . . . Thousands of copies of Hearst papers were torn from the hands of newsboys and burned in the streets . . . Emissaries of the *Sun* overran the entire country persuading clubs, libraries and other patriotic bodies to exclude them from the files. There was even an attempt made to induce Czolgosz to testify that he had been incited to his crime by reading them [Bierce's quatrain]— $10,000 for his family to be his reward; but this cheerful scheme was blocked by the trial judge, who had been informed of it."

Bierce was particularly enraged when Secretary of War Elihu Root joined the anti-Hearst crusade by stumping upstate New York to inveigh against Hearst's candidacy for the governorship (which was defeated). "The incident was not exhausted," Bierce recalled. "When Mr. Hearst was making his grotesque canvass for the governorship of New York the Roosevelt Administration sent Secretary Root into the state to beat him. This high-minded gentleman incorporated one of the garbled prose versions of my prophecy into his speeches with notable effect and great satisfaction to his conscience . . . If anyone thinks that Mr. Root will not go to the devil it must be the devil himself, in whom, doubtless, the wish is father to the thought."[3]

Historian Mark Sullivan in his multivolumed survey of the period credited Root's speech at Utica with having defeated Hearst's bid for the governorship and in effect the White House, which the publisher intended to occupy in its turn. "Root's arraignment of Hearst," Sullivan wrote, "had the combined impact of himself and his principal, Roosevelt. Root began by quoting passages from Roosevelt's first message to Congress, delivered after the assassination of McKinley, in which Roosevelt spoke of the assassin as inflamed 'by the reckless utterances of those who . . . in the public press appealed to the dark and evil spirits of malice and greed, envy and sullen hatred. The wind is sowed by the men who preach such doctrines, and they can not escape their share of responsibility for the whirlwind that is reaped. This applies to the deliberate demogogue, to the exploiter of sensationalism.' Root's speech defeated Hearst for Governor . . ."[4]

Bierce admitted that though the Hearst newspapers "had been incredibly rancorous toward McKinley," it was doubtless "my luckless prophecy that cost him tens of thousands of dollars and a growing political prestige."

He was amazed, as he had been on several previous occasions, by Hearst's forbearance toward a valued employe. "I have never mentioned the matter to him, nor — and this is what I have been coming to — has he ever mentioned it to me. I fancy there must be a human side to a man like that . . ."[5]

Bierce, less forbearing, could never forgive Theodore Roosevelt's manipulation of coincidence in the McKinley assassination. Subsequently he also detested Roosevelt, along with many of his cronies at the Army and Navy Club, for helping stop the Russo-Japanese War; Bierce and his friends believed that Russia would have won, despite Japan's brilliant victories on land and sea, if the war had been prolonged. That, in the opinion of Bierce and his fellow barroom strategists, would have been an excellent thing because they believed America would have to fight Japan one day and it might have helped if Russia had been allowed to curb the Japanese expansion in western Asia.

President Roosevelt, a *littérateur* whose equal was not to enter the White House for more than another half-century, had a mutual friend named Sam Davis urge that Bierce attend a presidential reception. Bierce balked at the idea; meeting rival celebrities, up to and including the President, had always been anathema to him, particularly if they did the receiving and he was required to make the semblance of obeisance.

Bierce, according to Walter Neale, was finally persuaded to accompany Davis to the reception, and received, but did not melt under, the famous Roosevelt treatment of a literary personage. "Well, well, well," Roosevelt exclaimed as Bierce appeared before him in the receiving line (as Bierce later told Neale), "so this is Ambrose Bierce — the man of all men whom I have longed to meet! Do you know, as I rode up San Juan Hill upon a very memorable occasion, I held firmly before my eyes the vision of a lone horseman — oh, you know the man! the man in your story, 'A Son of the Gods,' who went forward to reconnoiter, to find if the enemy were concealed behind a ridge! . . . I have called you here to tell you how you helped to make history — and to tender the thanks of a grateful nation!"

Bierce refused to thaw under the eupeptic Roosevelt personality, as he related the incident to Neale, because "both he and the President knew that the Rooseveltian ride had never taken place." Roosevelt, of course, had scrambled up San Juan Hill on foot along with the rest of the dismounted cavalry.[6]

The President, in Bierce's opinion, was a "timid blusterer," who would help bring on what he foresaw as "a war of vast destructiveness" inside a generation.

In this prevision of World War I, as in the verse which foretold (but did not necessarily subscribe to) the assassination of President McKinley, Bierce proved himself a prophet of formidable proportions.

The Walter Neale who supplied the above episode was a young Southerner who had set up his own publishing company in Washington and sought out Bierce shortly after his arrival in the capital. Neale was an almost daily intimate from 1901 to 1903, when he moved his editorial offices to New York, and a frequent visitor to the Bierce apartment thereafter. He not only set himself up immediately as the prospective Boswell to Bierce's Dr. Johnson, with the latter reveling in his appointed role, but pleased the older man mightily in coming years by publishing his *Collected Works*, all twelve volumes, a publishing venture which revitalized Bierce's ego.

Over food and drink, in long walks through Rock Creek Park, at chafing-dish orgies in the Iowa Circle apartment, Bierce, succumbing to the Polonius complex of his sixty years, was encouraged to discourse and philosophize by the attentive, note-taking Walter Neale. He stated his views on the poisonousness of the feminine influence on the life of a man of genius (for example, himself), on the unhappiness of fatherhood, on sex and seduction. Neale, using the older man's tender musings, not the most scientific means of measurement, estimated that Bierce had been sexually intimate with thirty to forty women in his life. Neale also covered page after page of his biography of Bierce, published in 1929, with quotations from Bierce on military affairs, politics, religion, literature.

Neale observed that without exception the women who edged their way into the Iowa Circle group, which took the place of the various Bierce Adoration Society branches in California, were unattractive. It seems to be the fate of literary incandescence to attract only the drabber species of moth. The leading acolyte of Bierce's later years was Carrie Christiansen, a thirtyish, spinster schoolteacher, whom he had met some years before in one of his retreats to the California mountains. Miss Christiansen, whom Bierce with no great tact called the "Ugly Duckling," served as his secretary, wailing wall, buffer against the world. His daughter Helen, with sweet condescension, described her as an "extremely plain little person whom he had taken from a dull small town in California." Carrie's great value to her father, she believed, was that "she took him for one of the gods"— a loving mistake which Helen herself avoided.[7] Drab though she may have been in personality, Bierce valued her presence so highly that he established her in the apartment on Iowa Circle. As Neale described that particular design for living, the apartment consisted of a half-dozen rooms, three of which were occupied by the landlord and his wife, two by Bierce, and one by Miss Christiansen, whose room was across the hall from Bierce's. Neale hinted that Miss Christiansen might have been permitted greater intimacies than the privilege of typing Der Grossmeister's manuscripts and listening to his fulminations against the stupidity of book publishers; he also believed that Bierce might have secretly married her, though she was almost thirty years his junior, before he took off on his final journey — but of that no evidence has ever been turned up. Certainly no one was closer to him in his later years than Carrie Christiansen.

Whatever success he had with women, according to Neale, Bierce attributed to his celebrity as a writer, wit and critic. Liter-

ary fame, however, didn't stand a chance in the amorous sweep-
stakes against notoriety. As Bierce put it to Neale, "I step out of
the ring when Jim Jeffries [the heavyweight champion of the
world] steps in. Fame wilts before Notoriety in the regard of
women. The woman doesn't live whose curiosity, whose sensu-
ality, whose fond love, whose spiritual essence is not more stimu-
lated by a prizefighter than by a writer. Fame means something
to a woman . . . but notoriety means a great deal more. It is her
life, her love, her hope of heaven."

In the early years of the century, literary realism as promul-
gated in varying degrees in the work of Frank Norris, Stephen
Crane, Theodore Dreiser and Jack London had begun to make
its presence felt. (The reaction of Crane and Bierce to each
other's work was diametrically opposed. Crane admired Bierce,
who did not return the compliment. The former was quoted by
his biographer, Thomas Beer, as saying of one of Bierce's short
stories: "Nothing better exists. It has everything." But Bierce said
of Crane: "I had thought that there could be only two worse
writers than Stephen Crane, namely two Stephen Cranes.") For
the realistic school he had no sympathy; nor with its fight against
censorship.

"Censorship?" he said in reply to a question of Neale's. "It is
essential and it must begin with the author himself . . . Some of
the literary soap-boxers, shrieking condemnation of literary censorship laws, are at the same time approving the law that inflicts
the death penalty for murder. A violation of good taste . . . out-
rages me more than does many a crime of murder committed
under the stress of some powerful and justifiable emotion."

In Neale's opinion — the opinion of a Virginian who believed
the wrong side had won the Civil War — Bierce had become
anti-Negro in his later years. He quoted Bierce as saying that he
might have joined the Confederate army if he knew as much
about the Negro then as he did now. No one else heard Bierce
express such sentiments; he was not a racist, even in a day when
racism was socially acceptable and intellectually not too unre-
spectable. Perhaps he had interviewed Bierce on the subject just
after the latter emerged somewhat battered from a midnight
encounter. A large muscular Negro, with robbery in mind, as-

saulted Bierce on his way home. He broke one of Bierce's ribs, but Bierce drove him off with repeated blows from a heavy walking stick he carried.[8]

Neale also shared with Bierce one of the lighter moments of his life in Washington. It concerned Dr. Adolphe Danziger, who had gone to Europe and while there had enraged Bierce by approaching Mrs. Phoebe Apperson Hearst and using Bierce's name, the way Neale recounted it, in an attempt to raise money.

Now Danziger was back in the United States, and as ready to make himself useful as ever. He had written Bierce in hopes of one more reconciliation, to which Bierce replied, ". . . There will be a few things for you to explain. I have had to pay some bills of yours, for one thing. And I have reason to think that you have been 'working' some of the persons whom you knew as my friends. In brief, it is up to you to show, if you can, that you are not an irreclaimable crook."

That was the last Bierce heard from his former collaborator, though not the last he heard of him.

One day he and Neale read in the newspapers that the great Italian tenor Enrico Caruso had been arrested for "jostling" a woman in the monkey house of the Central Park Zoo in New York City. Bierce was vastly amused; and Gertrude Atherton, for one, would have been even more amused at his amusement, recalling Bierce's own attempt at "jostling" her beside a pigpen years before.

An even greater source of merriment for Bierce and Neale was the fact that the ubiquitous Dr. Adolphe Danziger stepped forward in magistrate's court to testify that he had been present and no such unseemly act had occurred. Nevertheless Caruso was found guilty.

"Perhaps," Neale remarked between guffaws, "his testimony brought about Caruso's conviction."

"Monkey house!" said Bierce, roaring with laughter. "I have no doubt he was in the monkey house — in the cage!"[9]

Bierce apparently was contented with Washington and the new circle of friends and worshipers that gradually formed around him. In a club bar or his apartment he was, as always, the genial authoritarian. "There," recalled one of his new friends, "Bierce was a conversational autocrat: and his first look at a newcomer was unflatteringly appraising. It seemed to say, 'Show me your credentials.' He looked straight at you from under his frosty brows with a bright eye and a cynical smile, which said as plain as words, 'Now what kind of ass are *you* going to make yourself?' But, the moment you *did* show him that you belonged, the air was gone and you were admitted to his camaraderie in an instant, and on absolutely even terms, and for all time. Nobody could be more genial or more intellectually democratic. . . . He had no time and no use for men who had nothing to say, but was hail-fellow with any one who could talk . . . a wonderfully handsome man with talkative eyes and an eagle nose. I can see him at this moment, though I can't conjure up the face of the British Ambassador."[10]

Present concerns, however, did not entirely loosen his grip on the "pupils" he had left behind him. Unfailingly, he answered their letters, read the manuscripts they submitted, and criticized them in detail. Inevitably, however, many began slipping away from his influence once the Master had removed himself from their presence.

His greatest hopes had always been for George Sterling, with Herman Scheffauer, perhaps, a close second. For a year or two the younger men remained firmly in the Bierce orbit. Their continued devotion was evidenced in the spring of 1903, when they induced a San Francisco publisher to bring out a collection of his verse titled *Shapes of Clay*. Sterling raised the money and Scheffauer designed the jacket. The volume consisted of verse Bierce had written in various columns dating back twenty years or more, and was greeted by critics with little enthusiasm. The *Overland Monthly*, never one to overpraise him, characterized Bierce as a "has-been," adding that "Bierce has passed from the scene. He belongs to those unburied things that cry aloud for the undertaker."[11]

The poor sale of *Shapes of Clay*, he wrote Sterling, could not and did not distress him. "As to the pig of a public, its indifference to a diet of pearls — *our* pearls — was not unknown to me, and truly it does not trouble me anywhere except in the pocket."

He added, however, that he would not tolerate public indifference to Sterling's virtues as a poet and promised to "whack" the world into acceptance of his estimate of Sterling's powers. As Sterling's artistic guardian, his fierce and jealous protectiveness was displayed in all its light and heat, just as it never was with his own sons, untimely dead, and his daughter, who was similarly though not as traumatically affected. If there was one guiding star in Bierce's life, it was his conviction that poetry was the highest and purest form of the literary art, that great poetry was the most splendid thing humanity was capable of creating. Bierce considered himself, above all, a frustrated poet, and once told his fellow editor Jerome A. Hart, early in his career, that "When I was in my twenties, I concluded one day that I was not a poet. It was the bitterest moment of my life."[12]

When Sterling's first long poem, "The Testimony of the Suns," was published in 1902, Bierce informed his protégé, "You shall be the poet of the skies, the prophet of the suns." His enthusiasm was not entirely echoed by others. Sterling's work was ornate, glittering with elaborate images, but too literary and self-indulgent to convey a wide appeal (Gertrude Atherton somewhat cattily advised him to see more and read less). But to Bierce his literariness was no artistic handicap, quite the contrary. "To Bierce," as Dale L. Walker has written, "a poem was all *color*, remarkable words, vivid imagery . . ."[13]

Early in 1904, when Bierce received the manuscript of Sterling's newest work (and magnum opus, as it turned out to be), his enthusiasm soared like a skyrocket. The two-hundred-line poem was titled "A Wine of Wizardry," and on reading it Bierce wrote Sterling:

"No poem in English of equal length has so bewildering a wealth of imagination. Nor Spenser himself has flung such a profusion of jewels into so small a casket. Why, man, it takes away the breath!"

Even so, it could be improved, he indicated, by his own editorship and "I'll get at it with my red ink and see if I can suggest anything worth your attention." Awed by what he took to be evidence of Sterling's poetic genius, he became uncharacteristically diffident about offering advice, and would write Sterling,

266 AMBROSE BIERCE: A Biography

"Let me know how hard you hate me for monkeying with your sacred lines."[14]

For the next four years he would conduct a campaign on behalf of "A Wine of Wizardry" such as he had never waged for his own work. He was undeterred when *Harper's*, *Scribner's*, the *Atlantic Monthly* and other quality magazines rejected it. It was not to be published until 1907, when Bierce himself arranged for it to appear in Hearst's new acquisition, *Cosmopolitan*.

Convinced as he was of Sterling's blazing talent, he agonized all the more over reports reaching him from San Francisco that the younger man had fallen in with a group of Socialists, anarchists and liberal reformers. Worse, according to report, Sterling had taken up with that rambunctious young man, Jack London, an unruly tyke off the Oakland waterfront, whose abilities as a short-story writer were beginning to be trumpeted from coast to coast. Bad enough that London had arisen without Bierce's seal — he was also a fiery radical who had joined Coxey's army and been arrested as a teen-ager for mounting a soapbox in Oakland's City Hall Park and calling for a revolution.

Now George Sterling himself was making noises indistinguishable from the Socialist rabble. Bierce had been warning him for several years against being caught up in the illusion that mankind could be bettered by social and political reform. Late in 1902 he had admonished Sterling, "Let the poor alone — they are oppressed by nobody but God. Nobody hates them, nobody despises. The rich love them a deal better than they love one another." A short time later he argued, "Do away with the desire to excel and you may set up your Socialism at once. But what kind of a race of sloths and slugs will you have?"[15]

In the first letter in which Sterling mentioned his association with Jack London, the former asked whether it would be all right to show London one of his poems for criticism. Bierce replied that he considered London a "clever" young man and saw no objection, except that he doubted London's capacity for offering usable advice. "I should not think that . . . he is very critical."

Sterling obviously delighted in a situation in which two men of considerable talent would be fighting over possession of his conscience. In his introduction to a collection of Bierce's letters, Sterling many years later confessed that "it was my hope at one time to involve him [Bierce] and Jack London in a controversy on the subject [of socialism]," but that London "declined the oral encounter."

Bierce was further aggrieved to learn that Sterling, at London's urging, intended to leave his safe position in his uncle's real estate office and live the Bohemian life to the hilt. Nonsense, replied Bierce; having to work for a living was the "common lot," no matter how much it chafed poetic sensibilities. "I have chafed under the yoke for many years . . . It does not fit my neck anywhere. Some day perhaps you and I will live on adjoining ranches in the mountains — or in adjoining caves . . ."

But Sterling, as a slavish follower, was lost to him, and the realization of that loss caused Bierce many bitter reflections. Sterling recalled that his friends often accused Bierce of "laying a hand of ice on my muse." In time, he seemed to agree that Bierce's influence was somewhat inimical and that he would outgrow the Master. He could no longer accept all of Bierce's red-inked criticisms on the margins of his manuscripts. "When my unwillingness began unmistakably to show itself he was not without evidence of pique."[16] For all his growing belief that Bierce was, as his San Francisco enemies asserted, passé, George Sterling would never have a better, if also such an outrageously demanding, friend than Bierce. That was proved by the piddling inconsequentiality of the balance of his life, largely spent as the resident "character" of the Bohemian Club.

From human complications and the drudgery of turning out "The Passing Show" for the Hearst syndicate, Bierce escaped to the Cheat River country of what was now West Virginia to ramble through the mountainous countryside in which he had served as a young recruit with the Ninth Indiana Volunteers. Ever since the war, he wrote the secretary of the regimental reunion association, that country had been "a kind of dream-land," which he was reluctant to revisit out of fear of being disillusioned. Instead he found it the one youthful memory that survived the years. "The whole region is wild and grand, and if any one of the men who in his golden youth soldiered through its valleys of sleep and over its gracious mountains will revisit it in the hazy season when it is all aflame with the autumn foliage, I promise him sentiments that he will willingly entertain and emotions that he will care to feel. Among them, I fear, will be a haunting envy of those of his comrades whose fall and burial in that enchanted land he once bewailed."

He wandered through the Union cemetery at Grafton, reading the old gravestones and trying to connect them with the dim young faces of the men who lay buried there, and was outraged to find that the Confederates who had fallen in the skirmishes of the first year of the war had not been accorded a similar dignity. Several years later he was still so indignant over the treatment of the enemy dead that he wrote in a magazine article, concerning the Confederate graves he had searched out, "As nearly as I could make out there were from eighty to a hundred sunken graves, overgrown with moss and full of rotting leaves. Fewer than a dozen had headstones, with barely decipherable inscriptions rudely carved by comrades of the dead. These had mostly fallen into the excavations."[17]

On returning to Washington he wrote a San Francisco friend, "They found a Confederate soldier the other day with his rifle alongside. I'm going over to beg his pardon."[18]

More and more he had begun living in the past, the deep past before San Francisco. It now seemed to him that his San Francisco years, during which he had accomplished the most, had been largely a waste of time. What good had all his crusading done? San Francisco, he wrote Sterling, was now the "worst of all modern Sodom and Gomorrahs" and could use another shattering earthquake (this, of course, was a few years before the quake of 1906 which more than filled his prescription) or, better yet, "a steady tradewind of grapeshot."

Naturally he would not join in the nationwide chorus of praise for Jack London, whose *The Sea Wolf* had just been published to the highest critical acclaim. Sterling was anxious for Bierce's sanction of the novel and of its author, but Bierce would only admit to a qualified approval of London as a writer and a "deep contempt" for him as a "publicist and reformer."

As for *The Sea Wolf*, he conceded that it was a "rattling good story" and that the character of Wolf Larsen was a brilliant creation, but he could not go along with the opinion that Jack London had now joined the immortals. So it had climbed to the top of the best-seller list? Bierce was not the man to be awed by that illusory sort of eminence. "It is a most disagreeable book as a whole. London has a pretty bad style and no sense of proportion. The story is a perfect welter of disagreeable incidents. Two or three (of the kind) would have sufficed to show the character of the man Larsen . . . Many of these incidents, too, are impossible — such as that of a man mounting a ladder with a dozen other men — more or less — hanging to his leg . . . The 'love' element, with its absurd repressions and impossible proprieties, is awful. I confess to an overwhelming contempt for both sexless lovers."[19]

To that and all other of Bierce's criticisms London would reply that Bierce's ideas had calcified about the time he and Sterling were born, and that if he had been born later he would have made the fieriest sort of radical prophet himself. The San Francisco literary cliques were gleeful as word reached them of the infighting between London, their brightest new star, and Bierce, the old hetman of Pacific letters whose knout was losing its sting. Sooner or later Bierce and London would have to collide in person; both were violent characters, in word and deed, and the resulting set-to would be marvelous to watch. A half-dozen years later they did meet, with shots of whiskey at point-blank range.

For years Mollie Bierce had been living quietly in Los Angeles. She had cared for her mother until the latter's death in an old house on Figueroa Street, near the downtown section. Helen Bierce later wrote that she had often urged her mother to divorce Bierce and marry someone else, but Mrs. Bierce "only shook her head sadly and told me she could not love anyone but my father."

In the fall of 1904 Mrs. Bierce filed suit for a divorce from her husband on charges of desertion, because, as her daughter later related, "someone whispered he wanted a divorce so he might be free to remarry."

There may have been some truth in that whisper. During the summer of 1904, while spending a few weeks at the summer home of friends in Connecticut, Bierce had been strongly attracted to a handsome blonde woman and wrote to Sterling of the possibility of asking her to marry him. It was probably a fleeting impulse; certainly he did not pass along the word to Mollie that he was considering remarriage.

Mrs. Bierce was granted an interlocutory decree. Before the divorce became final, on April 27, 1905, after an illness of only a few days, she died of what was described on the death certificate as "heart failure." Perhaps that phrase was true in more ways than the clinical.

Her death was probably a harder blow than Bierce could allow himself to reveal, even to his closest friends. He did admit in a letter to Sterling that he was "upset" because death had been "striking pretty close to me again." Less than two months later, however, he was writing jocularly to the same correspondent of "being now (alas) eligible" to get married again.

Freedom could be disastrous, he jauntily added, because "I'm only a youth — 63 on the 24th of this month — and it would be too bad if I got started wrong in life."[20]

> Among what I may term "underground
> reputations" that of Ambrose Bierce is
> perhaps the most striking example.
> — Arnold Bennett
> *London New Age*, 1909

SIXTEEN *An Underground Reputation*

IN SEPTEMBER of 1905, William Randolph
Hearst decided that the curious talents of Ambrose Bierce would
be better displayed in the first of the chain of magazines he was
acquiring. The straphanging readers of his New York *Journal*
undoubtedly had not been as impressed with Bierce's barbed
comments on their civilization as Hearst had hoped. So "The
Passing Show" would become a monthly feature of *Cosmopolitan*,
the readers of which would presumably have more time to digest
him, and Bierce would have more time to compose his columns.
His salary would continue as it had for a number of years, one
hundred dollars a week.

Bierce had received fair warning of Hearst's intentions when
the publisher wrote, "I will have enough magazines pretty soon
to keep you busy in the magazine field, and then you won't have
to bother with newspapers. I imagine the magazine field will suit
you better anyway, as it is an opportunity for fuller discussion."[1]
Bierce did not balk, though his stablemates on *Cosmopolitan*
included a singular collection of the writers he particularly
abominated: the popular novelist and muckraker David Graham
Phillips, the saccharine poetess Ella Wheeler Wilcox, the cutrate
philosopher Elbert Hubbard, and Ellis Parker Butler — not to
mention a long and utterly banal series in which John Burroughs,

Edwin Markham and other public thinkers ruminated on the theme, "What Life Means to Me." Bierce was not asked to contribute to that series, with all its synthetic cheeriness. Safer that Bierce was established in the back of the magazine, where his voice could be heard growling up from the sub-basement as a murmurous background to the polite voices in the parlor above.

As observer of "The Passing Show" Bierce ranged widely over a number of fields, but with more emphasis on the cultural than before. He praised the early work of Ezra Pound, thus inadvertently placing himself in the avant garde, and Countess von Arnheim's *Elizabeth and Her German Garden*, and applied his cat-o'-nines to Upton Sinclair's *The Industrial Republic* and Marie Corelli's *Temporal Power*, which nevertheless sold 150,000 copies in a few weeks. He managed to demolish Shaw and Shakespeare in one paragraph, damning the former for boasting that he could outwrite the latter, and then taking Shakespeare himself to task for *Romeo and Juliet*. "All its men are blackguards, all its women worse, and worst of all is Juliet herself, who makes no secret of her passion for Romeo, but discloses it with all the candor of a moral idiot insensible to the distinction between propensity and sentiment. Her frankness is no less than hideous. Yet one may read page after page by reputable authors in praise of her as one of the sweetest of Shakespeare's heroines."[2]

The book-reviewing end of his chores, predictably, loosed his most savage energies. Time had not mellowed him as a critic of contemporary literature; his own commercial failures in that line were not calculated to make him gentler with the works of others. He once composed what may be the shortest, nastiest book review on the record by listing its title, author and publisher and adding the one-line comment, "The covers of this book are too far apart."

Occasionally, like an eagle swooping down on the carrion-littered plain of literature, he would quote one paragraph of a current novel as an example of hopelessly bad writing. Such as: "She remained inactive in his embrace for a considerable period, then modestly disengaging herself looked him full in the countenance and signified a desire for self-communion. By love's instinct he divined her purpose — she wanted to consider his proposal apart from the influence of the glamour of his personal presence. With the innate tact of a truly genteel nature he bade her good evening in French, and with measured tread paced away into the gathering gloom."

Contrarily enough, he could inveigh against the "sexlessness" of Jack London's lovers in *The Sea Wolf*, and all the coy evasions of other popular novelists who wanted to titillate but not offend the growing mass readership of the ten-cent magazines, and yet simultaneously proclaim to Walter Neale that Anthony Comstock, censor-in-chief of all he surveyed, had his "intellectual support."

The Hearst job, often as he derided it, actually was the comfort of his old age, the mainstay of such days as that on which he wrote a friend, "Today is my birthday. I am 366 years old." Difficult as he was for Hearst's executives to handle, he could not be easily lured off Hearst's payroll. A San Francisco friend of his named Robert Mackay announced the establishment of a magazine to be titled *Fiction*, and wanted Bierce to join his staff. Bierce turned him down, explaining, "Doubtless I shall be a salary man to the end of my days — what Hearst's papers call a wage-slave. The negro quarters are fairly comfortable, the pone and bacon tolerable and the overseer's whip can't reach me here in Washington. Sometimes I think I should like to be a free-nigger, but I dunno . . ."[3]

It must have been that fondness for the Hearst cornpone and side meat that persuaded him to participate in a public debate on the topic "Social Unrest" which was sponsored by *Cosmopolitan* magazine as a promotion designed to show it was concerned with serious problems. There was to be a round-table symposium on the causes of widespread unemployment and poverty in that spring of 1906. The radical remedies for the situation were to be presented by two prominent Socialists, Robert Hunter, the author of the widely read *Poverty*, a burden of statistics bent to Marxist purposes, and Morris Hillquit, a skilled debater and orator, more the activist than the intellectual. Bierce had practically no experience as a debater, except in barrooms, yet was persuaded to carry the banner of capitalism — or reaction, in the view of his ideological enemies — against two highly skilled dialecticians. Perhaps he agreed to enter the arena — the public room of a New York hotel — to escape from brooding over the quake and fire which had recently all but leveled San Francisco. (A few years before he had prescribed just such a remedy for its corruption, but when it happened he mourned that "*my* San Francisco is gone" and swore he would never visit the city rebuilt over its ruins, an "upstart bearing his [San Francisco's] name." He was cheered only by the fact that Sterling, Scheffauer and other friends, his brother Albert and his family had escaped with their lives.) His friends, at any rate, thought Bierce would be pulverized by two such expert millstones as Hunter and Hillquit. He was introduced to the assemblage as "a strenuous challenger of the optimists, a thinker whose views are the despair of the social reformer." Actually he presented himself as a spokesman for the elite, the intellectual as well as the economic aristocracy.

Immediately, however, he made it plain that he was not born into any privileged class but had won his position by scrambling away from the ruck of the unprivileged. "Nothing touches me more than poverty," he said. "I have been poor myself. I was one of those poor devils born to work as a peasant in the fields, but I found no difficulty getting out of it."

Hunter and Hillquit were pleased that he agreed that there was much poverty and material inequality in the country and immediately proposed a Socialist solution to the problem by reversing the position of the classes.

"I don't see," Bierce retorted, "that there is any remedy for this condition which consists in the rich being on top. They always will be. The reason that men are poor — this is not a rule without an exception — is that they are incapable. The rich become rich because they have brains."

That left the two Socialists an excellent opening. They could cite a hundred wealthy men, heirs to great fortunes, who were utterly brainless. "Well, sir," Hunter demanded, "how important do you conceive William Waldorf Astor to be to the City of New York? He lives in London; but he and his family extract from the people of New York interest on, let us say, four hundred million a year. Is he that valuable to the community? Is this because of his extraordinary brains?"

In that case, said Bierce, he should be "eliminated," a suggestion which could not have pleased any who hoped he would defend capitalism down to the last watery-eyed inheritor. "In this country every man has a vote. If he is not satisfied with conditions as they are, why doesn't he change them? If the workingman and the poor are in the majority, why can't they get together? Because they haven't sense enough. They can have any laws or any system they want."

That, replied Hillquit, was exactly why Socialism was working to educate the masses and to better their environment.

A better environment wouldn't improve their intelligence, which was acquired through heredity, Bierce countered. "I think it's very strange that you people who recognize the differences in dogs and horses don't recognize the differences in the human race . . . I don't believe in the greatest good to the greatest number. It seems to me perfect rot. I believe in the greatest good to the best men. And I would sacrifice a hundred incapable men to elevate one really great man. It is from great men only that the world gets any good. What do we owe to the artisans who laid the stones of the Parthenon? What to the gaping Athenians who stared at Plato?"

With that sort of attitude governing the ruling class, Hunter and Hillquit declared, there would inevitably be a bloody revolution in the United States.

"I haven't any doubt that a revolution is coming to this country," said Bierce calmly. It was one of his favorite hobgoblins, in fact. "It may or may not be suppressed. It will be a bloody one. I think that is the natural tendency of republican government. Undoubtedly we have to go over the whole Paris regime again and again."

Even the harsh repressions of the Czarist regime in Russia had not prevented the mass outbreak of 1905, the Socialists pointed out.

"The people," said Bierce with a wave of his hand, "are always doing silly things. They sail in and shed a lot of blood, and then they are back where they were before."

Mr. Hillquit permitted himself a sharkish smile. "You think civilization has not accomplished anything in recent years?"

"It has accomplished everything!" Bierce shot back. "But it has not made humanity any happier. Happiness is the only thing worth having. I find happiness in looking at poor men in the same way that I do in looking at the ants in an anthill. And I find happiness in looking at the capitalist. I don't care what he does, nor what the others do. It pleases me to look at them. Each man is concerned with his own happiness."

Mr. Hunter observed that Bierce's attitude reminded him of John D. Rockefeller, Sr.'s, and "I should say you were on a par with him in cleverness."

"I think him a damned fool in some ways," Bierce retorted.[4]

The debate ended as politely as it had been conducted, though those who knew Bierce well feared that he might lose his temper and even lay about him with his famous loaded cane (which had, in Washington's politer ambience, replaced the .45 revolver he had always carried in San Francisco). A letter to Sterling a month or so later indicated, however, that he had kept himself under control only with difficulty. Sterling had chided him for being so outspokenly reactionary, but Bierce haughtily replied that he didn't give a damn for the opinions of "babes and sucklings." Hunter, he said, was a "decentish fellow," but Hillquit was a "humorless anarchist." He had taken Hillquit to the nearest bar after the debate, he related. "When I complimented him on the beauty of his neck and expressed the hope of putting a nice, new rope around it he nearly strangled on the brandy I was putting down it at the hotel bar."[5]

Perhaps he was proving so cooperative with the Hearst management as to help along one of its promotional ventures because he was then pushing his campaign for publication of Sterling's "A Wine of Wizardry." After the sleetstorm of rejection slips which had greeted it, *Cosmopolitan* was about the only slick-paper magazine left to publish it. At any rate Bierce succeeded with his campaign and the poem was published the following year. Along with it was printed a long and somewhat defensive commentary by Bierce, which read as though he were trying to pour Sterling's vintage down the throats of the academic critics whether they gagged or not. "Whatever length of days may be accorded to this magazine," he wrote, "it is not likely to do anything more notable in literature than it accomplishes in this issue. . . . I steadfastly believe and heartily affirm that George Sterling is a very great poet — incomparably the greatest that we have on this side of the Atlantic." Regarding the poem itself, he wrote, "I hold that not in a lifetime has our literature had any new thing of equal length containing so much poetry and so little else . . . It has all the imagination of 'Comus' and all the fancy of 'The Faerie Queen.' "[6]

With that sort of sendoff, Sterling became so instantly celebrated that tourists took to stealing his firewood as souvenirs from his cottage at Carmel.

Other poets and critics, however, reacted sharply. A nation-wide controversy was stirred, in fact, which made Sterling's name all the better known. George Harvey, Gertrude Atherton, Ina Coolbrith and others differed rather violently with Bierce's tugging Sterling after him to the summit of Mount Parnassus. A San Francisco critic, Porter Garnett, questioned Bierce's credentials as a recruiting agent for the immortals on the grounds that he was no more than a "clever paragrapher" but lacked "both the catholicity and scholarship necessary to the making of a literary arbiter." He was more a "bigot" than a "critic" in literary matters, Garnett added for good measure. Arthur Brisbane, the Hearst papers' leading commentator in succession to Bierce, took issue with the poem and its sponsor even though it was published in a Hearst magazine: his complaint was that Sterling used too many words unfamiliar to a mass audience.

Undoubtedly Bierce was delighted by the big waves stirred by "A Wine of Wizardry." It was like the old days in San Francisco, when people cared enough about such matters to get embroiled, even though he was now in the defending rather than attacking position.

Tauntingly he titled his response to those who criticized his evangelizing on behalf of Sterling, in an article three months later, "An Insurrection of the Peasantry."[7]

A critic who complained of Sterling's reference in the poem to "the blue-eyed vampire, sated at her feast" because "Somehow one does not associate blue eyes with a vampire" was met with Bierce's riposte: "Of course it did not occur to him that this was doubtless the very reason why the author chose the epithet . . . 'Blue-eyed' connotes beauty and gentleness;* the picture is that of a lovely, fair-haired woman with the tell-tale blood about her lips. Nothing could be less horrible, nothing more terrible. As vampires do not really exist, everyone is at liberty, I take it, to conceive them under what outward and visible aspect he will; but this gentleman, having standardized the vampire, naturally resents any departure from the type — his type. I fancy he requires goggle eyes, emitting flame and perhaps smoke, a mouth well garnished with tusks — long claws, and all the other appurtenances that make the conventional Chinese dragon so awful that one naturally wishes to meet it and kick it."

To those who complained that "A Wine of Wizardry" was all precious imagery, Bierce replied that "Imagery is not only the life and soul of poetry, it *is* poetry." Another part of the audience disapproved of the grotesquerie that marked the poem. "What," demanded Bierce, "do you expect Wizardry to be? Sweet and sunny pictures of rural life? Love scenes in urban drawing rooms?"

He reserved his heaviest fusillade for Brisbane's objection that he, whose intellect was to be considered so weighty that fellow newspapermen would refer to him as "Old Double Dome," could not understand what Sterling meant. Brisbane had cited the passage "Infernal rubrics, sung to Satan's might/ Or chaunted to the Dragon in his gyre" in commenting "We confess that we had never before heard of a 'gyre.' Looking it up in the dictionary, we find that it means a gyration, or a whirling

---

* Bierce was half in love with the contemporarily fashionable view that the Anglo-Saxon physique, the blue-eyed blonde, was human beauty at its culmination. It may or may not have been significant that Bierce himself had blue eyes and once-golden hair.

around. Rubrics chanted to a dragon while he was whirling around ought to be worth hearing." Bierce was scornful of his colleague's obtuseness, and nominated Mr. Brisbane as one of the more abysmal peasants of his title. "Now whose fault is it that this distinguished journalist has never heard of a gyre? Certainly not the poet's. And whose that in very sensibly looking it up he suffered himself to be so misled by the lexicographer as to think it a gyration, a whirling around? Gyre means, not a gyration, but the *path* of a gyration, an orbit. And the poor man has no knowledge of a dragon in the heavens?— the constellation Draco, to which, as to other stars, the magicians of old chanted incantations? A peasant is not to be censured for his ignorance, but when he glories in it and draws its limits as a deadline for his betters, he is the least pleasing of all the beasts of the field."

Bierce was so pleased with his defense of Sterling that he included it in his *Collected Works* (and just about everything else but dunning letters and laundry lists). It made Sterling more famous, temporarily, than "A Wine of Wizardry" itself. But it did not make Sterling any more grateful or arrest his drift away from Bierce's tutelage. Soon Bierce was to be remarking on the fact that Sterling no longer submitted his work to the Master for approval and editing, and expressing fears that a semblance of success had spoiled his old protégé. Sterling, for his part, was offended because when he wrote Bierce of his concern over Jack London, the professional proletarian off on a South Seas cruise aboard his own yacht, being reported missing at sea for weeks, Bierce callously assured him that he need have no fears for London "because the ocean will refuse to swallow him."

About the same time as his number-one protégé was drifting rapidly into the shoals of Bohemianism and worse, his number-two protégé Herman Scheffauer earned himself banishment from the Bierce circle. Bierce had arranged for Walter Neale to publish a volume of Scheffauer's, and had been rewarded by reports that Scheffauer was talking against him to Neale and other New York publishers. He wrote Scheffauer a letter, in the fashion of those days, formally severing the bond between them. He indicated that he resented Scheffauer's remark that his (Bierce's) work "lacked soul." Scheffauer, he had come to perceive, was "not truthful, candid, without deceit, honorable." He left the door open, however, for a reformed and repentant Scheffauer: "If in the future you are convinced that you have become different, and I am still living, my welcoming hand awaits you. And when I forgive I forgive all over . . ."⁸

Fortunately new people and new interests were claiming his attention at the time his relations with the two young men for whom he had held such high hopes, labored over so long, were lapsing. One of the persons with whom a growing intimacy was forming was Percival Pollard, the Baltimore critic. Pollard, according to Walter Neale, came equipped with all the attributes — except possibly horns, tail and diabolic puffs of smoke — expected of a literary critic who specialized in wholesale demolition. He was "born sneering," was "mean, selfish and parsimonious." Neale was later outraged to learn that Pollard left an estate estimated at over a hundred thousand dollars, having "assumed that he was as poverty-stricken as he professed to be."

Bierce saw him in a kindlier light, possibly because the younger man did not conceal his admiration for Bierce and often invited him to his summer home at Sag Harbor, on Long Island Sound. Admittedly, to Bierce, Pollard was a "queer duck," but he was an oddly likeable one. He also liked Pollard's forthright style. As far back as 1896, in a "Prattle" column, he had called Pollard "that hard and ingenious explorer, that sun-eyed searcher of the intense mane, that robber-baron invader of literature's land oblivion, that painstaking chiffonier of fame's eternal dumping-ground . . ."⁹

Pollard was the literary critic of *Town Topics*, the weekly magazine edited by Colonel William d'Alton Mann, half society gossip sheet, half sharp-eyed comment on the cultural scene. The front of the book was devoted to gossip retailed by Colonel Mann, the pioneer in that field, who was revealed in 1905 to be something of an artist at blackmail: some of the mightiest figures in business and industry were buying immunity from the colonel and his staff of journalistic magpies. The back-of-the-book departments, however, were lively, unprejudiced, and not subject to the colonel's tendency to regard blackmail as a profitable by-product of journalism. James Gibbons Huneker, still regarded as a mighty influence on American culture, was its music critic, of whom Alfred Kazin wrote recently that he "brought the new currents of European art and thought to America and made them fashionable." He also wrote dramatic criticism, without which, H. L. Mencken said, Americans would "still be sweating at the Chautauquas and applauding the plays of Bronson Howard." It would be a "great absurdity and grave injustice," wrote Ludwig Lewisohn in his *Story of American Literature,* if *Town Topics*'s role in the development of American letters were ignored simply because its publisher happened to be a blackguard. Aside from the society gossip, its columns, Lewisohn added, "should one day be sedulously analyzed for the brilliant light that would thus be thrown on our cultural history during certain years." Those years were what Edmund Wilson termed "perhaps the most provincial and uninspired moment in the history of American society," the overstuffed Edwardian years.

Pollard, signing himself the "Ringmaster," was the *Town Topics*'s literary critic between 1897 and his death in 1911. As a tireless lambaster of the mediocre and insipid, he "showed the first American awareness of the great movements that were transforming continental literature." He kept pointing out to his readers that the greatest living American novelist was not F. Marion Crawford but Henry James. Most American writers, he said, were content to be "browsing forever on the complacent plains of mediocrity." Some of his more corrosive comments — which must have delighted Bierce — dismantled the artistic methods of the new realists without pity. Frank Norris's *McTeague,* he declared, was a gritty mixture of "dentistry, dust and alkali." Of the ultramasculine heroes created by Jack London in his own image, he wrote that the only conclusion to be drawn was that "If you want to succeed with women, you must wear the muscles of your neck outside of your collar." He also predicted George Bernard Shaw's future greatness at a time, as he said, when Shaw was a name "to frighten fools with," and translated some of André Gide's work for publication in *Town Topics,* its first American appearance.[10]

Of all his artistic convictions, however, the staunchest by all

odds was that Ambrose Bierce was the great, shamefully neglected figure on the American literary scene. He would stake
"my own critical reputation," Pollard wrote, on the prediction
that "no other American book written in the last fifty years"
would endure as long as In the Midst of Life,[11] as the newer
edition of Tales of Soldiers and Civilians was titled.

With comradeship like that, Bierce must have felt that he
could suffer a few defections among his fickle supporters in San
Francisco. Pollard's advocacy, in fact, inspired him to begin
writing short stories again, four of them in one month, which
found a home in Town Topics. H. L. Mencken, who was on the
staff of the Smart Set, a more literary periodical also published by
Colonel Mann, described Pollard as being "apparently without
the slightest affection for any human being."[12] The exception to
that judgment, apparently, was his fellow misanthrope in Washington.

Meanwhile there was a slight awakening of interest in Bierce
stirring in the New York publishing world. He lunched with the
editors of Doubleday, Page and Company in New York, and the
result of that three-hour session was a contract to compile The
Cynic's Word Book, later republished as The Devil's Dictionary,
with definitions clipped from his old "Prattle" columns and a
few new ones added. ("GARTER, an elastic band intended to keep
a woman from coming out of her stocking and desolating the
country." "DUTY, that which sternly impels us in the direction of
profit along the line of desire." "BORE, a person who talks when
you wish him to listen.") It failed to sell, Bierce believed,
because it lacked that touch of rural folksiness which other
Indiana-born authors, ironically, were so adept at conveying.
("Indiana novels," such as those of Booth Tarkington, and the
barefoot-boyhood verse of James Whitcomb Riley aroused his
most savage contempt. Of Riley, he wrote that "His pathos is
bathos, his sentiment sediment, his 'homely philosophy' brute
platitudes — beasts of the field of thought.") A short time later
his friend S. O. Howes of Galveston began collecting some of
Bierce's essays for a volume to be titled The Shadow on the Dial.

When Doubleday, Page promptly turned it down, Bierce commented that any publisher was a "mere tradesman," who would "doubtless willingly pay $50,000 a year to an infallible reader . . . I never feel any resentment when my stuff is turned down"[13]— a sentiment that certainly, if true, made him unique among literary men this side of heaven.

The Shadow on the Dial, containing some of his bitterest reflections on the quality of American life and occasionally prophetic musings on the future workings of an expanding, growingly permissive democracy, was finally published by A. M. Robertson of San Francisco. Of these forebodings, he wrote in an introduction to the essays:

"Formerly the bearer of evil tidings was only slain; now he is ignored. The gods kept their secrets by telling them to Cassandra, whom no one would believe. I do not expect to be heeded. The crust of the volcano is electric, the fumes are narcotic; the combined sensation is delightful no end. I have looked at the dial of civilization; I tell you the shadow is going back. That is of small importance to men of leisure with wine-dipped wreaths upon their heads. They do not care to know the hour."

The essays were widely but harshly reviewed. Their anger, said the *Bookman,* was only "the steam-heat of journalism." Bierce, commented the St. Louis *Mirror,* was "a Niagara running to waste." The *Nation* arraigned him on the charge that he "talks about matters he does not perfectly understand, says habitually more than he means."

In England, however, the volume caused enough interest for Arnold Bennett to identify Ambrose Bierce as a "striking example" of what he meant by an "underground reputation."

By then Bierce was quite certain that his status would always be that of an outsider, an esoteric commentator on times he found out of joint, an ikon to be revered by small and scattered groups who feared as he feared and hated as he hated — and so it has. Yet he may still be regarded in the future, if it should develop as he foresaw into an anarchic nightmare, as something more than a minor prophet, a disgruntled voice in the wilderness.

If the continuing experiment in democracy fails through inner stress or converging assault by historic circumstances, in a time of terror and disillusionment such as even he could not delineate, his words may be recalled with terrible emphasis. And the odds are all too good that they would be ripped out of context, misused and maltreated in some *Mein Kampf* of the future.

Any such prophet of reaction, by skillful mining, milling and smelting, would find a philosophic yield working over the tailings of his *Collected Works*. That twelve-volume behemoth was conceived in the spring of 1908, with Walter Neale, friend, biographer-to-be and publisher, as midwife. Bierce himself would be the editor, another mistake, since he was unable to perform the necessary excisions. A *Collected Works* of six volumes would have been twice as valuable. Instead Bierce did not really edit but threw in everything to make sure of coming out with an even dozen volumes. He was, as biographer Paul Fatout has written, so exhilarated by the prospect of being a collected author that it "made him drunker than any number of brandies ever did."

Neale had offered him one of the most generous contracts in publishing history — a twenty percent royalty on a limited edition (one hundred dollars a set) which was to be "printed on paper of high grade, in large style, leaded; the binding will be full Levant morocco, both sides and back decorated, bound by hand throughout, with double head-bands, and lining of moire silk, with gold edges all around."

Gorgeous it may have been — and less gorgeous the layers of dust it collects in the back stacks of libraries — but it was more of a monument to his ego than a twelve-gun salute to his talent. At times, during the several years of pasting the collection together, he seemed to sense that much of his journalism in particular was full of self-satisfied sound and puerile fury. "Indeed," he wrote Sterling, "my intellectual status (whatever it may be, and God knows it's enough to make me blush) was of slow growth — as was my moral. I mean I had not *literary sincerity*."[14] An overdue confession, it would seem, that much of the crusading and fulminating and moralizing of his San Francisco years — which, however, he could not bring himself to discard when editing the *Collected Works* — stemmed not so much from conviction as a desire to startle, annoy, harass, and thereby attract attention to himself.

The year 1908 saw his final severance from the Hearst organization, an event saddened more by the abrupt termination of his hundred dollars a week, which must have seemed almost like an annuity, than by the severance of sentimental ties to his employer. He would always concede, however, that Hearst was an almost eccentrically generous employer. The year before, writing Howes in Galveston, he recounted that he had been doing so little to earn his salary, "just *Cosmopolitan* stuff," that he had suggested that Hearst pay him less money. But he quoted Hearst as replying, "You haven't heard me shrieking about that, have you?"[15]

A few months later he was reacting ungratefully, from the Hearst viewpoint, to suggestions that he direct some of his sharper satiric shafts at Hearst's strongest competition in New York, Joseph Pulitzer and his *World*. He wrote Sam Chamberlain, then editor of the *Cosmopolitan:* "I don't like the job of chained bulldog to be let loose only to tear the panties off the boys who throw rocks at you. You wouldn't like it yourself in my place. Henceforth I won't bite anybody, a quiet life for mine — it is nicer and there is nobody to say me nay."[16]

The quieter life was arranged shortly after Hearst wrote him, "If you will kindly excuse me for saying so, you have devoted so much of your letter to soaking Mr. Chamberlain and proving that I am wrong in everything that I ever said or did, that the details of the arrangement have not received much attention. The Hon. William Randolph Hearst [Hearst had just been elected to Congress] is quite as anxious to do what is right and agreeable to you as Will Hearst ever was and I wish I could get you to believe that." According to Hearst's latest biographer, the publisher went all out in his efforts to keep Bierce and "would invite Bierce to lunch at his house, where there would be several ladies among the guests, reducing his opportunity for violent complaint, and he would be treated so royally that his anger would cool . . ."[17]

Finally, however, a Bierce resignation was proffered and accepted. Either Hearst's patience with his temperamental "chained bulldog" had dwindled, or he believed that Bierce at sixty-six really wanted to retire. The latter wasn't the case, according to Walter Neale. Bierce expected to be cajoled back on the payroll again, as Neale recalled it, and announced to his friends that he would return to his writing chores for the *Cosmopolitan* if Hearst would pay him the salary lost since his resignation — plus six percent interest. Neale also remembered Bierce's "telling me that he had got along all right with Hearst until his wife was given the *Cosmopolitan Magazine* as a plaything."[18] Bierce never heard from Hearst again.

Soon thereafter he was telling Neale that he intended to write a biography of the "Chief" which would expose him for all time as a man of dangerous ambition. He would not publish it, however, until the death of Mrs. Phoebe Apperson Hearst, the publisher's mother, whom he had always greatly admired and respected.

He didn't get around to the Hearst biography, but did leave several searing word portraits of his late employer which Hearst biographies have exhumed with relish. "But," he wrote, "the mental feat in which I take the most satisfaction, and which I doubt not is most diverting to my keepers, is that of creating Mr. W. R. Hearst, pointing his eyes toward the White House and endowing him with a perilous Jacksonian ambition to defile it. The Hearst is distinctly a treasure."[19] In that, of course, Bierce was claiming too much. Hearst was in every respect his own man, his own creation, and his ambition was notably self-propelled.

With a greater effort at fairness, he wrote elsewhere, in his "Thumbnail Sketch" of the publisher, "With many amiable and alluring qualities, among which is, or used to be, a personal modesty amounting to bashfulness, the man has not a friend in the world." However, he added, Hearst didn't deserve one because, "either congenitally or by induced perversity, he is inaccessible to the conception of an unselfish attachment or a disinterested motive. Silent and smiling, he moves among men, the loneliest man. Nobody but God loves him; and God's love he values only in so far as he fancies that it may promote his amusing ambition to darken the door of the White House. As to that, I think that he would be about the kind of President that the country is beginning to deserve."[20]

More or less voluntarily, Bierce had now entered upon semi-retirement. He continued with the editing of the *Collected Works*, the twelve volumes of which were published, without any great exultations from readers or critics, between 1909 and 1912. He also wrote stories and sketches from time to time— enough to maintain himself at the Iowa Circle apartment and pay his tabs at the Army and Navy Club — and kept up with his self-appointed duty of encouraging young writers, particularly poets, who submitted their work to him. Ezra Pound sent him "Goodly Fere" which, as Bierce wrote another protégé Samuel Loveman, was "highly commended by me."[21] Often he sent on such work to Mencken at *Smart Set* or other editors.

He considered moving back to California, perhaps to the new literary and artistic colony at Carmel where George Sterling was living, but insisted that he would not want to be identified with it because "I'm warned by Hawthorne and Brook Farm."

It would have been difficult, however, to detach himself from Washington and particularly from the bar of the Army and Navy Club, where he gathered daily with such cronies as General Fred C. Ainsworth, the head of the War Department's pension bureau. His friend Walter Neale couldn't understand the club's fascination for Bierce. "Always while there," Neale observed, "his inferiority complex was uppermost." The sense of inferiority, Neale believed, stemmed from his lack of a formal education. "He would sweat at the very thought of encountering a mature man ten years out of college." Thus Bierce also felt inferior because, though he remained very attached to his brevet rank of major, he was not a West Pointer, as most of the club's habitués were. Nevertheless whenever his out-of-town friends came to look Bierce up they always looked in at the Army and Navy Club first and usually found him holding forth in the bar. Neale, incidentally, was the only one to record Bierce's alleged feelings of inferiority about a lack of education.

In 1910 he decided to return to California, perhaps to see

whether living there the rest of his life might be feasible. Washington, with its damp heat, was not the best climate for his asthma. New York was too exhausting; it was, he wrote, "cocaine, opium, hashish." So in April 1910 he set out for California via the Panama Canal. Along the way, he wrote S. O. Howes, he would continue editing the later volumes of *Collected Works*. To Howes he expressed his disgust at the news that the British explorer Sir Ernest Shackleton had named a mountain after Sir Henry Lucy, the latter a name that popped out of his recollection of his years in England. "I knew Lucy very well — a little toady who afterward toadied himself into a title."[22]

Once arrived in California he repaired first the mountain cabin of his brother Albert — still affectionately called "Grizzly" — his nephew Carlton and the latter's wife Lora, to all of whom he was considerably attached. He was greatly alarmed to find that Carlton and Lora had become infected with social and political views — liberal, that is — which he detested. "Run after your false gods until you are tired; I shall not believe your hearts are really in the chase," he later wrote Lora Bierce.[23]

Later in the spring he repaired to San Francisco for night after night of wining and dining. He was greeted like a prodigal son. Then, at Sterling's urging, he visited the colony at Carmel where, above the white beaches and under the pines, various artists and writers were finding it heavenly to be established in an enclave far from the restrictions of a bourgeois society and the meaningless uproar of the marketplace. Not so Ambrose Bierce. He spent an evening listening to the young aspirants talking across a driftwood fire, and he was visibly unimpressed. So were the young people gathered around him. Mary Austin, a novelist of some stature, later described her impression of him as a man "secretly embittered by failure to achieve direct creation, to which he never confessed; a man of immense provocative power, always secretly — perhaps even to himself — seeking to make good in some other's gift what he had missed, always able to forgive any shortcoming in his protégés more easily than a failure to turn out according to his prescription. I thought him something of a poseur, tending to overweigh a slender inspiration with apocalyptic gestures."[24]

Bierce's verdict on Miss Austin and the others was briefer and more pungent. They were, he said, "a nest of anarchists."

After returning to his brother Albert's camp above the Russian River, he heard that the Bohemian Club was holding its midsummer outing, called the Annual High Jinks, at its camp nearby and that Sterling and his friend Jack London were among those disporting themselves. Thus the great confrontation, so devoutly wished by all who relished a good brawl, took place. Bierce summoned Sterling and announced that he wanted to meet London.

"Oh, you mustn't meet him," Sterling demurred, by his own account. "You'd be at each other's throats in five minutes."

"Nonsense," snorted Bierce, "bring him on. I'll treat him like a Dutch uncle."[25]

Word spread throughout the Grove that a celebrated literary feud was about to be resolved in blood, whiskey or words. A crowd of clubmen had gathered in the rustic bar where Sterling, in the wary manner of a referee, introduced Bierce to London. The latter was exactly half of Bierce's age of sixty-eight, but they appeared to be evenly matched unless fists were the chosen weapon.

What ensued, from the viewpoint of anyone hoping for spilled blood or at least a legendary slanging match, was hilariously anticlimactic.

The two contenders, after exchanging a few insults of low caliber and no great originality, settled down to a drinking contest.* They matched each other drink for drink, and with every shot fired down their own throats discovered, in boozy good will, that the other was a fine fellow.

Soon Bierce and London, with the disappointed spectators drifting back to their poker games, were standing at the bar with arms draped around each other's shoulders.

Later in the evening, according to Arnold Genthe, the photographer, he and Sterling, along with London and Bierce, left the

---

* A journalist present began his account, "Mr. Ambrose Bierce, the reddish [sic] haired vivisector of local reputations, met Comrade Jack London, special counsel for the enforcement of the United States Constitution, in a three-round bout at Bohemian Grove yesterday afternoon."[26]

bar for Sterling's camp and sat around a fire, talking and drinking until "none of us quite knew what we were talking about." Bierce's derby, Genthe recalled, was tipped over at an "alarming" angle.[27]

Around midnight the others decided to accompany Bierce back to his brother's cabin — a perilous journey for a quartet in their condition, since they had to negotiate the swift-running Russian River in a rowboat — largely because London couldn't bear to be parted from his new-found friend. They made it across the river, then proceeded along the railroad tracks above a steep embankment overlooking the river, all singing lustily and more or less in harmony. Bierce and London had their arms wrapped around each other's shoulders, with Bierce's hoary head nestling on London's shoulder.

Suddenly the other two heard London cry out: "Why, where the hell's Ambrose?"

On backtracking they found that Bierce's derby had fallen off his head and rolled down the embankment. Bierce had tumbled down after it and was found snoozing in a fern bed at the water's edge and "seemed content to lie there."[28]

The others helped him up the steep bank and hauled him to his brother's camp, where Bierce, whose stamina as a drinking man was remarkable even to such hardened boozers as London and Sterling, consumed a bottle of Martel's Three Star and talked the night away with London. In the morning Sterling found Bierce sleeping with his back against a tree trunk and his derby jammed over his forehead to keep the dawn light out, and London sprawled nearby.[29] No doubt the episode deserves its honored place in the long history of American literary drinking bouts. Bierce may not have been the most perceptive critic of American society, nor London its great novelist, but they would be hard to match as a two-man carousing team.

SEVENTEEN

Bierce and "My Dear Mencken"

MOST MEN of considerable talent break a path for others of greater or lesser significance. This path-breaking is usually unacknowledged, since their successors above all wish to be considered originals and gratitude, in any case, is seldom one of the more apparent virtues of literary men. The legacy of Ambrose Bierce would seem to include his contributions to the careers of H. L. Mencken and Sinclair Lewis, in particular, for their booming and relentless assaults in the 1920's on Mencken's "booboisie" and the Babbitts and Men Who Knew Coolidge of Lewis's imagination. Both selected the targets, such as Bible Belt fundamentalism, organized religion, general stupidity about politics and intellectual corruption, which Bierce had been aiming at a half-century before them. By then, of course, they were safer and more obvious targets thanks to Bierce's labors of enlightenment. An excellent recent monograph on Bierce's work remarks that Bierce's satire "finds an echo in H. L. Mencken and Sinclair Lewis" and "Certain scenes in *The Red Badge of Courage* and *A Farewell to Arms*, for example, remind us of Bierce. And a number of post-World War II novels have incidents recalling *In the Midst of Life*."[1] A number of other literary historians have noticed the similarity between Bierce and Mencken, in particular—among them Van Wyck Brooks, who observed that Mencken propounded many of Bierce's ideas "without his finesse and learning."

Mencken was rather shy about acknowledging whatever debt he may have owed Bierce, though he did concede that "For all our professed delight in and capacity for jocosity, we have produced so far but one genuine wit — Ambrose Bierce — and, save to a small circle, he remains unknown today."[2]

Mencken, no towering humanist himself, professed himself to be taken aback at the range and depth of Bierce's contempt for humanity and all its works. "So far in this life, indeed, I have encountered no more thorough-going cynic than Bierce was. His disbelief in man went even further than Mark Twain's; he was quite unable to imagine the heroic, in any ordinary sense. Nor, for that matter, the wise. Man, to him, was the most stupid and ignoble of animals. But at the same time the most amusing. Out of the spectacle of life about him he got an unflagging and Gargantuan joy. The obscene farce of politics delighted him. He was an almost amorous connoisseur of theology and theologians. He howled with mirth whenever he thought of a professor, a doctor or a husband."[3]

He did not lack a surgical objectivity when he set about dissecting the corpus of his predecessor's works. Bierce, he said, "followed Poe in most of his short stories" though was "less literary and more observant." His strong point, almost his only clear virtue as a writer, was his "devastating" wit. As both a critic and a storyteller Bierce suffered from serious infirmities: "Bierce's critical judgments were often silly, as when he put Longfellow above Whitman, and not infrequently they were strongly colored by personal considerations, as when he over-praised George Sterling's poem . . . He was too little read to be a sound critic of letters, and he lacked the capacity to separate the artist from the man . . . Writing of the trade he practiced all his life, he wrote like a somewhat saucy schoolma'am, and when another schoolma'am lifted his stuff the theft went almost undetected. His own style was extraordinarily tight and unresilient, and his fear of rhetoric often took all the life out of his ideas. His stories, despite their melodramatic effectiveness, begin to seem old-fashioned; they belong to the era before the short story ceased to be a formal intellectual exercise and became a transcript of life. The people in them simply do not live and breathe; Ring Lardner, whose manner Bierce would have detested, did a hundred times better in that direction. They are read today, not as literature, but as shockers. . . . Bierce's social criticism, like his literary criticism, was often amusing but seldom profound. It had, however, the virtue of being novel in its day, and so made its mark. He was the first American to lay about him with complete gusto . . . The timorousness of Mark Twain was not in him; no head was lofty enough to escape his furious thwack. Such berserk men have been rare in our history; the normal Americano, even when he runs amok, shows a considerable discretion. But there was no more discretion in Bierce than you would find in a runaway locomotive. Had he been a more cautious man, the professors of literature would be politer to him today."[4]

The personal link between Mencken and Bierce was the latter's friend Percival Pollard. Both Mencken and Pollard came from Baltimore and both served as literary critics for Colonel Mann's publications, Pollard for *Town Topics* and Mencken, on the floor below, for *Smart Set*, the editorship of which he took over with George Jean Nathan in 1911.

At first the relationship between Bierce and the much younger Mencken was mostly by correspondence and was based on their mutually savage delight in plucking examples of horrible writing out of the books they read. As one gourmet to another, Mencken would write Bierce: "Last night I struck one in which the heroine wants the hero to agree to preserve her virginity. He refuses and the marriage is postponed. A rival now sics a voluptuous wench upon him and he succumbs. Result: a hurry call for 606 [then the patented specific for arresting syphilis]. While he is being cured the rival marries the heroine and convinces her, by practical demonstration, that she was wrong about virginity. So she divorces him as a reward, marries the hero (cured by now), and the two go to the mat."[5]

Bierce and Mencken became closer acquainted in 1911 when

Pollard was stricken by his fatal illness. The approaching death of Pollard saddened Bierce more than most such events; he was losing his strongest advocate on the literary scene. Two years before, in his volume *Their Day in Court*, Pollard had praised Bierce as the great neglected genius of American letters. "He was the one commanding figure in America in our time," wrote Pollard, curiously relegating Bierce to the past tense. Side by side with Poe and Hawthorne, he was "sure to be heard of . . . when our living ears are stopped with clay." The fact that Bierce was his personal friend, he insisted, had nothing to do with this judgment. "Because he became my friend," Pollard concluded his chapter on Bierce, "was I to call his swans geese?"[6]

Pollard died in Baltimore on December 17, generally unloved to a degree remarkable even for a literary critic; the final ceremony, cremation, was attended by only a few persons. Among them were Bierce and Mencken. His friend's death, as was often the case, converted Bierce into a state of wild jocosity. As Mencken would recall almost fourteen years later:

"Bierce's conversation to and from the crematory was superb — a long series of gruesome and highly amusing witticisms. He had tales to tell of crematories that had caught fire and singed the mourners, of dead bibuli whose mortal remains had exploded, of widows guarding the fire all night to make sure that their husbands did not escape."

Bierce's mind was also hilariously engaged, on the surface, by suggestions for some practical use to which a critic's cinders might be put. Bierce, as Mencken recalled, "suggested that Pollard's ashes be moulded into bullets and shot at publishers, that they be presented to the library of the New York lodge of Elks, that they be mailed anonymously to Ella Wheeler Wilcox." To show his disdain for the presumed dignity of death, Bierce told his companion that he kept "the ashes of a near relative" on his writing desk. (It should be interpolated that both of Bierce's sons and his wife were sedately buried in California. Undoubtedly those were cigar ashes he kept on his table to enhance his reputation for ribaldry in the face of death.) "I suggested idly," Mencken wrote, "that the ceremonial urn must

be a formidable ornament." To which Bierce replied, "Urn, hell!
I keep them in a cigar box."[7]

It was all a false front, of course, for shortly thereafter he was
writing Sterling and admitting that he was "a bit broken up by
the death of Pollard . . . He had lost his mind, was paralyzed,
had his head cut open by the surgeons, and his sufferings were
unspeakable. Had he lived he would have been an idiot; so it is
all right — 'But, O, the difference to me!' "[8]

After the Pollard funeral, Bierce and Mencken saw each other
fairly frequently in New York and Washington. The latter
journeyed to Washington a number of times to linger at the bar
of the Army and Navy Club with Bierce.

The Bierce-Mencken correspondence, of which only Bierce's
portion is available, Mencken's letters being sealed for several
more years at this writing, indicated a growing friendship in the
year before Bierce enigmatically capped his career by vanishing
from life. At the outset Bierce addressed the younger man as
"Mr. Mencken," but in the last letters it was "My Dear
Mencken."

On May 1, 1913, in commenting on that fact that Mencken
had stopped by the Pacific colony and been repelled by it, he
wrote that "I too have visited Carmel and it left a yellowish taste
in my mouth." A short time later he was reproving Mencken for
insufficiently praising his ex-protégé in an article Mencken wrote
on George Sterling's poetry, but adding "I like the way you serve
up the poets." News of a fairly recent widow called forth his
usual acerb comment on the feminine nature: "Your news of
Mrs. Pollard surprises me. The last time I heard from her she
said she was coming to Baltimore soon, and asked me to go up
and meet her. And then she marries without my consent and
doesn't tell me about it! Alas, alas, for the fidelity of woman."

Mencken had proposed that Bierce join him on the staff of a
magazine which, as it happened, died stillborn. ". . . I fear I am
a bit too old and lazy for any regular connection with it — anything that would require consecutive work. I probably shall never
again write anything but stories, and then only when the spirit
moves me, or to fill a definite order. I *do* enjoy my idleness."

On April 25, 1913, he was already discussing his projected — and final — journey southward in a letter to Mencken. ". . . I shall go West later in the season — or rather Southwest — and may go into Mexico (where, thank God, there is something doing) and to South America. To that region if, in Mexico, I do not incur the mischance of standing against a wall to be shot."

He wrote of coming across two of Mencken's articles in *Smart Set* and was so enthusiastic that Mencken stood in imminent danger, it seemed, of being adopted as a Bierce protégé. "I like your work and want to tell you so; I had not known that you could write so devilish well. What particularly takes my attention and traps my approval is your view of the 'white slavery' — partly no doubt because of its conformity to my own notion, expounded many times in conversation but never written because I have now no 'organ' and don't write *anything*. Aside from that, your remarks are more than cleverly made — they charm."

On May 17, he was joshing Mencken on the title of the magazine he edited. "How would it be to start a mag. for women entitled *The Smart Sex?*" He added that he hoped Mencken wasn't annoyed by his flattery. "I hope you don't mind being 'discovered.' I have myself been discovered more frequently than any living writer, I think." He wanted to know "which of your books you are least ashamed of, that I may read it."

The last letter he wrote Mencken, dated May 25, 1913, thanked him for sending copies of his books: "they have delighted me." Mencken's attack on their mutual enemies and dislikes was "altogether admirable." The only fault he could find was that Mencken had been too "courtly" in his treatment of socialism. "I should myself not think of opposing a Socialist otherwise than by a cuff upon the mouth of him. . . . Observe that the fellow in jail for sending indecent matter through the mails is invariably a Socialist."

His final word to Mencken was a warning that "All the same, Socialism is going to get our goat."[9]

About a month later he was off on his roundabout journey, a sort of sightseeing tour of his past, to California, to the Southern battlefields of his youth, and finally to Mexico.

EIGHTEEN *"To Be a Gringo in Mexico..."*

THE GREATEST FAME that Ambrose Bierce achieved was by simply vanishing from life, whether deliberately or by mischance. Behind him he left the one thing guaranteed to keep him interesting to the rest of humanity — an unsolved mystery. As one of the more celebrated missing persons of history he joined the select spectral company of Judge Crater and Charlie Ross. He would have roared with Jovian laughter at that continuing irony of his nonexistence, to become more famous as a missing person than a living presence who did everything possible to call attention to himself. He would have been equally delighted that his disappearance caused the gainful employment of so many private investigators, freelance writers and others who set out to solve the mystery. For years an article introducing a new theory, no matter how fanciful, on what really happened to Bierce had a surefire sale in the magazines and newspapers. A truly amazing amount of nonsense was written on the subject. The palm, however, goes to Charles Fort (*Wild Talents*), who devoted his life to investigating various phenomena and explaining them to his own satisfaction. Mr. Fort noted that an Ambrose Small disappeared about the same time as Ambrose Bierce, and came up with the theory that some "daemonic" force was collecting Ambroses.

Almost everything, it seemed, was applied to the investigation except logic and good sense. Yet a few incontrovertible facts of his last few months in full view of his fellows speak clearer, if not louder, than all the rumors and the theories based on those rumors which have been collected in print. He was a man of seventy-one, ailing for years from asthma, which places a serious burden on the heart as well as the breathing apparatus. The alkali winds of the northern Mexico desert are not kindly to an asthmatic. He was fed up with life. He was an old man wandering around a countryside harsh in peacetime, terrible in the grip of a civil war. And he wrote of a man at his age and in his condition going to a Mexico in turmoil as a form of euthanasia.

If he did not actively seek death in the Mexican revolution, that death which had eluded him in his own war and which caused him to write enviously of those comrades it had claimed in their youth, at least he was not flinching from it. He was prepared to welcome it. Most significantly his daughter Helen, who did not approve of him but seemed to know him better than any of his other kinfolk, wrote of his attitude toward death: "When his hour struck he wanted to go quickly and with none of his friends near to look upon his face afterward."[1]

The last several months of his life, journeying to all the scenes of his earlier years except, with bitter significance, his family's home in Indiana, he was obviously taking leave of the past. All of it. He deliberately quarreled with George Sterling, the poet whose career had meant almost as much to him as his own, and even with his brother Albert, the only one he had remained on good terms with, and wrote them both off in such savage terms than neither was the same afterward. His last letter to Sterling addressed him as "Great Poet and Damned Scoundrel" and its tone, Sterling later wrote, was that of "God talking to a guttersnipe." The brutal last word to his brother, an amiable and even-tempered man whose affection Bierce had treasured since earliest childhood, was said to have hastened his death by apoplexy five months after it was received. Bierce's last will and testament to those he had loved was a characteristically bitter brew.

He left Washington in June of 1913, journeyed to California

and spent the summer there, even visiting St. Helena where he had lived with his wife and children during their brief years of domestic tranquillity. In September he returned East, stopping off in Bloomington, Illinois, to visit his daughter who, he wrote, "has a nice home, an auto and not many cares . . . And she didn't bore me with Christian Science."[2] With her he left a number of his personal papers for safekeeping. (Many of them ended up in the manuscript collection at the Huntington Library in San Marino, California, which was founded by the nephew of Collis P. Huntington.) He then returned to Washington to make final preparations for his trip south.

In all those final months in the United States he threw out hints of his purpose, many of which were contradictory but which could be summed up as an intense desire to get away permanently from a homeland he now detested. Many persons, later reconstructing his last words to them, must have asked themselves the question: Was he trying to tell us something? Perhaps. "Why," he demanded of his daughter, "should I remain in a country that is on the eve of prohibition and women's suffrage? . . . In America you can't go east or west any more, or north; the only avenue of escape is south . . . I'll take some letters [of introduction] with me and strike the border near El Paso. It will be easy enough to get along. I'm going to buy a donkey and hire a peon. I can see what's doing; perhaps write a few articles about the situation; and then pass to the West Coast of Mexico. From there I can go to South America, cross the Andes and ship to England. This fighting in Mexico interests me. I want to go down and see if these Mexicans shoot straight."[3]

To his nephew's wife Lora, however, he wrote in a more morbid vein: "If you should hear of my being stood up against a Mexican stone wall and shot to rags please know that I think it is a pretty good way to depart this life. It beats old age, disease or falling down the cellar stairs. To be a Gringo in Mexico — ah, that is euthanasia!"

He wrote Josephine McCrackin in a gentler vein, when she asked whether she might pray for him. "Why, yes, dear — that will not harm either of us. I loathe religions, a Christian gives me qualms and a Catholic sets my teeth on edge, but pray for me just the same, for with all those faults upon your head (it's a nice head, too) I am pretty fond of you, I guess. May you live as long as you want to, and then pass smilingly into the darkness, the good, good darkness."[4]

It was of course questionable whether he would seek the "good, good darkness" by the direct, suicidal route or that form of "euthanasia" which consists of placing oneself in the greatest possible danger of being killed. Yet he had often written approvingly of the idea of suicide, and it was a way out taken by many in the San Francisco literary world of the pre-World War I era. (Sterling and Scheffauer both killed themselves. So did Sterling's wife, despondent over his philandering. So did Jack London, in 1916, after making his own investigation of the Mexican revolution, finding it abhorrent and finally throwing over socialism because it tried to prevent United States intervention on the side of the Allies.) Twenty years before Bierce had written in a "Prattle" column that he agreed with Colonel Robert G. Ingersoll that suicide was an excellent remedy and too seldom used. "It is but a return to the wisdom of the ancients, in whose splendid civilization suicide had as honorable a place as any other courageous, reasonable and unselfish act. . . . The smug, self-righteous modern way of looking upon the act as that of a craven or a lunatic is the creation of priests, philistines and women. . . . No principle is involved in this matter; suicide is justifiable or not, according to the circumstances; each case is to be judged on its merits and he having the act under advisement is sole judge."[5]

In the essay titled "The Right to Take Oneself Off" in *The Shadow on the Dial*, he argued that "The time to quit is when you have lost a big stake, your fool hope of eventual success, your fortitude and your love of the game. If you stay in the game, which you are not compelled to do, take your losses in good temper and do not whine about them. They are hard to bear, but that is no reason why you should be."

Suicide, he maintained, is "always courageous." Many had a duty to end it all themselves; among whom he listed as candidates for self-destruction were those with an incurable disease,

those who were a burden to friends and family, those "irreclaim-
ably addicted to drunkenness or taking drugs," anyone who had
disgraced himself, one without "friends, property, employment
or hope." It was possible that he foresaw the time when he might
belong in one or more of those categories . . .

On October 2 he left Washington after sternly instructing
Carrie Christiansen, still his faithful unpaid secretary and sup-
porting herself by teaching in the public schools, to burn all the
letters he might send her on his journey.

For the next two weeks he toured the now green fields and
hills over which he and his comrades had fought a half-century
earlier: Shiloh, Stones River, Chickamauga, Kenesaw Mountain,
Franklin and Nashville. At each stop along the way he wrote
letters to Miss Christiansen, who dutifully destroyed them but
only after making notes on their contents.

On October 24, 1913, he arrived in New Orleans and was
interviewed by a reporter for the *States*, who described his eyes as
being "as blue and piercing as when they strove to see through
the smoke at Chickamauga" and as having "retained all the fire
of an indomitable fighter." Going over the old battlefields, he
told the reporter, convinced him that he "never amounted to
much since then," compared to his service as a soldier in the
Union army.

He was going to Mexico, he said, because "I like the game. I
like the fighting; I want to see it. And then I don't think Americans are as oppressed there as they say they are, and I want to get
at the true facts of the case.* Of course, I'm not going into the
country if I find it unsafe for Americans to be there, but I want
to take the trip diagonally across from northeast to southwest by
horseback, and then take shape for South America, go over the
Andes and across that continent, if possible, and come back to
America again.

"There is no family that I have to take care of; I've retired

---

* The Hearst papers then were proclaiming that Americans' property and
persons had been rendered unsafe by the Mexican revolution, and were
strongly advocating intervention. Hearst owned vast ranches and mining
interests in northern Mexico.

from writing and I'm going to take a rest. No, my trip isn't for local color. I've retired just as a merchant or businessman retires . . . But perhaps after I have rested I might work some more — I can't tell, there are so many things that might happen between now and when I come back . . ."

He reveled in the easygoing Creole atmosphere of New Orleans, even as he had as a young Treasury agent just after the Civil War, and considered it the loveliest of American cities, but pushed on to San Antonio, where, on October 27, he was given a dinner by old army friends at Fort Sam Houston. For several weeks he wandered up and down the border, almost as though hesitating over plunging in. On November 7 he was in Laredo and visited the nearby post at Fort McIntosh after writing his niece Lora, "There is a good deal of fighting going on over on the Mexican side of the Rio Grande, but I hold to my intention to go into Mexico if I can. In the character of 'innocent bystander' I ought to be fairly safe."[6] General Victoriano Huerta's troops, then representing the more or less legitimate government of Mexico, were guarding the bridge over the Rio Grande and preventing Americans from entering their country but he had heard that the border could be crossed at night, up or down the river, "almost anywhere." He added:

"I shall not be here long enough to hear from you, and don't know where I shall be next. Guess it doesn't matter much."

For some unknown reason Bierce left a trunk containing books and manuscripts in the hotel where he had been staying in Laredo. The trunk, according to his daughter, had simply disappeared from the hotel's storage room when she later tried to retrieve it.[7]

Late in November he finally crossed the border at Ciudad Juárez, across from El Paso, and was granted credentials as an observer with Pancho Villa's rebel army. Rail service was disrupted and he had to journey to Chihuahua, Villa's headquarters, on horseback. He was carrying at least fifteen hundred dollars in United States currency — almost an invitation to death in itself for a lone traveler through bandit-infested country in which law and order had vanished several years before. He arrived in Chihuahua City on December 16, eight days after it had been occupied by Villa's steeple-hatted legions.

At that point the Mexican revolution was simply a tigerish struggle for power among various contenders, none of them strong enough to seize it and hold it against his rivals. The revolution had begun with the overthrow of the dictator Porfirio Díaz. His successor was Francisco Madero, idealistic and ineffectual, who was murdered by his successor, the corrupt General Huerta. General Huerta had the will to win, but lacked the power to subdue the regional chiefs, Zapata in the south, Obregón in Sonora, Villa in Chihuahua. At present it was Villa, the robust bandit turned revolutionary, who was giving him the most trouble. Now Villa had taken the capital of Chihuahua State, and from there was preparing to strike north toward Ojinaga on the American border and Torreón far to the south.

At the time of Bierce's arrival in Chihuahua City, Villa's troop movements to the north had begun, train after train of boxcars swarming with his peon soldiery and their camp followers. The next big fight would be against the Federal garrison at Ojinaga, and Bierce evidently intended to be on hand to watch it. It was an exciting time, also a dangerous one. On Christmas Eve he sent a short letter to J. H. Dunnigan, an acquaintance of his, asking him to "pray for me — real loud."[8] If Bierce was suddenly turning religious, he must have felt the brush of premonition stronger than any that preceded it.

The last letter anyone received from him, also postmarked Chihuahua City and dated December 26, went to Carrie Christiansen in Washington. Before destroying it she noted its essence: "Trainload of troops leaving Chihuahua every day. Expect next day to go to Ojinaga, partly by rail."

After that, silence and mystery.

The sensible supposition would be that he did start for Ojinaga as he intended. Ojinaga is about one hundred twenty-five miles northeast of Chihuahua, across the Rio Grande from Presidio, Texas. It is possible that he caught a troop train and rode it as far as the gap in the rail sixty miles south of Ojinaga, from which he would have had to ride or walk — across the hot, dusty alkali plains — to join the Villa forces besieging the Huerta garrison. He could have arrived by the time the battle started, on January 1, 1914. The Villa forces, commanded by General Ortega, battered at Ojinaga with artillery and infantry assaults for seven days without taking the town. On January 7, Villa arrived on the scene and ordered the effort redoubled, though he had already lost a thousand men in the attacks. On January 10, the Federal garrison of four thousand slipped across the Rio Grande and was interned by the United States army while Villa occupied the shattered town. After that costly victory Villa returned to Chihuahua and began preparations for his successful descent upon the city of Torreón to the south, thus making himself supreme in the State of Chihuahua.

After Huerta was succeeded by General Venustiano Carranza in Mexico City, the Mexican government, at the request of the American government, made an investigation of Bierce's disappearance.* Carranza's investigator was a Major Gaston de Pridu, who showed a photograph of Bierce to many officers in Ortega's detachment of Villa's army. One of them, Second Captain Salvador Ibarra, identified it. Bierce, he said, had accompanied the Ortega detachment when it began the siege of Ojinaga; but he couldn't say what happened to Bierce.[9]

And that may well have been the soundest lead to Bierce's fate. An old man dying in the confusion of battle, then being dumped into an unmarked desert grave, would not have attracted much attention. Particularly if the person or persons who buried him found that money belt crammed with fifteen hundred dollars in American currency.

Of all the wild and wonderful stories that have cropped up since then, one of the earliest and most fantastic was the press report that Bierce had secretly gone to England, looked up Lord Kitchener, then war minister, and was advising him on how to conduct operations on the Western Front. Only the most diligent effort killed that rumor.

---

* That first inquiry was initiated by a letter from Carrie Christiansen in 1914 to Marion Letcher, United States consul in Chihuahua City.

The most persistent theme of all the later reports retailed in the newspapers and magazines was that Bierce joined Villa as a sort of staff officer, quarreled with him and was executed — "shot to rags against a Mexican stone wall," as Bierce himself had put it. This particular rumor would not die and kept cropping up, in different guises, in various "investigations" conducted through the years. It was first propounded by a correspondent named George F. Weeks, who admitted that he never saw Bierce or anyone resembling him around Villa's headquarters during the campaigning of 1914, in a story published in 1919. His story was that a Mexican officer told him Bierce was shot by orders of General Urbina, another of Villa's detachment commanders, in 1915. The next year the San Francisco *Bulletin* sent James H. Wilkins to conduct a thorough inquiry. The best he could do was to embroider on Weeks's theme. This time an unnamed informant, who claimed to have served with Villa, told of having accompanied a detachment which captured a Federal ammunition train. On it was a man he identified as Bierce, who was shot on the spot. Three years after that, in 1923, Dr. Danziger, who had now changed his name to De Castro, surfaced with a story that he had looked up Villa himself, then living in retirement, and badgered him until he admitted that he had had Bierce shot because he wanted to desert to Carranza's forces.*

All moonshine, of course, along with the stories peddled in the Twenties and Thirties by various "soldiers of fortune" who claimed to have served with or against Villa and had their own version, translated into salable prose by a ghost writer, of how Ambrose Bierce met a sudden and violent end.

After it appeared that Bierce would never turn up again, Carrie Christiansen left Washington and returned to California, set-

---

* Another interesting account of how Bierce met his death was contained in *20 Vibrantes Episodias de la Vida de Villa*, by Elias L. Torres (Mexico, D.F., 1934), a portion of which was translated by Miss Renée Quiroz of Texas Western College. Torres, who served with Villa and was close to him, wrote that Villa had Bierce shot to death after the latter announced that he was going over to the Constitutionalist (Carranza) side. After he was shot, by Torres's account, Villa smiled and remarked, "Let's see if this damned American tells his last joke to the buzzards on the mountain." The Torres account is generally believed in Mexico.

tling down at Napa, in the foothills where she first met Bierce. The fact that there was and is a state hospital for the insane at Napa gave rise to rumors that Bierce had never really journeyed to Mexico but had gone mad and been confined to the Napa hospital, that Miss Christiansen had moved there to be close to him. A search of the hospital records finally quieted that rumor.

Obviously Bierce never got close enough to Villa to incur his wrath and be shot by him or on his orders. If there was one thing Bierce detested more than a Socialist it was a revolutionary. That Bierce would "offer his services" to one is ridiculous. So is the suggestion that Villa would recruit a staff officer of seventy-one years, suffering from asthma, whose last military experience was almost fifty years in the past.

If he had been attached to Villa's headquarters, even as an "observer," for more than a few days, certainly he would have been noticed by one of the United States war correspondents accompanying Villa's forces, a group that included Frederick Palmer, Floyd Gibbons, John Reed, Gregory Mason, George Clements, William A. Willis and Edmund S. Behr. None of those reputable journalists remembered seeing or hearing of Bierce, except at secondhand. Gregory Mason recalled that two of the correspondents in the group became interested in trying to find out what happened to Bierce, a year or so after he disappeared, and that one of them told him "some Mexicans along our line of travel had seen an old gringo with a white beard who had come down to fight with Villa against the Federales" and "hopefully declared this *must* have been Bierce."[10] The only trouble with that report was that Bierce did not have a beard, white or otherwise. Timothy Turner, who was the Associated Press correspondent with Villa during the advance on Torreón, wrote a book about it but refrained from speculating on the Bierce disappearance, "being an honest man and refusing to play on my imagination," as he recalled in 1957.[11]

Another man who would have known if Bierce had joined Villa, as a number of Americans had, was George Carothers, a State Department representative. Carothers was attached to

Villa's headquarters at a time when the United States was hopeful that Villa would become less anti-American. He never saw or heard of Bierce, but once asked Villa if he knew anything about him. Villa, one of whose virtues was a brutal frankness, simply replied that he couldn't remember any such person.* Some years later the State Department launched an inquiry, as thorough as possible at that late date, part of which consisted in showing Bierce's photograph to twelve men who had been close to Villa. None of them could identify it.[12]

The search for some tangible evidence of what happened to Bierce has continued, against all discouragements, into the present.

A little more than two years after Bierce vanished, the United States, retaliating for Villa's raid on Columbus, New Mexico, sent a ten-thousand-man punitive expedition into Mexico under General John J. Pershing. No member of that expeditionary force, so far as is known, came across any clue to Bierce during the months of campaigning throughout the State of Chihuahua. Recently Professor Haldeen Braddy of Texas Western College at El Paso, a leading authority on the Pershing expedition and an expert on the Bierce disappearance, sent a questionnaire to all surviving members of the punitive force and the Villistas opposed to them while doing research for a history of the 1916 campaign. One of the questions he asked was, "What were Villa's true inner feelings about such Americans as Tracy Richardson, Ambrose Bierce, Sam Dreben and other adventurers?" None of the men circularized could supply a scrap of information, not even a fresh rumor, about any connection Bierce might have had with Villa.

Nor has Villa's last surviving wife, Señora Soledad Seanez de Villa, of Ciudad Juárez, been able to recall that Villa ever mentioned Ambrose Bierce.

All that is known for sure is that Bierce was in Chihuahua the day after Christmas 1913 and that he had announced his inten-

---

* An investigation was also conducted by Major General Frederick Funston, commanding the United States forces along the border, when reports began circulating that Bierce had disappeared.

tion of joining the movement on Ojinaga. It is likely that he did set out for the beleaguered town on the border. It is possible that he reached the scene of battle. But the trail really ends in Chihuahua City the day after Christmas.

Of all who have investigated the few facts and analyzed their possible significance, Edward H. Smith, whose speciality was missing men, probably came up with the most sensible conclusion: "My own guess is that he started out to fight battles and shoulder hardships as he had done when a boy, somehow believing that a tough spirit would carry him through. Wounded or stricken with a disease, he probably lay down in some pesthouse of a hospital, some troop train filled with other stricken men. Or he may have crawled off to some waterhole and died, with nothing more articulate than the winds and stars for witness."[13]

It was at least a fitting end for Ambrose Bierce. Perhaps he chose it himself, as much as any man can. It had just the right touch of sardonic unconcern.

Yet there could have been a happier ending, such as Bierce seldom wished upon any of his fictional characters. It might go something like this: Instead of going off to see one more ghastly fracas between human beings who had little idea of what they were fighting about, he slipped away from Chihuahua City and headed south, east or west. Then, on reaching the coast, he took a ship bound for South America. On arrival he struck out for some village high in the Andes, where the sun and clear air would be kindly to his asthma. And there he lived out his days. The inevitable dullness of his days would be relieved, from time to time, by contemplating fresh evidence of the fame he had won, greater than in forty years of literary striving, by simply not being around any more. After some years of the peace hitherto denied him, he finally met that unseen character in most of his stories, Death.

That was an ending only a well-wisher could contrive for him. Bierce would have scorned it as bad art.

Notes

1. THE FIRST DISASTER

1 From his column in the *Wasp*, November 3, 1883.
2 Data on Bierce ancestry has been collected by the Connecticut State Library.
3 The anecdote is told in Carey McWilliams, *Ambrose Bierce*.
4 The subject of Spiritualism in Ohio is covered in Emma Hardinge, *Modern American Spiritualism*. An account of the Abby Warner trial was published in the Cleveland *Plain Dealer*, December 28, 1851.
5 Letter of Albert Bierce to his sister Alameda, July 20, 1909.
6 Bierce column in San Francisco *News-Letter*, October 2, 1869.
7 San Francisco *Examiner* column, January 8, 1899.
8 Walter Neale, *Life of Ambrose Bierce*.
9 *Ibid.*
10 McWilliams, *op. cit.*
11 San Francisco *Examiner* column, May 9, 1897.
12 Akron *Beacon*, December 7, 1859.
13 Carey McWilliams, "Ambrose Bierce and His First Love," an article in the *Bookman*, June 1932.

2. IN THE MIDST OF WAR

1 Marcus Cunliffe, afterword to the Signet Classic edition (1961) of *In the Midst of Life*, originally *Tales of Soldiers and Civilians*.
2 Indianapolis *Journal*, July 27, 1861.
3 "On a Mountain," *Collected Works*, Vol. I.
4 *Ibid.*
5 "The Crime at Pickett's Mill," *Collected Works*, Vol. I.
6 "What I Saw of Shiloh," *Collected Works*, Vol. I.
7 *Ibid.*
8 *Ibid.*
9 Elkhart *Review*, December 20, 1862; February 21, 1863; and February 28, 1863.

10 Article by Maurice Frink, 1952 *Brand Book*, published by the Westerners, Denver.
11 *Argonaut*, December 21, 1878.
12 "One Kind of Officer," *Collected Works*, Vol. I.
13 "The Crime at Pickett's Mill," *op. cit.*
14 "A Little of Chickamauga," *Collected Works*, Vol. I.
15 *Ibid.*
16 *Ibid.*
17 Bierce column, *Wasp*, February 13, 1886.
18 *Examiner*, November 14, 1888.
19 Carey McWilliams, "Ambrose Bierce and His First Love," *Bookman*, June 1932.
20 "The Crime at Pickett's Mill," *op. cit.*
21 Carey McWilliams, "Ambrose Bierce and His First Love," *op. cit.*
22 "Four Days in Dixie," *Collected Works*, Vol. I.
23 *Ibid.*
24 "What Occurred at Franklin," *Collected Works*, Vol. I.
25 *Ibid.*
26 *Examiner*, August 17, 1890.

3. WITHOUT A CARPETBAG TO HIS NAME

1 "Way Down in Alabam," *Collected Works*, Vol. I.
2 *Ibid.*
3 *Ibid.*
4 *Ibid.*
5 *Ibid.*
6 *Examiner*, May 9, 1897.
7 Notes from Bierce's Civil War notebook.
8 "Way Down in Alabam," *op. cit.*
9 "Across the Plains," *Collected Works*, Vol. I.
10 *Ibid.*
11 *Ibid.*
12 "A Sole Survivor," *Collected Works*, Vol. I.
13 "Across the Plains," *op. cit.*
14 *Wasp*, September 2, 1881.
15 *Argonaut*, May 31, 1879.
16 "Across the Plains," *op. cit.*

4. SAN FRANCISCO: FIRST INTERLUDE

1 "Across the Plains," *Collected Works*, Vol. I.
2 *Ibid.*
3 Carey McWilliams, *Ambrose Bierce*.
4 *Argonaut*, March 9, 1878.
5 Oscar Lewis, *Bay Window Bohemia*.
6 *Examiner*, January 22, 1893.
7 Franklin Walker, *San Francisco's Literary Frontier*.
8 Mock prayers included in the collection *Nuggets and Dust*.

9 Paul Jordan-Smith, *On Strange Altars.*
10 *Examiner*, March 3, 1899.
11 *News-Letter*, February 19, 1870.
12 Adolphe Danziger, *Portrait of Ambrose Bierce.*
13 *News-Letter*, February 5, 1870, as quoted by Paul Fatout in *Ambrose Bierce: The Devil's Lexicographer.*
14 Bierce to Stoddard, Huntington Library collection of Bierce's letters.
15 Fatout, *op. cit.*
16 Bierce to Stoddard, January 5, 1872, Huntington Library collection.
17 Poem quoted in Carey McWilliams, *Ambrose Bierce.*

5. A SEA CHANGE OR TWO

1 *News-Letter*, March 9, 1872.
2 *Argonaut*, February 9, 1879.
3 *Wasp*, February 14, 1885.
4 Walter Neale, *Life of Ambrose Bierce.*
5 Adolphe Danziger, *Portrait of Ambrose Bierce.*
6 *Ibid.*
7 *Examiner*, September 4, 1887.
8 *Alta California*, October 3, 1872.
9 Bierce to Stoddard, Huntington Library collection.
10 *Ibid.*
11 Bierce to Stoddard, September 28, 1872, Huntington Library collection.
12 Carey McWilliams, *Ambrose Bierce.*
13 Danziger, *op. cit.*
14 *Argonaut*, April 6, 1878.
15 "Working for an Empress," *Collected Works*, Vol. I.
16 *Ibid.*
17 *Ibid.*
18 *Ibid.*
19 *Ibid.*
20 *Ibid.*
21 *Ibid.*
22 Danziger, *op. cit.*
23 Harold T. Wilkins, *Strange Mysteries of Time and Space.*
24 "A Sole Survivor," *Collected Works*, Vol. I.
25 Bierce to Stoddard, quoted in Carey McWilliams, *Ambrose Bierce.*

6. AN UNCOMMONLY ACERB PRATTLER

1 Clifton Fadiman, introduction to *The Collected Writings of Ambrose Bierce.*
2 "The Socialist—What He Is and Why," *Collected Works*, Vol. IX.
3 Paul Fatout, *Ambrose Bierce: The Devil's Lexicographer.*
4 Carey McWilliams, *Ambrose Bierce.*
5 Adolphe Danziger, *Portrait of Ambrose Bierce.*
6 *Ibid.*
7 *Ibid.*
8 *Ibid.*

9 Introduction to *Selections from Prattle*, edited by Carroll D. Hall.
10 *Argonaut*, May 26, 1877.
11 Jerome Hart, *In Our Second Century*.
12 *Argonaut*, May 18, 1878.
13 *Ibid.*, April 1, 1877.
14 *Ibid.*, June 23, 1877.
15 *Ibid.*, February 2, 1878.
16 Carey McWilliams, *Ambrose Bierce*.
17 *Argonaut*, October 12, 1878.
18 *Ibid.*, April 22, 1877.
19 Carey McWilliams, *Ambrose Bierce*.
20 *Argonaut*, April 27, 1878.

7. INTERLUDE IN ROCKERVILLE

1 Robert J. Casey, *The Black Hills*.
2 Carey McWilliams, *Ambrose Bierce*.
3 *Ibid.*
4 Quoted by Paul Fatout in his *Ambrose Bierce and the Black Hills*.
5 "A Sole Survivor," *Collected Works*, Vol. I.
6 *Ibid.*
7 *Ibid.*
8 *Ibid.*
9 Paul Fatout, *Ambrose Bierce and the Black Hills*.
10 *Ibid.*
11 Adolphe Danziger, *Portrait of Ambrose Bierce*.

8. ALMIGHTY GOD BIERCE

1 "Epigrams," *Collected Works*, Vol. VIII.
2 C. Hartley Grattan, *Bitter Bierce*, one of the four Bierce biographies published in 1929, which included McWilliams, Danziger and Neale, by a freakish coincidence.
3 "Prudery in Letters and Life," *Collected Works*, Vol. VIII.
4 *Ibid.*
5 Quoted by Carey McWilliams, *Ambrose Bierce*.
6 *Ibid.*
7 Adolphe Danziger, *Portrait of Ambrose Bierce*.
8 Carey McWilliams, *Ambrose Bierce*.
9 *Examiner*, September 3, 1889.
10 *Wasp*, June 24, 1881.
11 New York *Sun*, December 29 and 30, 1883.
12 *Wasp*, April 9, 1881.
13 *Ibid.*, October 21, 1881.
14 Carey McWilliams, *Ambrose Bierce*.
15 Danziger, *op. cit.*
16 Vincent Starrett, *Buried Caesars*.
17 *Examiner*, July 11, 1897.
18 *Wasp*, December 5, 1885.

19 Helen Bierce, "Ambrose Bierce at Home," *American Mercury*, December 1933.

9. A HEARSTLING IS BORN

1 William A. Swanberg, *Citizen Hearst*.
2 Mrs. Fremont Older, *William Randolph Hearst, American*.
3 "A Thumbnail Sketch," *Collected Works*, Vol. XII.
4 Swanberg, *op. cit.*
5 Oscar Lewis, *The Big Four*.
6 Swanberg, *op. cit.*
7 Jerome Hart, *In Our Second Century*.
8 *Examiner*, March 18, 1888.
9 *Ibid.*, September 18, 1887.
10 Edmond D. Conlentz, *Ambrose Bierce, Stepfather of the Family* (a pamphlet).
11 Vincent Starrett, *Buried Caesars*.
12 C. Hartley Grattan, *Bitter Bierce*.
13 *Collected Works*, Vol. XI.
14 *Examiner*, November 17, 1887.
15 *Ibid.*, November 30, 1887.
16 "Epigrams," *Collected Works*, Vol. VIII.
17 Helen Bierce, "Ambrose Bierce at Home," *American Mercury*, December 1933.
18 *Ibid.*
19 *Ibid.*
20 "Epigrams," *op. cit.*
21 Helen Bierce, *op. cit.*
22 Chico *Enterprise*, August 12, 1889.
23 Account of Day Bierce's death, Chico *Enterprise*, July 26, 1889; San Francisco *Examiner*, July 27, 1889.
24 Chico *Enterprise*, July 27, 1889.
25 *Argonaut*, August 5, 1889.
26 Carey McWilliams, *Ambrose Bierce*.

10. "NOTHING MATTERS"

1 *Examiner*, October 19 and 26, 1890.
2 *Collected Works*, Vol. X.
3 *Examiner*, October 12, 1890.
4 *Ibid.*, November 8, 1891.
5 *Ibid.*, March 23, 1890.
6 "Epigrams," *Collected Works*, Vol. VIII.
7 Quoted by C. Hartley Grattan, *Bitter Bierce*.
8 Gertrude Atherton, *Adventures of a Novelist*.
9 *Ibid.*
10 *Ibid.*
11 Carey McWilliams, *Ambrose Bierce*.
12 Robert A. Wiggins, *Ambrose Bierce* (a pamphlet).

13 Joseph Lewis French article, *Pearson's* magazine, August 1918.
14 Atherton, *op. cit.*
15 Walter Neale, *Life of Ambrose Bierce.*
16 William A. Swanberg, *Citizen Hearst.*
17 Quoted in Adolphe Danziger, *Portrait of Ambrose Bierce.*
18 Carey McWilliams, *Ambrose Bierce.*

11.   "DEAR MASTER"

1 C. Hartley Grattan, *Bitter Bierce.*
2 Gertrude Atherton, *Advantures of a Novelist.*
3 Joseph Lewis French article, *Pearson's* magazine, August 1918.
4 Grattan, *op. cit.*
5 Adolphe Danziger, *Portrait of Ambrose Bierce.*
6 Grattan, *op. cit.*
7 Danziger, *op. cit.*
8 *Ibid.*
9 Carey McWilliams, *Ambrose Bierce.*
10 *Jack London: A Biography*, by the author.
11 *New Masses*, November 1926.
12 George Sterling, introduction to *The Letters of Ambrose Bierce.*
13 *Ibid.*
14 Danziger, *op. cit.*
15 *Examiner*, August 30, 1891.
16 Danziger, *op. cit.*
17 *Examiner*, May 8, 1892.
18 *Ibid.*, July 3, 1893.
19 *Ibid.*, July 23, 1893.
20 *Ibid.*
21 *Ibid.*, August 13, 1893.
22 Danziger, *op. cit.*
23 *Ibid.*
24 Carey McWilliams, *Ambrose Bierce.*
25 Danziger, *op. cit.*
26 *McEwen's Letter*, May 25, 1895.

12.   "HOW MY FAME RINGS OUT"

1 Paul Fatout, *Ambrose Bierce: The Devil's Lexicographer.*
2 Clifton Fadiman, introduction to *The Collected Writings of Ambrose Bierce.*
3 Thomas Beer, *The Mauve Decade.*
4 *Ibid.*
5 Clifton Fadiman, *op. cit.*
6 Vincent Starrett, *Buried Caesars.*
7 *Ibid.*
8 Bierce to Blanche Partington, *The Letters of Ambrose Bierce.*
9 *Jack London: A Biography*, by the author.
10 *Examiner*, May 20, 1894.

11 *Ibid.*, March 4, 1894.
12 *Ibid.*, March 11, 1894.
13 "On Trusts," *Collected Works*, Vol. IX.
14 "On Newspapers," *ibid.*
15 "The Socialist—What He Is and Why," *ibid.*
16 Oscar Lewis, *The Big Four.*
17 Mark Sullivan, *Our Times*, Vol. II.
18 William A. Swanberg, *Citizen Hearst.*
19 The poem was published in the *Examiner*, January 15, 1899.
20 *Examiner*, January 22, 1899.
21 Bailey Millard, "Personal Memories," *Bookman*, February 1915.

13. DON AMBROSIO CRUSADES AGAINST THE "RAILROGUES"

1 *Examiner*, February 1, 1896.
2 Quoted in Adolphe Danziger, *Portrait of Ambrose Bierce.*
3 *Examiner*, February 22, 1896.
4 *Congressional Record*, 54th Congress, 2nd Session, Part I.
5 *Congressional Record, op. cit.*
6 Paul Fatout, *Ambrose Bierce: The Devil's Lexicographer.*
7 Willis J. Abbot's autobiography, *Watching the World Go By.*
8 *Examiner*, January 10, 1897.
9 *Hampton's* magazine, September 1910.

14. A LESS THAN TOTAL PATRIOT

1 *The Shadow on the Dial.*
2 *Examiner*, August 7, 1898.
3 *Ibid.*, July 31, 1898.
4 *The Shadow on the Dial.*
5 Bierce to S. O. Howes, May 14, 1899, Huntington Library collection.
6 Bierce to S. O. Howes, November 29, 1899, Huntington Library collection.
7 *Examiner*, December 14, 1898.
8 *Ibid.*, January 14, 1900.
9 Essay in *The Shadow on the Dial.*
10 *Ibid.*
11 *Ibid.*
12 *Ibid.*
13 *Ibid.*
14 Bierce to Amy Cecil, January 2, 1901, quoted in Carey McWilliams, *Ambrose Bierce.*
15 Quoted by Paul Fatout, *Ambrose Bierce: The Devil's Lexicographer.*
16 Quoted by Adolphe Danziger, *Portrait of Ambrose Bierce.*
17 Carey McWilliams, *Ambrose Bierce.*
18 Bierce to Danziger, September 28, 1900, in Danziger, *op. cit.*
19 Bierce to Danziger, December 12, 1900, in Danziger, *op. cit.*
20 Walter Neale, *Life of Ambrose Bierce.*

21 Helen Bierce, "Ambrose Bierce at Home," *American Mercury*, December 1933.

15. THE BULLET THAT SPED EAST

1 William A. Swanberg, *Citizen Hearst.*
2 "A Thumbnail Sketch," *Collected Works*, Vol. XII.
3 *Ibid.*
4 Mark Sullivan, *Our Times*, Vol. III.
5 "A Thumbnail Sketch," *op. cit.*
6 Walter Neale, *Life of Ambrose Bierce.*
7 Helen Bierce, "Ambrose Bierce at Home," *American Mercury*, December 1933.
8 Neale, *op. cit.*
9 *Ibid.*
10 Quoted in Carey McWilliams, *Ambrose Bierce.*
11 *Overland Monthly*, November 1903.
12 Jerome Hart, *In Our Second Century.*
13 Dale L. Walker, introduction to *A Wine of Wizardry*, privately published.
14 Bierce to George Sterling, February 5, 1904, *The Letters of Ambrose Bierce.*
15 *Ibid.*
16 Jerome Hart, *In Our Second Century.*
17 *Cosmopolitan*, May 1906.
18 Bierce to George Sterling, February 18, 1905, *The Letters of Ambrose Bierce.*
19 Bierce to George Sterling, December 3, 1905, *ibid.*
20 Bierce to George Sterling, June 16, 1905, *ibid.*

16. AN UNDERGROUND REPUTATION

1 Quoted in Carey McWilliams, *Ambrose Bierce.*
2 *Cosmopolitan*, December 1905.
3 Bierce to Robert Mackay, August 20, 1906, Huntington Library collection.
4 The debate was extensively covered in *Cosmopolitan*, July 1906.
5 Bierce to George Sterling, August 11, 1906, *The Letters of Ambrose Bierce.*
6 *Cosmopolitan*, September 1907.
7 *Ibid.*, December 1907.
8 Bierce to Herman Scheffauer, *The Letters of Ambrose Bierce.*
9 *Examiner*, July 26, 1896.
10 Andy Logan, *The Man Who Robbed the Robber Barons.*
11 Percival Pollard, *Their Day in Court.*
12 H. L. Mencken, *A Book of Prefaces.*
13 Bierce to S. O. Howes, February 19, 1909, Huntington Library collection.
14 Quoted in Carey McWilliams, *Ambrose Bierce.*
15 Bierce to S. O. Howes, February 19, 1907, Huntington Library collection.

16 Quoted in Carey McWilliams, *Ambrose Bierce.*

17 William A. Swanberg, *Citizen Hearst.*

18 Walter Neale, *Life of Ambrose Bierce.*

19 "A Mad World," *Collected Works,* Vol. XII.

20 "A Thumbnail Sketch," *Collected Works,* Vol. XII.

21 *Twenty-one Letters of Ambrose Bierce,* edited by Samuel Loveman.

22 Bierce to S. O. Howes, March 7, 1910, Huntington Library collection.

23 Bierce to Lora Bierce, November 11, 1910, *The Letters of Ambrose Bierce.*

24 Mary Austin, "George Sterling at Carmel," *American Mercury,* May 1927.

25 *American Mercury,* October 1925.

26 J. B. Cassell in the San Francisco *Bulletin,* undated clipping.

27 Arnold Genthe's autobiography, *As I Remember.*

28 *Ibid.*

29 George Sterling account in *American Mercury,* October 1925.

17.   BIERCE AND "MY DEAR MENCKEN"

1 Robert A. Wiggins, *Ambrose Bierce* (a pamphlet).

2 Quoted by C. Hartley Grattan, *Bitter Bierce.*

3 H. L. Mencken, *Prejudices: Sixth Series.*

4 *Ibid.*

5 Quoted in Carey McWilliams, *Ambrose Bierce.*

6 Percival Pollard, *Their Day in Court.*

7 New York *World,* March 1, 1925.

8 Bierce to Sterling, December 27, 1911, *The Letters of Ambrose Bierce.*

9 The letters from Bierce to H. L. Mencken were supplied by Betty Adler of the Enoch Pratt Free Library in Baltimore.

18.   "TO BE A GRINGO IN MEXICO . . ."

1 Helen Bierce, "Ambrose Bierce at Home," *American Mercury,* December 1933.

2 Bierce to Lora Bierce, November 12, 1912, Huntington Library collection.

3 Quoted in Carey McWilliams, *Ambrose Bierce.*

4 Bierce to Josephine McCrackin, September 13, 1913, *The Letters of Ambrose Bierce.*

5 Quoted in Adolphe Danziger, *Portrait of Ambrose Bierce.*

6 Bierce to Lora Bierce, November 6, 1913, Huntington Library collection.

7 Article in *Esquire,* February 1936, by Tom Mahoney, then a reporter in El Paso, who undertook a thorough investigation of all the Bierce disappearance reports.

8 *Ibid.*

9 *Ibid.*

10 Letter from Gregory Mason to Haldeen Braddy, June 17, 1957.

11 Letter from Tim Turner to Haldeen Braddy, June 13, 1957.

12 Undated clipping from *El Heraldo de Chihuahua,* University of Chihuahua Library.

13 Edward H. Smith, *Mysteries of the Missing.*

Some Observations of Ambrose Bierce

On public and private morality:
The gambling known as business looks with austere disfavor upon the business known as gambling.

If man's notions of right and wrong have any other basis than this of expediency; if they originated, or could have originated, in any other way; if actions have in themselves a moral character apart from, and nowise dependent on, their consequences — then all philosophy is a lie and reason a disorder of the mind.

Christians and camels receive their burdens kneeling.

The money-getter who pleads his love of work has a lame defense, for love of work at money-getting is a lower taste than love of money.

One whose falsehoods no longer deceive has forfeited the right to tell the truth.

*　*　*　*

On modern music:
They are experimenting in New York with modern music as a cure for madness.

> If modern music cures the mind
> The remedy cannot be had

> For that — though I grieve to say it —
> Requires a lunatic to play it.

*   *   *   *

On women:

To woman a general truth has neither value nor interest unless she can make a particular application of it. And we say that women are not practical!

Empty wine-bottles have a bad opinion of women.

When God makes a beautiful woman, the devil opens a new register.

Do not permit a woman to ask forgiveness, for that is only the first step. The second is justification of herself by accusation of you.

If women did the writing of the world, instead of the talking, men would be regarded as the superior sex in beauty, grace and goodness.

A virtuous woman is the most loyal of mortals; she is faithful to that which is neither pleased nor profited by her fidelity.

Remembering that it was a woman who lost the world, we should accept the act of cackling geese in saving Rome as partial reparation.

In order that the list of able women may be memorized for use at meetings, Heaven has considerately made it brief.

Women and foxes, being weak, are distinguished by superior tact.

*   *   *   *

On love and marriage:

Love is a delightful day's journey. At the farther end kiss your companion and say farewell.

A bad marriage is like an electric thrilling-machine: it makes you dance, but you can't let go.

*   *   *   *

On the human condition:
Cheerfulness is the religion of the little.

Gratitude is a dog licking the hand of the bread-giver. There may be a few crumbs adhering to the fingers.

Let him who would wish to duplicate his every experience prate of the value of life.

If public opinion were determined by a throw of the dice, it would in the long run be half the time right.

To the eye of failure success is an accident with a presumption of crime.

From childhood to youth is eternity; from youth to manhood, a season. Age comes in a night, and is incredible.

Acknowledgments

BY ONE of those coincidences which give publishers an occasional nightmare, four books about Ambrose Bierce
were published in one year, 1929. They were written by Carey
McWilliams (*Ambrose Bierce: A Biography*), who was given
cooperation by the Bierce family; by C. Hartley Grattan (*Bitter
Bierce*), who concerned himself mainly with his subject's work;
Adolphe Danziger (De Castro) whose *Portrait of Ambrose Bierce*
was a collation of reminiscence and rumor, some of it far off the
mark; and Walter Neale (*Life of Ambrose Bierce*), who was
Bierce's publisher and knew him well in his later years. There
has also been an excellent later work, Professor Paul Fatout's
Ambrose Bierce: The Devil's Lexicographer, published in 1951.
To all of these works the author is greatly indebted.

I was also assisted in many ways, and without stint, by my
friends Dale L. Walker and Dr. Haldeen Braddy of the University of Texas at El Paso. Dr. Braddy's thesis for his master's
degree was on the subject of Bierce. Both helped me as though
the work were their own; neither bears any responsibility for the
use I made of their contributions.

I am also indebted to the following persons and institutions:
Mary Isabel Fry and Janet Hawkins of the Huntington Library

at San Marino, California, where most of the Bierce papers are collected.

Tom Caton, city editor, and Agness Underwood, assistant managing editor of the Los Angeles *Herald-Examiner*, and Jack C. Smith of the Los Angeles *Times*.

Jack Wallace, Sunday editor of the San Francisco *Examiner*, which published so much of Bierce's newspaper work.

Samuel Stark, the San Francisco theater historian.

Dr. James De T. Abajian of the California Historical Society in San Francisco.

Betty Adler of the Enoch Pratt Free Library, Baltimore, for letters from Bierce to H. L. Mencken.

The Berg Collection of the New York Public Library.

Mrs. Frances Buxton of the California Room of the Oakland Public Library.

Ralph W. Ashley, curator of the Charlotte Ashley Felton Library of Stanford University.

J. R. K. Kantor, the reference librarian of the Bancroft Library, University of California at Berkeley.

Robert Woodward, of the Bangor Public Library, who was of great help in obtaining books on loan from other libraries.

Donald C. Gallup, curator of the Collection of American Literature at Yale University.

Miss A. J. Lewis, Department of Manuscripts at the British Museum.

Selected Bibliography

Abbot, Willis J., *Watching the World Go By*, Boston, 1933.
Atherton, Gertrude, *Adventures of a Novelist*, New York, 1932.
Beer, Thomas, *The Mauve Decade*, New York, 1926.
Bierce, Ambrose, *Can Such Things Be?*, New York, 1893.
———, *Cobwebs from an Empty Skull*, London, 1874.
———, *Collected Works* (12 volumes), New York, 1909–1912.
———, *Fantastic Fables*, New York, 1899.
———, *The Fiend's Delight*, London, 1872.
———, *The Shadow on the Dial* (edited by S. O. Howes), San Francisco, 1909.
———, *Shapes of Clay*, San Francisco, 1909.
———, *Tales of Soldiers and Civilians*, San Francisco, 1891.
———, *Twenty-one Letters of Ambrose Bierce* (edited by Samuel Loveman), Cleveland, 1922.
Brooks, Van Wyck, *Emerson and Others*, New York, 1927.
Casey, Robert J., *The Black Hills*, Indianapolis, 1949.
Cummins, Ella Sterling, *The Story of the Files*, San Francisco, 1893.
Danziger, Adolphe, *Portrait of Ambrose Bierce*, New York, 1929.
Fatout, Paul, *Ambrose Bierce: The Devil's Lexicographer*, Norman, Okla., 1951.
———, *Ambrose Bierce and the Black Hills*, Norman, Okla., 1956.
Grattan, C. Hartley, *Bitter Bierce*, New York, 1929.
Hall, Carroll D. (editor), *Selections from Prattle*, San Francisco, 1936.
Hardinge, Emma, *Modern American Spiritualism*, New York, 1869.
Hart, Jerome A., *In Our Second Century*, San Francisco, 1931.
Hazen, W. B., *A Narrative of Military Service*, Boston, 1885.
Jordan-Smith, Paul, *On Strange Altars*, New York, 1924.
Lewis, Oscar, *Bay Window Bohemia*, New York, 1956.
———, *The Big Four*, New York, 1938.
Logan, Andy, *The Man Who Robbed the Robber Barons*, New York, 1965.
Lovecraft, Howard Phillips, *Supernatural Horror in Literature*, New York, 1945.
McWilliams, Carey, *Ambrose Bierce: A Biography*, New York, 1929.

Mencken, H. L., *Prejudices: Sixth Series*, New York, 1927.
Murdock, Charles A., *A Backward Glance at Eighty*, San Francisco, 1921.
Neale, Walter, *Life of Ambrose Bierce*, New York, 1929.
Noel, Joseph, *Footloose in Arcadia*, New York, 1940.
O'Connor, Richard, *Bret Harte: A Biography*, Boston, 1966.
———, *Jack London: A Biography*, Boston, 1964.
Older, Mrs. Fremont, *William Randolph Hearst*, New York, 1936.
Parry, Albert, *Garrets and Pretenders*, New York, 1933.
Pollard, Percival, *Their Day in Court*, New York, 1909.
Rice, Harvey, *Pioneers of the Western Reserve*, New York, 1888.
Smith, Edward H., *Mysteries of the Missing*, New York, 1927.
Starrett, Vincent, *Ambrose Bierce*, Chicago, 1920.
———, *Buried Caesars*, New York, 1923.
Sterling, George, *A Wine of Wizardry* (with introduction by Dale L. Walker), Fort Johnson, Texas, 1964.
Swanberg, William A., *Citizen Hearst*, New York, 1961.
Tallent, Annie D., *The Black Hills*, St. Louis, 1899.
Walker, Franklin, *San Francisco's Literary Frontier*, New York, 1934.
Wilkins, Harold R., *Strange Mysteries of Time and Space*, New York, 1958.
Wilson, Edmund, *Patriotic Gore*, New York, 1962.
Woodruff, Stuart C., *The Short Stories of Ambrose Bierce*, Pittsburgh, 1964.
Ziff, Larzer, *The American 1890s*, New York, 1966.

NEWSPAPERS

Chico (California) *Enterprise*
El Heraldo of Chihuahua, Mexico
Elkhart (Indiana) *Review*
Indianapolis *Journal*
Los Angeles *Examiner*
Los Angeles *Times*
New York *American*
New York *Journal*
New York *Sun*
New York *Times*
Sacramento *Union*
San Francisco *Bulletin*
San Francisco *Chronicle*
San Francisco *Examiner*
Washington *Post*
Washington *Star*

MAGAZINES

Alta California
American Mercury
American Notes and Queries
Argonaut
Bookman
Cosmopolitan
Esquire

Hampton's magazine
New Masses
Overland Monthly
Pearson's magazine
Wasp
Wave

Index